DISCARD

FREDERIC C. DUMAINE
Office Boy to Tycoon

ARTHUR M. KENISON

Based on Dorothy Wayman's Unpublished Work
Dumaine of New England, Circa 1958

Frederic C. Dumaine

FREDERIC C. DUMAINE
Office Boy to Tycoon

ARTHUR M. KENISON

PUBLISHED BY SAINT ANSELM COLLEGE PRESS
SAINT ANSELM COLLEGE
MANCHESTER, NEW HAMPSHIRE

Published by Saint Anselm College Press
Saint Anselm College
100 Saint Anselm Drive
Manchester, NH 03102-1310

Printed and bound in Canada.

January 2000
First Edition

ISBN 0-9629547-2-1

Library of Congress Data applied for.

Kenison, Arthur M.
   Frederic C. Dumaine : Office Boy to Tycoon / Arthur M. Kenison – 1st ed.
   p.   cm.
   Includes bibliographical references and index.
   ISBN 0-962-95472-1
   1. Dumaine, Frederic Christopher, 1866-1951 – Biography. 2. Capitalists and financiers – United States – Biography. 3. Amoskeag Manufacturing Company – History. 4. Textile manufacturers – New Hampshire – Manchester – History. 5. Waltham Watch Company – History. 6. New York, New Haven, and Hartford Railroad Company –History. 1. Title.
   CT275.D86 K46 2000

For my grandchildren
Rachel and Summer,
who have brought new joy to my life.

Acknowledgments

In the fall of 1998, having completed the major portion of the work on my book, *Dumaine's Amoskeag: Let the Record Speak*, dealing with an analysis of the factors leading to the closing of the Amoskeag Manufacturing Company, I began writing about the life of Frederic C. Dumaine. I had developed a genuine admiration for Mr. Dumaine as a result of my study of Amoskeag. I wanted to enhance my understanding of the individual behind the business decisions and share my findings in this current book.

From my prior research, I knew that F.C. kept an extensive diary about his personal and business affairs. I felt that access to these diaries would be critical to the current work. Having met several members of the third generation of Dumaines in my research for *Dumaine's Amoskeag*, I requested access to the diaries. While the family was eager to provide me access, all but three years of F.C.'s diaries were either lost or destroyed. They did provide me, however, with galley proofs of a manuscript by Dorothy Wayman, now deceased and a onetime writer for the Boston Globe. Written in 1958 at the request of the second generation of Dumaines, the manuscript, for a reason unknown, was never published. It was based on Dumaine's diaries, from which she quoted extensively.

While chagrined at not having direct access to the personal pen of F.C. Dumaine, my disappointment was somewhat offset by the fact that the Wayman work was based, in part, on interviews with many of

Dumaine's business associates and family members who are now deceased. At this time, some forty-five years after Dumaine's death, I could not expect to have the perspective given by the interviews that Ms. Wayman had in her earlier work. To a great extent, this book owes its existence to the Wayman manuscript on which I must trust the accuracy of the quotations from the diaries. In addition, many of her observations of his personal life are directly incorporated into this book.

In addition to the Wayman manuscript, the book relies extensively on material from Charles W. Moore's *Timing a Century: History of the Waltham Watch Company*, Vincent P. Carosso's *More Than a Century of Investment Banking: The Kidder, Peabody & Co. Story*, John L. Weller's *The New Haven Railroad: Its Rise and Fall*, and my own research as published in *Dumaine's Amoskeag: Let the Record Speak*. Countless newspaper and magazine articles were also reviewed in preparation for this writing.

Last, but not least, this book includes a substantial amount of family folklore that has been passed down in the form of oral history to Dumaine's grandchildren. Of particular value have been the contributions of Dudley B. Dumaine, one of F.C. Dumaine's grandsons, who at one time also was the president of the Amoskeag Company. While these sources are subject to potential historical error, the risk is more than offset by the reward of the texture that the family history adds to the portrait of Dumaine.

I wish to extend my appreciation to the Reverend Peter S. Guerin, O.S.B., who has been particularly encouraging to me to complete this book, and to Professor Emeritus Austin Conley, the Reverend Mark A. Cooper, O.S.B., John Cox, Richard L. Fortin, Marianne Lake, Loretta Martineau, Leslie Nesky, and Barbara Miller, who have been advisers. I particularly want to thank John Greene for his excellent work in organizing, editing, and publishing the book.

Moreover, any conclusions expressed in this book are those of the author and not necessarily those of Ms. Wayman, Dr. Moore, Mr. Carosso, or the Dumaine family. In addition, the author assumes full responsibility for any errors in this writing.

Arthur M. Kenison
Manchester, New Hampshire
January 1, 2000

Contents

F.C. working in Manchester to learn the business.

C H A P T E R   I

Son of a Broom Maker

Frederic C. Dumaine was born into a working class Canadian family that had immigrated to the United States prior to his birth. His father died before F.C. reached his teen years. The younger Dumaine went to work to help support his widowed mother. Beginning as an office boy, he eventually became the chief executive officer of the Amoskeag Manufacturing Company, the world's largest textile firm. It was in his original apprenticeship and his gradual assumption of increasing responsibility that Dumaine learned the creed of the "Boston Associates," who were various old New England families given credit for the origin and development of the industrialization of the American economy. This industrialization was accomplished through the construction of textile mills on the rivers throughout New England.

The "Boston Associates" creed exemplified the best of the profit system. They were investor managers who were not interested in the "quick buck." Rather, they invested for the long term. When they adapted the manufacturing system they had seen in Great Britain, they took measures to lessen the negative aspects of the factory life as it existed in England. When they built factories, they also built quality housing for their workers. They invested heavily in parks and other recreation enhancements for the towns and cities in which they located their factories.

Some sixty years after being introduced to this method of investing, F.C. would give his grandchildren the following lecture:

1

You take care of your assets and they will take care of you. Always remember that the most precious assets you have are the people who work for you.

Dumaine went on to become one of Boston's most noted businessmen of the late 19th century and first half of the 20th century. In due course, F.C. Dumaine's name would become associated with the Fore River Shipyard, the Waltham Watch Company, and the New Haven Railroad.

Dumaine, however, was more than merely a major player in the Boston business community. He served on corporate boards with J. Pierpont Morgan, dealt with Henry Ford and Charles Schwab on a first-name basis, was openly welcomed in the financial houses of New York, and was offered J.P. Morgan, Jr.'s interest in the House of Morgan when the younger Morgan died.

F.C. became the friend and confidant of several United States presidents and statesmen. In the gray years leading to World War II, U.S. Supreme Court Justice Felix Frankfurter referred to Dumaine as one of three individuals with the best understanding of world conditions. The other two were President Franklin Delano Roosevelt (popularly called FDR) and Great Britain's Prime Minister Winston Churchill. Of particular interest was Dumaine's relationship with FDR during both the Great Depression and World War II. Once, when visiting Roosevelt, in an effort to give comfort to the president who was concerned with public opinion on his recent decisions, Dumaine quoted Abraham Lincoln:

> If I were trying to read, much less answer all the attacks made on me, this shop might well be closed for any other business. I do the best I know how, the very best I can and mean to keep on doing it to the end. If the end brings me out all right, what is said against me will not amount to anything. If the end brings me out wrong, ten angels swearing I was right would make no difference.

The president liked the quotation and, upon returning to Boston, Dumaine had a copy framed and sent to FDR.

While the quotation was part of Dumaine's creed, it illustrates why many individuals in the past and present never gave Dumaine the credit he deserved. Dumaine surely read and was told of the many criticisms of him, but he generally paid no heed. Instead, he simply did the best he could and let the record speak for itself.

During the 1922 strike at Amoskeag and the 1924 strike at Waltham

Watch, both of which were in response to wage cuts, it was easy to label Dumaine the enemy of labor. Both cuts, however, were attempts to equalize the local labor costs with those found in other sections of the country. To provide employment in the long run, a firm's wage rate must be competitive. While Dumaine would have preferred to see wages in other mills and factories rise to the levels at Amoskeag and Waltham, he had no control over those rates. The introduction of competitive rates — even if this meant a drop in the hourly wage — would ensure employment.

When the Amoskeag Manufacturing Company was forced to close in 1936, most people put the blame on Dumaine. A careful examination of the record vividly illustrates that Dumaine's devotion to his most precious assets, the workers, caused him to expand production and employment in New Hampshire in the early quarter of the century, at time when other firms were closing their mills and opening new factories in the South.

If Dumaine is to be criticized, it should **not** be for his lack of concern for his work force but for "dreaming the impossible dream," for trying to maintain employment for his workers when the more prudent course, as history has proved, would have been to move or close the enterprise.

The life of Frederic C. Dumaine should be mandatory reading for all current and future business people. Dumaine's life serves as a case study for today's executive in balancing a firm's fiduciary responsibility to the shareholders with its social responsibility to the labor force.

Until recently, there was little known about the ancestry of Frederic Christopher Dumaine. This is not as odd as it may seem. Frequently, the preference of many families emigrating from Canada to the United States in the middle of the 19th century was to alter their names. Even the correct spelling of Dumaine's father's name is uncertain. What Frederic Dumaine did know was that his father, Christopher Dumaine, was born on July 13, 1835, of French-Canadian parents in the Province of Quebec. He was one of three brothers. Apparently, Christopher was baptized a Catholic. F.C.'s mother, Cordelia Roberts, was also born in Canada in 1831. Her parents were Charles and Lucille Roberts. Cordelia attended the Congregational Church. At the age of sixteen, Cordelia Roberts married Barrett Stone. This marriage produced three daughters: Elizabeth, Relenia, and Georgia. Barrett Stone, Cordelia's first husband, died, leaving her with the three young children.

On May 14, 1858, in Chelsea, Massachusetts, Christopher Dumaine married the widow Cordelia, who had also emigrated from Canada. They were residing in Hadley, Massachusetts, when their only son, Frederic, was born. The uncertainty of the spelling of the name Dumaine comes from Frederic's birth certificate, which states in part: "I hereby certify that the birth of Charles Frederic Domain son of Christopher Domain and ___ Domain born at Hadley, on the 6th day of March, in the year 1866," appears in the record for that year. The misspelling likely resulted from the difficulty the clerk had in spelling an unfamiliar French-Canadian name. Frederic Dumaine never bothered to correct the error in his name as recorded on the document.

Only recently, through the efforts of Richard L. Fortin, a genealogist in Manchester, New Hampshire, has Dumaine's ancestry been traced to the original immigration to Canada from France. Louis-Michael Maingot, F.C.'s great-great-grandfather, arrived in Quebec in the spring of 1755. He was a soldier assigned to the French Regiment from Guyenne. In 1760, after the fall of Montreal to the British, Louis-Michael was discharged from the service. It was during his military service that he acquired the "dit," or "also known as" "Dumaine." It was common practice for French soldiers to adopt a second surname, often to specify their geographic origin. Louis-Michael was thus identifying himself as from the French Province of Maine.

Following his release from the army, Louis-Michael settled in Rouville County in the Province of Quebec, where he married Marie-Anne Fontaine. One of their grandchildren was Francis-Xavier Maingot-dit-Dumaine, F.C.'s grandfather. Francis-Xavier married Adeline Lescaolt. This marriage would produce two daughters (Philomena and Stephanie) and three sons (Joseph, Pierre, and Christopher, F.C.'s father).

Francis-Xavier did not live to old age. The grandfather of F.C. Dumaine became a casualty of the 1837-38 Rebellion. He was a member of the "Patriots," who rose up, under the leadership of Louis Joseph Papineau, against the perceived injustices of the British Government. Many French-Canadians associated with the rebellion fell away from the Catholic Church when the local bishops did not support their movement. On November 25, 1837, Francis-Xavier lost his life when the government forces attacked and destroyed the village of St. Charles. It appears unlikely that F.C. was ever aware of the role that his grandfather played in the rebellion.

Christopher Dumaine, F.C.'s father, was a broom maker by trade. In 1868, the family moved to Dedham, Massachusetts, where Christopher was employed as a foreman in David Baker's broom factory. They lived

Christopher Dumaine   *Cordelia Dumaine*

in a pleasant, middle-class neighborhood. The only plumbing in the house was a cast-iron water pump in the kitchen sink.

One day when Fred was four years old and sunshine followed a shower, the tot was allowed to go outside. It was warm. He was sent out in a new outfit. Horses were drawing loaded wagons on the dirt road in front of his house.

As children are wont to do, Dumaine moved close to the road just as a wagon wheel splashed through black mud. He was covered. Whether out of fear from the punishment that he anticipated from his mother for getting his new outfit soiled or angry from the insult of being covered with the mud, he let out a series of curses. It was never explained exactly how the young Dumaine had come to learn such expressions. The commotion caused the driver to stop and return to assist young Fred, motivated first to be sure that the child was not hurt, then to see if he could assist in the cleanup. When the driver and other bystanders saw that Fred was not hurt, they chuckled in amusement over the sight. As might have been expected, their amusement made the lad angrier. In this early incident, Dumaine illustrated the gritty attitude that he would demonstrate throughout his life.

The broom factory must have paid good wages for the times, as Christopher Dumaine supported his wife, three stepdaughters, and son. By 1874, when Elizabeth and Relenia had married, Dumaine was able to send the third stepdaughter, Georgia, to secondary school at Antioch College in Yellow Springs, Ohio.

In addition to his job at the broom factory, Christopher Dumaine was also active in the community. He was a member of the local volunteer fire department. While his father's membership in Engine Company Hero Number One of the Upper Village brought Fred and his family great pride, it would also bring a great family tragedy that would force Fred to leave school to help support the family.

On the evening of January 7, 1878, when Fred was eleven years old, the local volunteers responded to a fire near Dedham Square. The temperature was below zero, making the fire difficult to fight. When Christopher returned home the following morning, he was soaking wet and direly chilled. Pneumonia quickly set in.

There was no real method of treatment for the illness. The only remedy of any type was to feed the patient alcohol. Doctors merely would monitor pneumonia cases to see what would come on the ninth day. If the patient lived that long and if the fever "broke," there was a chance for recovery.

Cordelia, sensing that her husband was near death, asked if Christopher wanted her to fetch the local priest. Christopher, who had not been an active member of the church for many years, responded: "No, I came this far alone. I guess I can go the rest of the way by myself." Whether Christopher's disassociation with the Catholic Church was a result of the French bishop's lack of moral support for his father's role in the Rebellion, his marriage to Cordelia, a Protestant, or simply a lack of interest, cannot be determined.

Young Fred assisted his mother in the nursing of his father. The elder Dumaine would sit in his armchair because he had difficulty breathing when lying flat in bed. On the eighth day, Christopher succumbed. Fred would always remember the way his father died. When Fred Dumaine was nearing his death some 73 years later, he asked to be helped to Christopher's chair, which he had kept. It was his desire to die in his father's chair.

Cordelia Dumaine went to work as a midwife and also took in washing. The family was forced to move into a smaller house. A few months later, young Fred, by then twelve years old, quit school to help support the household by working at a local dry goods store.

One of his children's and grandchildren's favorite stories of Fred prior to his landing the job at Amoskeag was when he was the proud owner of a mongrel Boston bull terrier, which he loved dearly. The dog went everywhere with him, following him to and from work.

6

F.C. about age 10

To get to the general store where he worked, Fred and his dog had to pass the town bully's house, which was set back from the road. The bully was Fred's senior by 14 or 15 years and he owned a ferocious half-hound, half-collie, which was a noted fighter. The bully boasted his dog could lick any dog in town. Fred's Tiger had the reputation of being able to hold his own. One day the town bully and his dog met Fred and Tiger. The bully encouraged a fight. When it started, young Fred said, "I told you that you one day would see that my dog could and would lick your dog."

Tiger shook the 'bejabbers' out of his opponent. Fred gathered up his scattered belongings, and with triumphant Tiger at his heels, ran home, while the bully unmercifully beat his dog with a stick.

A few days later the town bully, whose dog had recovered, waited for a chance to spot Tiger without his young master. A fight between the dogs ensued and, as an excuse to stop the fight, the town bully shot Tiger.

Fred reported the bully to the police and inquired as to how he could have him sued for killing his dog. He sued the bully, who contested, claiming that Dumaine should be fined for having had such a dog that was a fighting nuisance that attacked all the other dogs in town.

Fred was served notice to appear in the Dedham Court House. He had no money and did not want to ask anyone for help. Determined to vindicate his faithful Tiger's good name, he hit upon a plan and boldly went to work doing extra errands to fund his idea. With his earnings, he took Tiger to a taxidermist and had him stuffed.

The day young Fred was called to court he went to the attic where he had hidden Tiger carefully in an old trunk. He wrapped the dog in newspaper tied together with string and carried his bundle to the Dedham Court. He was ushered in by a policeman, who took him to the front of the courtroom. His case was just being called. Frightened but determined, Fred weathered the preliminaries and, wide-eyed, stood his ground.

After the complainant's version of Fred's ferocious, savage, attacking dog was heard by the court, the judge asked the defendant where his lawyer was. Fred said he couldn't afford one and preferred to argue his own cause.

The judge asked, "How can you prove anything? Your dog is dead." Fred squared his shoulders, looked the judge in the eye, then asked if he could call two witnesses. With the judge's permission, Fred called for the town bully to bring his dog on a leash into the court. While the complainant was fetching his dog (he lived a block or so away), Fred lay his package on a wooden bench in the front of the courtroom and began to untie the strings and loosen the newspaper. Just as the bully returned with his ferocious dog, Fred opened the paper. The bully's dog took one look and savagely flew across the room, grabbing the stuffed Tiger, and shook the daylights out of it, causing a great commotion in court room. Fred dissolved into tears and rage at seeing his Tiger being savaged again. He pounded the bench and poured out his claim to the judge that his dog was not the aggressor. The judge found in Fred's favor and went on to encourage Fred to defend himself and stand up to injustices, but with some wisdom in gathering his facts for his testimony.

Young Fred profited by the advice. In later years, he studied law with his uncle-by-marriage, the prominent Boston lawyer Richard Olney, gaining a deep grasp of legal principles and procedures.

As an adult, Dumaine would become an avid diary keeper. At that time, he recorded in his diaries his activities following his father's death:

> My father died the fourteenth of January and one or two months after I went to work for Henry Pettingall in a little dry goods store which he kept. After a year I left him because he would not give me more pay and, for the balance of the school term, went to school. During the summer, I got a job with a screen

man named Pedrick, and in the fall went into McLaughlin's haberdashery where I stayed until the following spring when Mrs. Rodman got Steve Weld to find me a place in the city.

Stephen Weld, a former general in the Civil War, lived in Dedham and operated a cotton brokerage office in Boston. Weld knew of Dumaine from his sister-in-law, Harriet Rodman. Dumaine would supplement the family income by picking and selling blueberries. One of his best customers was Mrs. Rodman. Dumaine always remembered the kindness shown by her. In later years, he would name one of his daughters Harriet in her honor. He also handled Mrs. Rodman's estate following the death of her husband in 1910.

Apparently the meeting with the general occurred on an evening when Weld, returning home from Boston, came across Fred Dumaine, who was in the process of leaving home to find employment in the city.

Weld stopped, inquired where Dumaine was heading and offered assistance. He contacted T. Jefferson Coolidge, treasurer of the Amoskeag Manufacturing Company, Weld's best customer. Apparently Coolidge was looking for an office boy and, as a result of that chance meeting, Dumaine was hired. Thus, in a boyhood that reads like a story from a Horatio Alger, Jr. book, Frederic C. Dumaine began his career with Amoskeag Manufacturing Company.

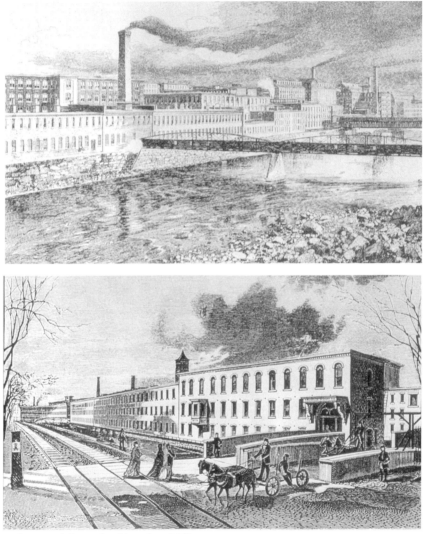

19th century lithographs of Amoskeag Mills

C H A P T E R   I I

Early Amoskeag Years

On June 15, 1880, fourteen-year-old Frederic Christopher Dumaine entered the employ of the Amoskeag Manufacturing Company at its Boston office on 50 State Street. General Stephen Weld had recommended Dumaine to his best customer for cotton, T. Jefferson Coolidge, treasurer of the world-famous Amoskeag Mills. New England textile firms followed the English tradition of calling the chief executive officer of the corporation the treasurer. Freddy was hired as a messenger boy at $3 a week. He borrowed $4 to purchase a three-month commuter ticket from Dedham to Boston and began a career with Amoskeag that would span 70 years. He would eventually succeed T. Jefferson Coolidge as treasurer at a salary of $100,000 a year.

The Amoskeag Mills in Manchester, New Hampshire, were a sight to behold when Fred first saw them in the 1880's. There was beauty of landscape, magnitude of construction, and dynamic activity of accomplishment.

At that time, half a century after the Amoskeag Manufacturing Company had been incorporated in 1831, one looked upon the broad Merrimack River, roiling down a quarter of a mile from the dam that reined in the water power, and then to canals carefully designed to work in favor of the mills.

Forested green hills surrounded the valley. On the east bank of the river were massed tall mill buildings of red brick, set in orderly rows around cobbled yards. Belting towers (specifically built to transmit the maze of rope belting required to power machinery) rose like cupolas to beautifully adorn the architecture. Green lawns with shrubbery hedges and flower beds of bright geraniums lay between mills and river. Through the yards moved great wagons with bales of cotton or wool, and boxes and bundles of woven goods, drawn by powerful draft horses.

Fred would wonder why the peculiar sounding name Amoskeag (pronounced Am'-oh-skag) was selected for the name of the company. The name was from the Indian word meaning "high place for fish," referring to the salmon that leapt up the falls of the Merrimack River. When the Boston men acquired the land early in the 19th century, there were only fifty inhabitants. The Amoskeag Manufacturing Company had a plan drawn for a city and gave free sites for a town hall, library, schools, churches of several denominations, and many green parks. Perhaps the most significant commentary to illustrate the civic responsibility with which owner-managers of New England textile firms were imbued was written in 1902. A British journalist traveling in the United States wrote:

> None of the manufacturing towns in New England pleased me as much as Manchester in New Hampshire. Unlike its great godmother (Manchester, England), it has clean air, clear water, and sunny skies; almost every street is an avenue of noble trees... Certainly the most impressive buildings are the Amoskeag and Manchester Mills... rising sheer out of a deep, clear, swift flowing stream... they need little more than to be silent to masquerade successfully as ancient colleges.

The history of Amoskeag in the 19th century is really a history of five separate corporations that shared common stockholders and overlapping management. All of these corporations were ultimately merged together in the next century. Amoskeag was by far the largest of the five. In addition to manufacturing cotton textiles, Amoskeag also constructed and operated the canal system, built its own mills and the mills of its sister corporations, and maintained an extensive machine shop and foundry for the production of textile machinery, which it sold throughout New England. The other four corporations were Stark, which specialized in the manufacture of cotton duck cloth; Manchester Print Works, which produced delaines or printed cloth; and Langdon and Amory, which both produced cotton textiles. The general practice of the "Boston Associates," a name given to the various groups of Massachusetts investors who organized the development of mill communities

12

throughout New England, was to form new corporations when they planned a substantial capacity increase or when they moved into the production of a different type of cloth. Usually the new corporations had many overlapping stockholders with the older corporations in the same community.

In addition to building mills, Amoskeag also built housing for the workers. Since Amoskeag originally followed the "Lowell System" of recruiting young women from rural farm families to tend the looms in the mills, most of the residences were boarding houses. The corporation imposed strict rules for the residents. There was a ten o'clock curfew. Alcoholic consumption was prohibited. Moreover, weekly church attendance was mandatory. While these regulations seem prohibitive by today's standards, they provided a sense of security to the Yankee families considering sending their daughters to Manchester to work in the mills.

By the latter part of the 19th century, when immigrant families replaced the "mill girls" as the primary source of workers, these boarding houses were converted to tenements suitable for family residences. Even after the conversion to tenements, the corporation maintained a paternalistic outlook, with conditions of employment stating, "The company will not employ anyone who is habitually absent from public worship on the Sabbath, or who uses profane or indecent language in the mills or elsewhere, or who uses ardent spirits as a beverage."

The Amoskeag ginghams, cotton goods, woolens and worsteds, and A.C.A. ticking, were unsurpassed in quality. Abraham Lincoln in 1845 in Springfield, Illinois, bought "four and a half yards of Gingham" for $1.50 to have a shirt made. The Amoskeag machine shop and foundry— in addition to servicing the mills — built locomotives and steam fire engines for America, Europe, South America and the Far East. During the Civil War they manufactured muskets for the Union cause. Amoskeag had the only lathe large enough to turn big brass rings for the turrets of the *Monitor*, the armored vessel that would become famous in the history of the Civil War.

Unlike most mills of the era, Amoskeag did not borrow and pay interest on cash for purchases and payroll. Amoskeag was proud that it had on hand its own "quick capital" [working capital] of $6 million, in addition to the money invested in buildings, machinery, and land.

Wages were low. Workers averaged $6 a week. However, the company boardinghouses lodged unmarried workers and fed them for $2.25 a week, while company houses for married workers rented for a dollar a

13

month per room. By this time, Amoskeag had reduced the hours of labor per day from fourteen to ten. Children under sixteen, by New Hampshire law, had to show a school certificate to be permitted to work in the mills.

Manchester had charm in those early days when Dumaine first knew it. The city was prosperous. A good proportion of inhabitants owned their own dwellings, with a lawn and a garden patch. The Amoskeag deeds to land in the inner city carried a stipulation for fire-resistant construction. The inner city was characterized by red-brick and gray-granite buildings topped with slate roofs. Amoskeag had built the city on virgin ground and therefore did not inherit any slum-like conditions. In the employment provided and the rhythm of life set in its factory bells and whistles, Manchester was largely synonymous with Amoskeag. The annual payroll had risen steadily from $36,296 in 1831 to $2.4 million by 1890.

The story of the Amoskeag Manufacturing Company is not properly understood until identification of the mills with the families that labored there is made clear. The mill hands would begin working part-time while still in school. After leaving school, they would take full-time positions in the Amoskeag. Often they married someone they had met in the mills. Their offspring would then continue the cycle.

In a similar manner, the first generation of stockholders risked their capital and poured into the planning their vision, ability, and energy. Their sons grew up hearing Amoskeag discussed at the dinner table. They, in their turns, went into the mill or countinghouse to learn the business, then to take on the responsibility as directors or treasurers.

When Fred started working for Coolidge, the old Amoskeag office in Boston was still heated by open coal fireplaces. Slanted desks were breast-high and the clerks stood while transcribing minutes of directors' meetings or bookkeepers' figures into immense ledgers. A battery of equally high, flat-topped tables was strewn with samples of cotton and wool, lengths of shirting, tickings, ginghams, and worsteds. Dumaine was still using one of those tables in his own office fifty years later.

During his first few years working for Coolidge at Amoskeag's Boston office, Dumaine continued to live with his mother and stepsister in Dedham. On the way home from the commuter train stop, Dumaine would pick up laundry from neighbors. His mother would do the washing that night and young Fred would deliver it the following morning on the way to the train station.

14

According to Dumaine family legend, it was about this time that F.C. Dumaine first met James Michael Curley, the boy who was to become one of Boston's most famous mayors.

Curley, eight years younger than Dumaine, sold newspapers on a street corner where Fred often passed while delivering documents around town for Amoskeag. He got to know Curley. One day someone gave Fred an apple and he was eating it on the way back to the office. He passed James Michael, who yelled at him, "Fred, what's you gonna do with the core?" F.C.'s answer was, "Ain't gonna be no core."

"Ain't gonna be no core" became a mainstay comment for Dumaine, maybe even a motto, because it represented a habit of frugality that F.C. Dumaine would practice throughout his life.

But we must return to those formative years when Coolidge took on Fred. Coolidge and his manager, Lucius Manlius Sargent, soon noticed the keen mind and willing spirit of the new messenger boy. They developed an affection for Dumaine, a trust in him that endured through their lifetimes. As the years went by, the intimacy was more apparent, with Dumaine calling Mr. Coolidge "Grandpa" and being named the executor of the estate and a trustee of the Coolidge family millions.

Gossip-loving Bostonians created a whispered legend that Dumaine was an illegitimate son of T. Jefferson Coolidge. There was a touch of Boston Brahmin snobbery in the legend: Those Yankees from Boston's Back Bay would not credit the son of a French-Canadian broom maker with such financial astuteness; there had to be some distinguished Coolidge blood coursing through those veins to account for his ability, they guessed.

Actually, the genes of Christopher and Cordelia Dumaine are entitled to all the credit for their son's success. T. Jefferson Coolidge, with his wife and three daughters, went to Europe early in 1865, at the end of the Civil War, and stayed there for three years. It was geographically impossible for T. Jefferson Coolidge to have fathered the boy born in Hadley, Massachusetts, on March 6, 1866.

Most likely, however, the boy did transfer a father-image to the kindly and distinguished man who treated him like a son. T. Jefferson Coolidge was a hero to a boy beginning a career in business. A great-grandson of President Thomas Jefferson, Coolidge's high forehead, aristocratic nose, trim mustache and "imperial" beard, together with a slender, stately figure, gave him a patrician air inherited from the best bloodlines of old

15

Virginia and colonial Boston. In later years, Dumaine commissioned a portrait to be done of Coolidge to hang in F.C.'s office. Mr. Coolidge spoke French and German fluently; his mind was enriched with the resources of books, art and travel made possible by inherited wealth. He was a princely patron. The Jefferson Physical Laboratory was an out-right gift to Harvard in 1884. In addition, he had built a beautiful library that was his gift to Manchester-by-the-Sea, where Coolidge had his summer estate beginning in 1873.

In 1880, as Dumaine joined the Amoskeag office, Mr. Coolidge be-came president of the Atchison, Topeka and Santa Fe Railroad, a tem-porary assignment that Coolidge undertook. At the request of Kidder, Peabody and Co. and various other Boston financial interests, Coolidge assumed the responsibility of reorganizing the financially troubled rail-road. In 1889, his close friend President Benjamin Harrison made him a delegate to the Pan-American Congress to discuss the question of gold or silver as legal tender. In 1892, Harrison named Coolidge the United States Minister to France.

Such outside interests often took Coolidge away from the office. It was his son-in-law, Lucius Sargent, whom Dumaine saw daily. Sargent had every advantage that Dumaine lacked. After graduating from Harvard in 1870, he had studied in French and German universities. He was handsome with a full brown mustache that Fred Dumaine imitated as soon as he could raise one. Sargent had an estate at Magno-lia, north of Boston. He sailed his yacht, rode pedigreed horses, and pursued foxes with the Myopia Hunt Club. When he died in 1890, Dumaine recorded in his diary:

> Mr. Sargent was ideal to my mind but one day he fell from his horse and, after apparently getting well, had a relapse from which he died. This came as the saddest thing in my life up to this time. I remember him with the greatest love. His judgment was always good and he was always fair. He was a boy's ideal and I never expect to know another man for whom I shall have so much respect.

In 1887, the year that Fred Dumaine turned twenty-one, Sargent gave him his first vacation. He spent it in the Maine woods with young Arthur G. Staples, who later would become the editor of the Lewiston Journal. While they were camping at Passadumkeag, twenty-five miles northeast of Bangor, Dumaine had an attack of acute indigestion. His friend took him to a doctor in Bangor who diagnosed it as a heart attack.

T. Jefferson Coolidge   Lucius Manlius Sargent

"Young man," said the doctor, "you have a terrible heart condition. Get home to your mother as fast as you can for you cannot live much longer. Above all, don't smoke or drink any liquor."

Dumaine's reaction, as soon as they left the doctor's office, was to ask where, in the prohibition state of Maine, he could buy a quart of whiskey. He took it back to Passadumkeag and resumed fishing. He lived sixty-three years longer and drank some whiskey and smoked several cigars every day.

During his early years in the Boston office, Dumaine was observing the routine business practices that made for efficient operations and provided the skills necessary for advancement. More important, he was trained in Amoskeag's policy relative to the treatment of its most important asset, its labor.

Of particular interest was the construction of two mills, one in 1886 and the second some three years later. The first mill, called the Jefferson in honor of Coolidge's great-grandfather, is significant because its looms were steam driven. Amoskeag had outgrown the water power generated by the Merrimack. This policy was demonstrated more vividly in 1889 when the corporation built Mill No. 11. It was located on the west side of the river. Since there were no canals on that side, it could never be powered by water. More significant than the exhausting of water power was the growing labor cost advantage of the South. Amoskeag was following this policy of expansion in Manchester fully aware of the conditions in the South. In the annual report of 1886, the year that the Jefferson Mill was constructed, Coolidge was quoted as saying:

17

The Southern Mills have of late years succeeded in making coarse yarns as cheap or cheaper than the New England Mills, and have compelled [us] to abandon in a great measure the manufacturing of heavy goods for the home market... [The Southern Mills] bought their cotton at least half a cent lower and their greater comparative production caused by a longer day's labor has been an important element in their success.

In the 1889 Annual Report to the stockholders, the same year that Mill No. 11 was constructed, Coolidge noted:

We are now barely holding our own and unless some improvement takes place the next year will be unprofitable... We must not forget the growth of the Southern Mills which has been marvelous... We shall be obliged to yield to them the coarser kind of manufacturing.

Two years later, while reporting on Amoskeag's performance, Coolidge cautioned:

Considering the extreme competition which is caused by the enormous growth of Mills at the South, the past year has not been an unsatisfactory one. We must not, however, disguise from ourselves that the competition of the Southern Mills becomes more severe every year. They have the advantage over us in paying... less for the raw material, decidedly lower wages, and what is of still more importance, they run twelve hours against our ten.

While many New England mills at that time had decided to have all of their expansion take place in the South, which had the advantage of cheaper transportation and labor costs, Amoskeag was not following this practice. It described itself as a Manchester company that planned to continue to operate and expand in the city, even if greater profits could be made elsewhere. This was a practice that Dumaine never changed.

Sargent and Coolidge were grooming the youngster for future responsibilities. They encouraged him to take night courses in accounting at a Boston business college. This meant he could no longer commute from Dedham, so he moved into Mrs. Whittlesey's boardinghouse on Beacon Hill. He had grown a mustache, cultivated in imitation of Lucius Sargent, who was keeping a fatherly eye on his young protege. When Dumaine was drawn into an affair with an older woman at the boardinghouse, Sargent saw to it that the woman was expelled by the landlady. Dumaine was transferred to work in the Jefferson Mill of the Amoskeag Company in Manchester, New Hampshire. He was to learn the textile business from the bottom up, all the operations, from generating steam to carding, spinning, warping, slashing, drawing, and weaving. Apparently Fred found this tenure in Manchester beneficial. A generation later he would send his eldest son Buck for a similar exposure to the mills.

While in Manchester, F.C.'s weekly wage was just over $6. Sargent arranged that he take a room in the parsonage with the widowed Unitarian minister, the Reverend Cyrus W. Heizer.

One Sunday afternoon, Mr. Heizer took his boarder driving and introduced him to the future Mrs. Dumaine. The reverend was calling on Mrs. Isaiah Thomas, whose husband had recently died of tuberculosis, leaving her a twelve-year-old daughter, Elizabeth. Dumaine was twice the age of the shy young girl. It was an uneventful meeting, a curious prelude to the romance that would be both the greatest happiness and greatest tragedy of Frederic Dumaine's life.

In August 1890, Coolidge and President Harrison stayed overnight in Manchester at the home of the New Hampshire Governor, P. C. Cheney. The next morning, Dumaine saw his first president in the flesh, driving in a carriage with Coolidge through the Amoskeag mill yards, a further prelude to the associations he would have with Presidents Taft and Roosevelt.

An even more curious prelude to Dumaine's business career occurred during his tenure in Manchester. Beginning in October 1890, a Pan American delegation of representatives of the International Congress of American Nations toured businesses in the eastern United States. While in New England, in addition to Amoskeag and its sister mills in Manchester, they also visited Waltham Watch and traveled on the New Haven and Boston and Maine rails. Dumaine eventually would play a vital role in all three businesses.

Coolidge and Sargent kept young Dumaine in the mill at Manchester only one year before promoting him to be a buyer of cotton and wool. Intoxicated at the prospect of traveling through the South and West with such responsibility and a large raise in pay, Dumaine reported so promptly in Boston that he forgot to collect his weekly check at the paymaster's office of the Jefferson Mill. Three decades later, as treasurer of the Amoskeag Manufacturing Company, he discovered that the bookkeeper was still carrying "in suspense" that uncollected amount of $6.05.

In his haste to advance his career in the Boston home office, Fred Dumaine had left a core.

19

Bessie and the kids

C H A P T E R   I I I

Courtship and Marriage

After a couple of years experience as a buyer of the raw materials for textiles, young Dumaine was transferred back to the Boston office of the Amoskeag Mills for training in selling and accounting. He boarded in Boston's Back Bay on Dartmouth Street. On his daily walk to the State Street office, he noticed with interest a beautiful young girl on her way to school. He had no way of knowing that she was Elizabeth Thomas, to whom the Unitarian minister had introduced him in Goffstown, New Hampshire, six years earlier. However, fate took a hand.

Fred Dumaine had bought a bicycle and joined a club of young men. On Sundays they would set off for the country, pedaling their high-wheeled vehicles, attired in knickerbockers and striped flannel blazers.

One Sunday afternoon when he was riding by the white Unitarian Church in Wayland, twenty miles from Boston, Fred Dumaine saw lettered on a sign the name of his old Manchester friend, the Rev. Cyrus W. Heizer. Impulsively, he waved his companions on and stopped to inquire as to the whereabouts of the parsonage. Mr. Heizer, he learned, had bought a farm nearby and combined raising horses with his pastoral duties. Dumaine rode his bicycle up a country lane to the house.

To his surprise, by the gate holding a horse by the bridle stood the beautiful girl of Commonwealth Avenue in Boston. Dumaine was so

21

flabbergasted that he lost control of the bicycle, which toppled, pinning him.

The Reverend Heizer came hurrying out, dusted off, Dumaine and reintroduced him to Bessie Thomas, who was now the minister's step-daughter. Elizabeth Thomas was a direct descendant of Isaiah Thomas of Revolutionary War fame, hailed as a publisher of the Massachusetts Spy and for denouncing the oppression of the colonies by the British government as well as for his participation in the Battle of Lexington. Her grandfather had been a Massachusetts Supreme Court judge and her uncle was Richard Olney, a noted attorney who served as President Cleveland's secretary of state.

Much to the dismay of Reverend Heizer, Dumaine began courting Bessie. A penniless French Canadian youth already supporting his widowed mother and invalid stepsister was no match for her, in the opinion of the reverend.

Dumaine was twenty-nine and Bessie Thomas only eighteen, but they fell deeply in love. Aunt Mary Thomas in Boston was romantically sympathetic.

Elizabeth Thomas and Frederic C. Dumaine were married on April 13, 1895, at Mary Thomas' apartment in the old Hotel Guilford on Dartmouth Street, Boston. Uncle Richard Olney gave the bride away. T. Jefferson Coolidge's wedding present was a collar of pearls and rubies made in Paris. Dumaine's gift to his bride was a beautiful saddle horse and Aunt Mary gave her a habit of blue broadcloth, skirted to drape over a sidesaddle.

The next twenty years were the happiest of Dumaine's life. T. Jefferson Coolidge, who had kept a diary from 1857, commended the practice to his protégé. When Dumaine began the first volume in 1904, he made his marriage its starting point:

> On the 13th of April, 1895, I married Elizabeth Thomas. This was the turning point in my life. It brought me the happiness of a home life, gave the companionship of a true woman, which filled me with responsibility and ambition; and from that time I commenced to know life as it is. My future success, if there be any for me, dates from that event.

Their first home was a simple one near the railroad tracks in Concord. The rent was $25 a month. Dumaine was still supporting his mother and stepsister in Cambridge.

22

F.C. and Bessie, circa 1905

During their courtship and early years of marriage, Bessie was teaching Fred to ride horseback. She herself had been used to horses from childhood. He soon became as keen about riding as she. With his marriage began his invariable pattern of riding every morning before breakfast. As the children came along, they would join the morning ride.

Altogether, the children numbered seven. They soon acquired nicknames. First came Mary, named for Aunt Mary Thomas, but always known as either Polly or Jackie. She was born on April 19, 1897.

Rapid promotion with increases in salary enabled Dumaine to buy, in 1899, a small, shingled house on Garfield Road, Concord. Born in this house were Elizabeth (Betty), January 3, 1900; Harriet (Hatsie), March 12, 1901; Frederic C., Jr. (Buck), September 5, 1902; Cordelia (King), February 17, 1907; Christopher, April 6, 1910; and Thomas Park, whose name was legally changed to Pierre (Spike), August 21, 1912. Except for Cordelia, all the children were tall like their mother; Cordelia bore more resemblance to Dumaine's mother, for whom she was named.

Dumaine's mother died of an abscess in her throat on June 23, 1900, shortly before her sixty-ninth birthday. She had lived in the Cambridge home at 14 Porter Road that he had maintained for her. From his first earnings in the dry goods store at Dedham to the date of her death, Fred had given his mother one-half of his earnings. She wore on a chain

23

around her neck with a five-dollar gold piece that was the first director's fee he had received. She was buried in the village cemetery at Dedham beside her husband Christopher. Four years later her invalid daughter Georgia joined them there.

Marriage brought out in Dumaine all the French inheritance of his blood. He expected to be the head of the house. He was passionately fond of his young and beautiful wife and devoted to the children as they came along in swift succession. Due to the long hours he worked, he rarely saw his family except for those early morning rides. The children remembered him chiefly as a strict disciplinarian. When they were caught in mischief, they would hear the classic threat, "Wait till your father comes home!" Upon his arrival, he would whip off his leather belt and say brusquely, "Hold out your hand!" Of the seven children, only Betty, by intuition or nature, sensed the real tenderness he had for them and knew from infancy how to cajole him. The others never looked back to the old days in Concord without seeing little Betty beside him, clinging to his finger.

Bessie Thomas Dumaine, by birth and upbringing, fitted naturally into the social life of Concord. On the other hand, Fred was too occupied with business to be at ease with the leisured, literary people who came to dinner.

F.C. at the shore with daughter Mary.

During this period, not only the mills in New Hampshire absorbed his time, thinking, and energy, but, more and more, the aging Coolidge called on Dumaine's loyalty and ability. In 1902, Dumaine found himself in the shipbuilding business because Mr. Coolidge had $2 million tied up in the Fore River Ship and Engine Company, which was in trouble. There were also the Bay State Fishing Company, the Arkwright Club, an association of New England manufacturers of which he became president in 1910, and the railroads. From 1908, Dumaine was a director of the Boston and Maine, sitting at the board table with J. Pierpont Morgan. The same year, he was elected a member of the board of the Old Colony Trust Company.

Frederic Dumaine, under the tutelage of those "Proper Bostonians" Lucius Sargent and T. Jefferson Coolidge, had unconsciously and permanently absorbed a new identification. He was the first outsider not related by blood or marriage to the directorate dynasty to be elected to the high position of treasurer, which in reality and responsibility meant chief executive officer.

No accolade could have been more thrilling to him or more permanently cemented his loyalty than being made treasurer of the Amory Mills, one of Amoskeag's sister mills in Manchester. The Amory Mills had acquired the Langdon Mills in 1887, a merger that brought the number of separate corporations producing textiles in Manchester from five to four. With the merger, the number of Amory employees increased to 1,400. In 1898, Frederic Dumaine became its treasurer.

The "Boston Associates" intended Dumaine's appointment as treasurer of Amory to be a trial run, to test the young man's mettle. His ability was already recognized. He had been offered a partnership with a guaranteed minimum profit of $100,000 a year in the well-known factoring firm of Bliss, Fabyan. The firm provided credit to textile mills by purchasing their accounts receivables, a practice Amoskeag did not resort to because of its strong financial position. Although Dumaine was paid only $15,000 a year by Amoskeag, he loyally told George F. Fabyan, the senior partner, that he could not leave Mr. Coolidge after he and Mr. Sargent had been so kind to him.

About a year later Mr. Fabyan died and another partner, Cornelius Bliss, came from New York for the funeral. After the services he called on T. Jefferson Coolidge at the State Street office. As Bliss left to take the five o'clock train for New York, Mr. Coolidge beckoned Dumaine to his private office.

25

"Bliss just offered me a $100,000 salary to join their firm," he said. "Of course, I was not interested."

"Well, Mr. Coolidge, I guess I can tell you now," answered Dumaine. "George Fabyan made me the same offer a year ago."

Dumaine took over management of the Amory Mill in the year the Spanish-American War began. The hostilities were precipitated by the explosion in Havana harbor that blew up the *U.S.S. Maine* on February 15, 1898. Boston, in those days before radio and airplanes, was unable to learn the location of the Spanish fleet. The city feared attack and not without logic, since the Watertown Arsenal, the Navy Yard at Charlestown, and the Fore River shipyards were all likely military targets.

Mr. Coolidge's complete confidence in young Dumaine was illustrated at the time. He sent for Dumaine, handed him a key, and gave him instructions.

"I want you to remove all the securities and cash from the vault and take them to Manchester."

Dumaine took the key, procured a couple of suitcases, then went to the Milk Street station of the Boston police to secure a bodyguard. He and the officer went to the vault, packed $15 million in cash and negotiable securities, rode in a hackney cab to the railroad station, and took the train to Manchester, where Dumaine placed the securities in two safe-deposit boxes. Following the end of the war, he returned the securities to Boston.

In 1901, the Stark Corporation, another Amoskeag sister corporation in Manchester, was absorbed into the U.S. Cotton Duck Corporation. Prior to the sale, Stark continued to share a close working relationship with Amoskeag. Throughout most of these years both corporations employed the same selling agents. Coolidge had served as treasurer of both corporations. At the time of the merger, Sidney Coolidge, his brother, was Stark's treasurer. Many of Amoskeag's shareholders owned stock in Stark. This relationship was severed when the directors accepted a cash offer of $1,500 per share. Prior to the merger, the book value of Stark was $1,800 per share while the market price was $975. The fact that Stark was selling at approximately 50 percent of its book value is indicative of the competition found in the textile industry at that time.

U.S. Cotton Duck had been formed the prior year through the merger of mills in Maryland and Connecticut in the North, and South Carolina, Alabama, and Georgia in the South. This was one of the first attempts to form a trust in a section of the textile industry. The goal of the 1900 merger was to form a cartel in the manufacture of heavy duck cloth. The rationale behind the move was similar to most trust formations at the time, which was to gain some market power in an extremely competitive industry. However, like many of the industries in which entry was possible, the raising of prices by the trust firms led other firms in peripheral industries to alter their products to fill the demand of the market left by the monopoly pricing. Stark specialized in the manufacturer of light weight duck cloth. It was a relatively simple procedure to alter the manufacturing process to produce a heavier weight cloth. This was the primary reason that U.S. Cotton Duck was willing to pay such a substantial premium over the market price to gain control of the Stark Mills. In retrospect, U.S. Cotton Duck gained little market dominance from either the 1900 or the 1901 merger due to new firms moving into the heavy duck cotton market.

The competitiveness of the textile market in general is an important point to understand. While competition resulted in better prices for the general public, it also meant that, for a firm to survive and thus be able to continue to provide employment to its workers, its costs must be in line with the most efficient in the industry. As more and more textile mills were constructed in the lower labor cost areas in the South, the severity of this problem for Northern mills increased. This was the challenge Dumaine would have to face in his attempt to keep Amoskeag's Manchester Mills open.

THE STARK MILLS, MANCHESTER, N.H.

Following his appointment as treasurer, Dumaine did so well reorganizing and streamlining the production at the Amory that he was able to return $430,000 in excess capital to the stockholders. Based on his accomplishments with Amory, T. Jefferson Coolidge gave him responsibility for another mill complex, this one in serious trouble. Dumaine was named treasurer of the Manchester Mills in March 1903.

The Manchester Mills had an up-and-down fortune in the manufacture of delaines and prints from their opening in 1846 until sold by Amoskeag interests in 1874. At the end of the nineteenth century, the mills were in financial difficulty, and T. Jefferson Coolidge suggested Dumaine as the doctor. He called him into his private office.

"I am about to sail for Europe," he said, "but I hear that the firm of Minot, Hooper and Company have a lien of more than $2 million on the Manchester Mills and may foreclose. We of Amoskeag do not want other interests to control the Manchester Mills because it would interfere with our waterpower rights on the Merrimack and possibly compete with our labor supply. Neither, for the sake of the people in the city of Manchester, do we want to see those mills go out of business. I have deposited $2.5 million in your name in the bank. I want you to purchase those mills for Amoskeag."

Mr. Coolidge went to Europe and Dumaine took over the affairs of the Manchester Mills in addition to the Amory Mill. He redeemed the liabilities to Minot, Hooper and completely refurbished the mills with new equipment where needed.

Two years later, Dumaine was also appointed treasurer of the Amoskeag. One of his first major acts was to merge the Amory and Manchester Mills with the Amoskeag operations. In December 1905, the Amoskeag Manufacturing Company bought the Amory for $1.6 million paying $175 cash to stockholders for each outstanding share, while the Manchester Mills were bought for $3.5 million, or $140 a share to stockholders. Most of the Amory and Manchester stockholders elected to exchange their ownership in the Amory and the Manchester for shares in Amoskeag.

The transaction brought to Amoskeag Manufacturing Company all the cotton manufacturing plants of Manchester, New Hampshire, except the Stark Mills. Much of the credit went to Frederic Dumaine. He made this observation in his diary:

> I spent a lot of time, after my marriage, studying law under my
> wife's uncle, the great Richard Olney [He served in President

Richard Olney

Cleveland's cabinet, first as attorney general, later as secretary of state]. I think I could have passed the bar examinations but I never did. However, in that Manchester Mills business, I handled the contracts myself. There weren't any lawyers in it. Today, in a transaction of that size, you'd have to have four or five lawyers in and pay their fees.

F.C. (second from right) at the launching of the U.S.S. Rhode Island

U.S.S. Rhode Island

C H A P T E R   I V

Setting a New Course at Fore River

Dumaine went into the shipbuilding business because the Old Colony Trust Company and the Coolidge family stood likely to lose $2 million advanced to the Fore River Ship and Engine Company at Quincy, Massachusetts. Dumaine reorganized the company. He assumed the role of executive vice president. Dumaine convinced Admiral Francis T. Bowles, the Navy's chief of construction, to resign his commission to accept the appointment as president and operations manager at Fall River. A quarter of a century later, Dumaine recorded in his diary:

> August 3, 1927: Frank-Admiral-Bowles died today, 69. He was chief constructor under [Theodore] Roosevelt and, when appointed was the youngest man ever held the position. In 1903 I engaged him for president of the Fore River Shipbuilding Company. He was a strong character and a natural leader but not a great success as the head of a business institution. I went to London with him to secure the contract for the Argentine battleships and one, the *Rivadavia*, was built at Quincy.

There was a showdown in the spring of 1904 when the U.S.S. *Rhode Island* was nearing her launching from the Fore River yards. Beside her, the sister battleship U.S.S. *New Jersey*, was half completed and the blueprints for the even larger U.S.S. *Vermont* were already on the drafting boards.

Dumaine, when he took over direction of the Fore River Ship and

31

Engine Company, assumed the responsibility for the completion of the *U.S.S. Rhode Island,* a fifteen-thousand-ton steel battleship. The contract dated from December 1900. The *Rhode Island* was to be 435 feet long, 70 feet in beam at the widest point, and capable of 19 knots, a significant speed at the time. Payment of $3.5 million from the government was conditional upon the ship's launching. As the ship neared completion, a strike was under way.

The strike was in response to Bowles' call for one additional hour in the work week. On April 17, 1903, the Boilermakers Union called for a strike vote. Two thousand of the 2,700 men on the Fore River payroll voted to go out on strike. Following the strike vote, the union conducted an orderly picketing outside the company. However, the remaining 700 Fore River shipbuilders, with the assistance of men from other yards in need of work, elected to cross the picket line and succeeded in completing the ship.

While the men honoring the strike vote were disappointed in the progress being made in the completion of the vessel, they took consolation in the belief that the scabs at Fore River had neither sufficient skills nor manpower to successfully launch the huge vessel.

Bowles devised a plan that he felt would enable Fore River to launch the ship, receive the $3.5 million payment from the government, and at the same time succeed in breaking the will of the strikers. Dumaine acquiesced to the strategy.

Bowles had established relationships with all of the shipyards on the Atlantic Coast during his tenure with the Navy. He recruited two hundred expert shipwrights at Groton, Connecticut. Dumaine arranged for a special train to transport them to South Braintree. From there a barge ferried them to the Fore River yard. In addition, a yard gang of millwrights from Amoskeag were imported from Manchester by a second train.

On May 24, much to the dismay of the strikers, the gates to the shipyard were opened to allow entrance of directors, city and state officials, officers and smartly dressed women. Among the women was Bessie Dumaine, described by the Daily Ledger as "a striking blonde, wearing a blue costume with a corsage of violets, a white straw hat trimmed with black velvet, and a large pink rose."

At 11:30, Bessie Dumaine smashed a bottle of champagne against the steel hull as she cried, "I christen thee *Rhode Island.*" In response to her christening, the workers used their mauls to knock out the wedges that held the hull in place. The great ship began to slide, accelerating until it hit the water. The force of the weight caused the *Rhode Island* to continue until her stern hit the mud bank on the Weymouth shore. Later that day, when the tide was right, tugs pulled her free and towed her down to deep water. The launching was a success.

With the successful launch, Fore River received payment from the government and the strikers returned to work. Following the completion of the *Rhode Island*, the shipyard was operating at capacity. In the fall of 1904, the *U.S.S. New Jersey* was launched. The following summer, the *U.S.S. Vermont*, a $4 million project, was completed.

In November 1905, the same year that the *Vermont* was completed, Fore River finished the steam trawler *Spray*. Unlike the prior three ships, the *Spray* was not built for the government. It was built for commercial fishing and was considered somewhat experimental by American standards. A Norwegian inventor came to Dumaine's office in 1905. He was looking for financial backing for his design of an otter trawler. The experimental nature of the ship would bring F.C. Dumaine into yet a new industry, that of commercial fishing.

While there was some experimental fishing with steel powered vessels using nets to catch ground fish by the British and Scandinavians, the practice was not in use in the United States. The fishing industry was still carried on largely in sailing vessels. Once these ships arrived at the fishing grounds, the men would board dories and fish by hand line or set the twenty-fathom trawler lines with a baited hook every six feet. The method was dangerous. Many men lost their lives. In addition, it lacked the productivity that the new technology offered.

Dumaine bought the rights to the invention for $11,000. He directed Admiral Bowles at Fore River, a former student at the Royal Naval College in England, to contact British friends to design a vessel suited for trawling. The schematics cost $3,000. Another $56,000 was spent building the *Spray* at Fore River. The *Spray* was the first beam-trawler in the United States. It was owned and operated by Bay State Fishing Company. Dumaine was the organizer and treasurer.

Because American fishermen were not familiar with this method of fishing, a foreign crew was brought over to work on the project. They fished for two years ⁓ and caught practically nothing. Dumaine was the butt of native fishermen's jokes. Dumaine's friends advised him to write off the project.

In the fall of 1908, a Gloucester fisherman who had lost his schoo-

33

ner came to see Dumaine. Captain Michael Greene had sold his ship to pay for expenses associated with illness in his family.

"Trouble with the *Spray* is that those limeys don't know where the fish school over here," he told Dumaine bluntly. "Send me out as pilot and I'll show 'em where to catch fish."

On October 16, 1908, the *Spray* returned to port after its first voyage under Greene with a hundred thousand pounds of fish. The bulk of the catch was deep-sea flounder. The mysterious fish was new to New England markets. The few flounders brought to Boston had been thrown away or sold to hand cart peddlers at two thousand pounds for a dollar. Under the direction of Captain Greene, the otter trawler had reached down to the banks where flounders habitate.

What was Dumaine to do with this near worthless catch? He hired a group of young boys and directed them to deliver the iced fresh fish to the leading Boston hotels, "compliments of Mr. Dumaine."

"Tell the chef this is a sample of the best English sole, famous in all European restaurants," he told the boys.

The fish were well received by the patrons of the restaurants and the *Spray* began making two trips a week to the fishing grounds. Mike Greene became fleet captain of the Bay State Fishing Company, the now profitable flounder fishing fleet.

Dumaine built, out of earnings, some eight more trawlers, all constructed at Fore River: the *Foam* and the *Ripple* in 1910; the *Crest*, 1911; the *Swell* and the *Surf* in 1912; the *Wave*, the *Billow*, and the *Breaker* in 1913.

In 1916, a group of New Yorkers organized a Maine corporation and purchased the Bay State Fishing Company. The original stockholders received $500,000 in cash, another $500,000 in preferred stock and still another $500,000 in common stock, while the new company assumed liability for three trawlers still under construction.

Following an initial investment of under $100,000 and two years of unsuccessful operations, the original shareholders made a profit of $1.5 million. In addition, the fishermen employed had both higher wages and safer working conditions. Finally, the Boston market was supplied with this new gourmet food. All in all, not a bad catch.

In January 1909, Dumaine combined business related to Fore River with pleasure on a trip to London. When he sailed to England, Mrs. Dumaine accompanied him. This was the first time in thirteen years that the couple took a significant holiday together. The time seemed right. They had five children. Polly, the oldest, was twelve years old and Cordelia, the most recent baby, was two. They could afford to bring in competent care for the children, leaving Bessie free to enjoy the voyage.

However, Dumaine was becoming increasingly uncomfortable with the general practices associated with the international armament trade. In November of the same year, he made the following diary notations, expressing his views on the expected payments to government officials in order to receive contracts:

> November 27, 1909: Bowles at meeting of Fore River Executive Committee, having landed the 26th from London. Explained he had agreed to pay Argentine commissioners 1 percent. I left for Washington and with Meyer saw the president who ordered Secretary of State Knox to send message to Minister at BA [Buenos Aires].

> November 29, 1909: Notified Executive Committee Fore River could not subscribe to payment of commission. Intense discussion. Referred matter to TJC [Thomas Jefferson Coolidge]. He advised letting Bowles return to London, assuming he would not secure the contract any way and that such a thing should never again be done.

Whatever arrangement the admiral had to make with the foreign commissioners, Fore River did secure the contract to build the *Rivadavia*. This battleship, with her sister ship the *Noreno*, built in New York, was a 30,000-ton ship with a speed of 23 knots and equipped with twelve 12-inch and twelve 6-inch guns. As the *Rivadavia* and *Noreno* neared completion, there was talk of an order for a third battleship to be built.

About this time Dumaine was informed by an associate in New York that a certain individual in the government had told the Argentine officials that the U.S. Government would be favorably disposed if the contract for the third battleship were placed with the New York Shipbuilding Company rather than being purchased on a competitive basis. Dumaine responded by traveling to Washington. His diary recorded the situation:

> Acting upon this information... I took the train for Washington and on Friday morning, after considerable delay, I got the president's [Taft] ear and made him fully aware of the existing conditions, and he agreed that *** should be pulled out if he was interested in the thing; and that it was the intention of the government to take no part as to which shipyard should secure the business.

Five days later, apparently after a flurry of consultations in Washington, Dumaine received a long letter from the White House.

December 29, 1910

My dear Mr. Dumaine:

Immediately after your visit to me the other day, I spoke to Mr. Knox on the subject and he answered most emphatically that he himself notified everybody connected with the State department, or with the letting of ship contracts for Argentina, that he would take no part whatever as between American shipyards; and that Mr. *** was fully advised of his position in that regard, and that he had not the slightest idea that Mr. *** had done anything of the kind indicated in your conversation; and Mr. Knox gave the Department to understand that if anyone in the service took any part in the matter, it would be cause for immediate removal. Mr. Knox was especially sensitive on this point because in years past, he had some interest in a New York shipbuilding company and parted with it because he considered that difficulties might arise which would embarrass him in the discharge of his public duties. Nevertheless, he told Mr. *** what you said to me, and he ascertained from Mr. *** that there is not the slightest foundation for your suggestions or statements. Mr. *** has fully understood Mr. Knox's position and has not taken the slightest part in attempting to influence the Argentine or anyone acting for them, in what particular shipyard the Argentine should patronize in the letting of the contract for the third battleship.

I write this full statement to you because I think Mr. *** is entitled to have from me a statement completely exonerating him from the charge which you made against him to me.

Sincerely yours,

Wm. H. Taft

A year later, President Taft would invite the Dumaines to be guests at the White House, so there was no breach in their relations. In the meantime, the New York Shipbuilding Company, through Admiral Bowles, began negotiations for a merger with Fore River.

Dumaine was not satisfied with Bowles' management nor with his negotiations with the New York Shipbuilding Company. And he was more and more dissatisfied with the political and financial complications of securing international contracts. F.C. and Charles M. Schwab of Bethlehem Steel began negotiations. The conversations were apparently informal and confidential. Neither man left any preliminary records. When, in the spring of 1913, the transaction was agreed upon, the price was four times what the New York Shipbuilding Company had offered a year before through Admiral Bowles. The date of the transfer of Fore River to Bethlehem was June 30, 1913. The purchase was effected by issuing $600,000 in gold bonds at par and $750,000 of bonds at $90.

The decision to sell Fore River was partially based on the excellent selling price and partially on Dumaine's uneasiness in conducting business on an international basis which sometimes resulted in dealing with public officials from other countries that expected payoffs. F.C.'s business creed in that respect is illustrated by a sermon that he would quote to his grandchildren in later years:

> America is the greatest country ever devised by man because in every set of rules, whether it is the simple game of baseball or the Constitution of the United States, in its rules it has a rule to change the rules. So if you want to play the game, find out what the rules are and play like hell. But, if you don't like the rules, change them, <u>but change them according to the rules</u>.

As for building ships for an international market, Dumaine did not like the rules, could not change the rules according to the rules, so elected to withdraw from the game.

Coolidge Mill southwest corner under construction, May 1909.

Power Plant under construction, September 1909.

C H A P T E R   V

Dumaine Reorganizes Amoskeag

As treasurer of a textile mill, Dumaine was the chief executive officer and the liaison between the board of directors and the mill agent. The treasurer's authority and responsibility were not limited to finances but encompassed all departments of the business. The agent was responsible for manufacturing operations of the business. The titles were adopted from the early English mills.

When Dumaine became the treasurer, the agent of the Amoskeag Mills was Herman F. Straw, whose father, Ezekiel A. Straw, had the office before him. Herman's son, William Parker Straw, in turn would hold the position. Thus, for most of the years from 1856 to 1929, three generations of the Straw family headed mill operations.

Dumaine kept the treasurer's office in Boston, since Boston was the New England capital for banking, finance, cotton, and wool brokers. It was also the chief port and railroad terminal, with quick access to New York and Washington, two cities that he visited frequently to conduct business. It was simpler for Dumaine to go to Manchester, when necessary, than to move his office to Manchester and have to be away on Amoskeag business most of the time.

Following the successful merger of the Amory and Manchester Mills into Amoskeag in 1905, the company experienced a period of steady sales and profitability. In 1909, Dumaine built a new power plant and constructed the Coolidge Mill, substantially increasing capacity.

39

Amoskeag was aware of the possibility of constructing these plants in the South, thereby taking advantage of the lower labor costs. However, Dumaine had learned the lesson of corporate social responsibility from his predecessors. On the other hand, the directors were practical businessmen. In addition to having a desirable goal, that of maintaining employment in Manchester, they must have felt that it would continue to be profitable. To be successful in the long run they needed equal labor costs.

One rationale for not building the Coolidge mill in the South could have been to assume that the superior skills of New England mill workers would allow Amoskeag to compete at the hourly rate differential. To this day, critics of Dumaine cite this as a reason why the hourly difference was not a sufficient cause to close Amoskeag in the Great Depression. It seems unlikely that Amoskeag's management would have fallen a victim of this error. Dumaine had already seen Amoskeag's own workforce shift from imported Scottish weavers and Yankee farm girls to include immigrant Irish, Franco-Canadian, Polish and Greek workers. Each ethnic group successfully integrated into the mill setting as a response to the economic incentives.

It is more likely that Amoskeag's directors expected that the white workers employed in the Southern mills and the black workers who would soon follow them would respond to the same economic incentives and soon reach the quantity and quality equivalent of a New England mill worker.

A second rationale for believing that Amoskeag could be successful in this corporate social policy would be to assume superior administrative skills in Boston. This factor, combined with the potential for increased organizational costs operating over a wider geographical area, made a move to the South seem risky. This also appears unlikely, however. Improvements in transportation and communication now made the effective distance from Boston to the South much less than from Boston to Manchester when Amoskeag was first organized.

A more probable explanation for Amoskeag's optimism for its long-term competitive ability was to presume that labor market forces in the South would result in wage pressures that over a relatively short time would bring about near-wage equality. With the advantage of hindsight, this was as unlikely as the two alternative explanations.

Regardless of the basis for the optimism, Amoskeag built the facilities. Critics of the free market system applauded this as an instance in which the conscience of the corporation caused it to make a socially beneficial investment earning "satisfactory profits" rather then pushing for maximum profits. In retrospect, one might question whether this was truly in society's best long-term interest. The future expansion of mill construction in the South would ultimately cause the market price of textiles to drop to a point where Amoskeag's "satisfactory profits" turned into "unsatisfactory losses," due to the labor cost disadvantage in the North. These losses would not have occurred had the firm acquiesced to the greed of profit maximization.

In May 1911, the organization of Amoskeag was changed from a corporation to a trust. The change was motivated as a means of reducing tax obligations. In addition, the twelve trustees, consisting of the former eight directors and four new members, had greater latitude in the management of the corporation. At the same time that the organization's form of business was changed, Amoskeag's capital stock was increased through a five-for-one split. Each of the 57,600 shares of $100 par value common was replaced with three shares of no par common paying $3 dividend each, and two shares of 4.5 percent $100 par preferred. The net effect of this change was that a former shareholder, who had been receiving $12 on an old share, now was receiving a total of $18 on the five new shares.

The significance of the increase in dividends associated with the stock split was that the trustees felt the prosperity experienced during this period could be expected to continue and that they would be able to maintain the dividend payout in the future without dipping into surplus.

In the five years following the May 1911 change to a trust organization, Amoskeag experienced its greatest physical output and employment. The profits were sufficient to pay the dividend increase associated with the trust formation. However, the profit margin, or income per dollar of sales, was beginning to be squeezed by pressure on selling prices as a result of increases in Southern production of textiles due to its labor cost advantage.

Dumaine believed that if Amoskeag were to be successful in continuing to operate in New Hampshire, everything needed to be done to minimize the wage rate differential. One method would be to expand its corporate welfare system. This responsibility was left to W. Parker Straw, who currently held the title of superintendent.

In 1910, the Textile Club was organized to provide additional recreational, educational and social activities for the employees. About the same time, the company began the publication of a semimonthly paper called the "Amoskeag Bulletin." In addition to printing newsworthy information about the activities of the Textile Club, the paper provided management with a means of informing the workers of the increased benefits provided. Finally, the paper served as a mechanism to dispense the Amoskeag philosophy, aimed at generating greater employee loyalty.

The Textile Club organized a school that provided courses in various subjects, including mechanical drawing, shorthand, typing, mathematics, weaving, and automobile maintenance. In addition, the club sponsored both a glee club and a dramatics society.

The company constructed the Textile Field, complete with a stadium. To commemorate the dedication of the park, a baseball game was played between an all-star team from Manchester and the Boston Red Sox. In addition, a bowling league was formed, and a nine-hole golf course was built for the employees. An extensive recreational program was also created for the children of Amoskeag employees. It included a summer camp and scout troops for the boys and a domestic school for the girls. The company also built a playground, complete with recreational equipment and a wading pool, and provided land for children's gardens.

Amoskeag also developed a medical program that was quite extensive for the time. There was an accident department with a resident nurse and the availability of a doctor to treat industrial accidents. The company also provided a visiting nurse to tend to sick employees and their families. In that respect, the company also employed a housekeeper who would assist in the running of residences in which the homemaker was ill. Finally, the medical program provided for free dental care for all of the children of the company's employees.

In February 1912, Treasurer Dumaine circulated a plan to the employees illustrating how a worker could become a stockholder of Amoskeag. The plan allowed employees to purchase shares through a down payment of $5. At this point the company would purchase the share in the employee's name. Thereafter, $1 would be deducted from each biweekly pay envelope until the share was paid off. Any dividend earned during that time would go to offset the total cost. Following the payoff of the loan, the stock would be turned over to the worker. The intention of the plan appears to be twofold. First, it would allow employees to share in Amoskeag's profitability. Second, it promulgated greater loyalty to the company.

An example of one edition of Amoskeag's employee newspaper.

Perhaps the most dramatic aspect of the benefit program was introduced on March 12, 1912, when the company initiated a program for those employees who had been employed for five years or more. For no money down, they could purchase house lots from the corporation. Amoskeag would require neither principal nor interest payments as long as the worker remained an Amoskeag employee. The mortgage would be subordinated to any loan that the individual was able to obtain from the local banks. The subordination allowed the employee to borrow sufficient funds to build his own home with little or nothing down.

If the individual remained employed with Amoskeag for a second five-year period, the company would surrender half of the mortgage for the payment of $1. If the employee remained for a third five-year period, a second $1 payment would totally eliminate the land mortgage. In effect, the employee would acquire the lot for a total cost of $2.

The following year, Dumaine initiated a pension program that called for the agent to nominate elderly candidates with a long history of employment. Upon approval of the board of trustees, the monthly pension was continued until the individual's death.

It is difficult in this day and age to assess the scope of the benefits provided by Amoskeag under Dumaine's leadership. On one hand, Amoskeag could be classified as too paternalistic in the broad mixture of non-wage compensation given to its employees. On the other hand, it is important to evaluate the various programs based on the era that they were put into effect. While company-sponsored stock savings plans are prevalent today, they were almost unheard of when introduced by Dumaine. The pension program, limited though it may have been, preceded the federal introduction of Social Security by some twenty years. Moreover, the Amoskeag program required no contribution by the employees.

The programs for free dental care and home nursing care demonstrated a corporation with a genuine interest in the welfare of its employees. The playgrounds and various youth programs reflect an interest that is usually associated with today's government and nonprofit associations.

Obviously, one intention of the sale of house lots for $2 was to create an environment in which employees would develop a long-term relationship with Amoskeag. However, the program is indicative of the gains made by mill workers. When the first mills were constructed, workers could expect to live in boardinghouses. In later years, the workers lived in apartment houses. Now, under Dumaine's leadership, the dream of owning one's own home was within the average worker's grasp.

At the same time, it is important to recognize that such programs had an intrinsic value to Amoskeag. The programs were introduced to ensure that the corporation would have a workforce that was proud to be associated with the company. Amoskeag knew well that a contented workforce was a productive workforce. This was essential for the company to successfully compete with output from lower-wage-rate regions.

While Amoskeag experienced its maximum production and sales in terms of material in the prewar years, it was during the war years that it recorded its greatest dollar revenue and profit. In prewar years the profit averaged $1.1 million. For the three years ending May 1920 the average was $5.8 million. Such is the nature of a wartime economy. Two incidents illustrate the particular problems and opportunities associated with wartime production.

In August 1915, the Amoskeag Mills were shut down for three weeks for lack of dyes from Germany. Some years later, Dumaine told Frank Knox, "The Germans knew how to make dyes but not how to dye

44

cottons. We took German dyes and made blue shirtings. The only complaint we had was from junk-dealers. They wrote they could not bleach out the blue from Amoskeag cottons."

The second incident began in July 1917, when the War Industries Board was created to set up priorities and fix prices for essential raw materials. Dumaine, like every other manufacturer, was having a difficult time acquiring an adequate supply of coal, which was essential not only for operation of the mills but for heating the mill operatives' residences. He liked to tell of one experience he had in those days.

A New York jobber, Harry Bonties, who was in charge of purchasing textiles for the Army, telephoned Dumaine to say that he needed a million yards of olive-drab worsted shirting. Dumaine said he would come to New York that night to see Bonties first thing in the morning. After consultation with the accountants and Agent Straw relative to costs and possible deliveries, he concluded that he could take the order at 80 cents a yard. He let Bonties open the conversation the next morning.

"Fred, I've already contracted for a million yards, a hundred thou-

Amoskeag was a leader in providing benefits for employees.

45

Amoskeag's flag for World War I

sand from this mill, another lot from so-an-so. I'm counting on Amoskeag for this other million. What's your offer?" said Bonties.

"Well, Harry, I don't want to cut prices, nor do I want to ask a figure above the market. What are you paying?"

"I've paid an average of $1.30," replied Bonties.

"I can't guarantee delivery unless you can guarantee I'll get my coal," stipulated Dumaine. "People have been waylaying my coal in transit. If you can arrange that I'll get my coal at Manchester, I'll let you have a million yards at the price you named."

It was based on such a wartime economy that Amoskeag was able to come out of the war years with $40 million in surplus, much of which was invested in U.S. government Liberty Bonds.

Not all the credit for the manufacturing achievement of the Amoskeag Mills in those years was due to Dumaine, and he would have been the first to acknowledge the skill and efforts of all, from executives to the youngest operative. However, a large factor in the surplus accumulated was Dumaine's ability in sales, purchasing of raw materials, and investing surplus cash. In the dozen years from 1912 to 1925, the income of interest from investments totaled $7 million.

Based on this wartime profitability, in 1920 the Amoskeag Manufacturing Company paid a 100 percent stock dividend on its common stock.

46

The operatives had benefited, too. In 1917, pay raises figured at 15 percent; in early 1918, another 10 percent; in June, 12-1/2 percent. Meanwhile the employees still had the advantage of board at $5 a week and furnished rooms from $1.25 to $3.50 a week in company board-inghouses; rent at one-half the market price for houses or apartments in company-owned property; and the cancellation of mortgages for ten-year occupancy in a house built on land bought from the company after 1912.

In 1921, when 15,000 men and women were on the payroll, the weekly average pay was $16.77. Skilled operatives, like weavers, warpers, and slasher tenders, could earn up to $25 or $35 a week without over-time, while Southern mills had a wage scale of half as much. While the cost of living in the war years increased by almost 100 percent, the wage scale of Amoskeag Mills had increased by 150 percent. In effect, the workers' standard of living increased some 25 percent.

For the owners, managers, and laborers of Amoskeag, these were the best of times. However, Dumaine was not complacent. He observed the expansion of mills in the South which had the advantage of substan-tially lower production costs as a result of cheaper wage rates. Dumaine, like his fellow Amoskeag trustees, had been aware of this fact for three decades. They saw themselves as a New Hampshire firm with a genu-ine interest in maintaining employment for its current workers. In one interview, grandson Dudley B. Dumaine was quick to point out that not all of the credit for the loyalty to Manchester should be given to his grandfather. Dumaine needed the support of the other trustees. Dudley suggests that one reason that the Amoskeag took a different path from New England textile firms that moved their production to the South was because of the strategic importance of Amoskeag to Manchester. Manchester was not just a one-industry town, rather for all practical purposes it was a one firm town.

At the same time, Dumaine and the other trustees were realists enough to know that it was only a matter of time before the increased Southern production, in combination with the decrease in overall de-mand due to the end of the war, would result in the lowering of the price at which textiles could sell and dangerously impact Amoskeag's profit margin.

Bessie

48

C H A P T E R   V I

Growing Apart

Dumaine's circle of acquaintances was constantly widening. He had not the slightest ambition for political office and no desire for appointment to the cabinet or to an ambassadorship. Despite his inclinations, he was brought into the company of many men who aspired to high office. His sincere interest in the welfare of the country, his keen mind and practical advice, and his own compelling personality often ripened acquaintance into friendship.

Originally it was T. Jefferson Coolidge who introduced Dumaine into such circles. Coolidge was an admirer of Theodore Roosevelt. Another director, George von L. Meyer of Boston, was more intimate with and an ardent admirer of President Roosevelt. Meyer was an Amoskeag director in 1904. Meyer also was friendly with William Howard Taft, with whom he played golf at the Myopia Hunt Club. Meyer introduced Dumaine to Taft.

Dumaine's files contain receipts totaling $10,000 which "generously contributed toward the legitimate and necessary expenses of the campaign of the Republican Party for 1908." Following Taft's election as president, George von L. Meyer was appointed secretary of the Navy.

Two and a half years later, F.C. Dumaine received the following letter:

The Secretary of the Navy
Washington

October 21, 1911

My dear Mr. Dumaine:

I shall review the Atlantic Fleet of 102 vessels on November first at New York, and I hope to have the pleasure of your company and that of Mrs. Dumaine on that day. Launches will be waiting at a landing stage, foot of West Twenty-third Street at 9:30 A.M. sharp, to take you to the Mayflower. Luncheon will be served on board.

Very sincerely yours,
G. von L. Meyer

It must have been a pleasure for Bessie and a delight to Dumaine that no one had a handsomer wife present. Long, sweeping skirts, picture hats with ostrich plumes or flowers, set off her tall, slender figure, her marcelled blond pompadour, her chiseled features. Dumaine enjoyed her pleasure in the fashionable outing. When he himself was invited to the White House, he demurred unless he could bring her, as the following correspondences illustrate.

The White House
Washington

Personal

March 13, 1912

My dear Dumaine:

If you find that you can come down to Washington some day the latter part of next week, I should be glad to have you break bread with me and spend the night at the White House. Let me know if and when you can come.

Sincerely yours,
Wm. H. Taft

Dumaine promptly responded:

President William Howard Taft

March 16, 1912

My dear Mr. President:

It will give me the greatest pleasure, as you can well imagine, to go to you Friday, Saturday, or Sunday of next week. Will you be good enough to let me know which day will be most convenient, and may I bring Mrs. Dumaine?

Sincerely yours,

F. C. Dumaine

To which Taft replied:

The White House
Washington

March 17, 1912

My dear Mr. Dumaine:

We shall be delighted to see you and Mrs. Dumaine on any day most convenient to you — Friday, Saturday, or Sunday. We are going to the opera on Saturday night and perhaps it might be pleasant for you to come then.

Let us know when you arrive and we will send to the station for you.

Sincerely yours,
Wm. H. Taft

Dumaine's response to this second invitation is even more surprising, demonstrating his lack of desire to humor the president and his devotion to his own children.

March 19, 1912

My dear Mr. President:

We are planning to leave New York on Friday, reaching Washington on the train over the Pennsylvania Road, due at 3:15.

It was most kind of you to suggest Saturday night and the opera, and it is a great temptation, but as we have a very large family of small children and this is home week from school, it is rather essential we should be back on Sunday.

I am looking forward to this opportunity of seeing you with the greatest anticipation for, certainly, these are perilous times and require most perfect teamwork.

I have been watching each one of your receptions here with the greatest interest, and the enthusiasm and affection the people are showing is the greatest satisfaction to me.

Mrs. Dumaine heard your address before the [Massachusetts] legislature yesterday and says it was perfectly splendid. I was not in New Hampshire, preferring to allow the natives a free hand, but I think every possible arrangement has been made for your trip there and I know you will be pleased with the result.

With kind regards, believe me, as always

Most devotedly yours,

F. C. Dumaine

The reader might question whether Mrs. Dumaine approved of her husband's decision to cut short the White House visit to be at home in Concord for Sunday with their children. In retrospect this could be the first sign of the rift developing in his marriage. He personally cared nothing for high society life; he hobnobbed daily, at luncheon or in directors' meetings, with important figures of national life of his day; he was neither educated in nor fond of music. For him, foremost was to have one day of the week when he could be with his children.

It is easy to contemplate what the feelings of a woman in her early thirties must have been. She was in the midst of returning to social life after years of being tethered to a nursery. Her opportunity to wear a new evening gown and to mingle with official Washington had been dashed. Without consulting her, her husband had refused an invitation to the opera in the president's box in Washington. The discussion surely was lively.

The Dumaines did go to Washington, had tea and dinner at the White House, then went home on the express train to Boston, arriving at midnight so that Frederic did not miss the Sunday morning ride with his youngsters. He was very proud of the horsemanship they were developing.

The elder Coolidge had undergone a serious operation in July 1911 and was handicapped by increasing deafness. More and more he depended on Dumaine. In 1913, Mr. Coolidge made up his mind to retire from financial and business cares.

He executed a deed of trust, committing his millions for the rest of his life, his children's lives, and until the fiftieth birthday of the youngest grandchild, to the stewardship of Frederic C. Dumaine and Philip Dexter as the original trustees.

Dumaine's friends and business associates found Frederic cordial, generous, understanding, and stimulating. Most of his friendships were lifelong. Office executives, personal secretaries, grooms, gardeners, and chauffeurs remained in his employ for forty, even fifty, years.

He was not as successful in marriage, however, and to the pangs of an upcoming separation and divorce was added his genuine bewilderment as to the causes of the failure. Divorce in that era was so unusual that it evoked social condemnation. The experience would leave a permanent scar on the personality of a proud and sensitive man.

There was the slow and bitter realization that the woman he loved was no longer "in love" with him. There was the strain of "keeping up appearances" for the sake of the children and the community. Above all, there was, for Dumaine, the plunge into the emptiness of the home he had worked so hard to maintain. Underneath it all was a gnawing self-analysis to discover why he had failed to keep the loyalty and affection of his beautiful wife. Added was the difficult daily challenge of a father to rear seven children of whom F.C. would eventually be awarded custody.

Dumaine would never be the same after the divorce. He developed an abrupt and coarse manner. It was his unconscious defense against the feeling that his Bessie and her social world had repudiated him because of his proletarian birth and his lack of formal education. Beneath this brusque exterior, he tried to conceal the heart that remained as passionately affectionate, as broadly generous, as innately understanding, as ever. Those who retained, and those who gained his friendship in later years, knew that his rough exterior and his profanity were only a bluff.

Perhaps the rift between Dumaine and Bessie was inevitable. The Reverend Heizer would probably have claimed that he had foreseen it when he opposed their marriage in 1895. The eleven years of difference in their ages became increasingly important. Perhaps she was too young in the beginning to make friends with his aging mother or with his stepsisters. He might have been too old, too concentrated on the heavy demands of his business, to slip easily into the new circle of friends she made in Concord.

Bessie Thomas Dumaine emerged from fourteen years of consecutive childbearing as a mature woman of thirty-two, strikingly beautiful, and indoctrinated with the feminist spirit of her contemporaries. She found herself married to a millionaire nearing forty-five, immersed in business problems and responsibilities, and conservative in outlook and politics.

The Dumaines were not the only couple to feel the tensions of those times. Households across the country in 1912 were divided in the three-cornered ideological conflict between stand-pat Republicans, traditional Democrats, and surging Progressives, symbolized by William Howard Taft, Woodrow Wilson, and Theodore Roosevelt. There was no doubt where Dumaine stood; he had been and remained the loyal supporter of Taft.

Not even the trip Dumaine had arranged for her at the White House could shake Bessie Dumaine's allegiance to the feminist cause. The town of Concord where the Dumaines voted, although predominantly conservative, had a militant, small group of suffragists who insisted on holding an unofficial election in protest at being denied the ballot, and Bessie Dumaine was one of the leaders. Her husband objected, protested. She persisted. High-spirited as the horses she rode, Bessie Dumaine was spurred to open demonstration by her husband's disapproval. When the suffragists staged their big parade in Boston on May 2, 1914, she marched up Beacon Hill bearing the American flag at the head of the parade. The Boston Globe article covering the parade stated:

> ...Margaret Foley was conspicuous at the head of the line carrying another suffrage banner, and Mrs. Frederic C. Dumaine of

Concord, carrying Old Glory, marched at the side of Miss Foley...
the women marchers started to sing with a vim their new battle
hymn [to the tune of "It's A Long Way To Tipperary"].

It's a long way to women suffrage:/It's been a long way to go./
It's been a long way to women suffrage/By the straightest way
we know./Then it's good-bye to old traditions;/Farewell, doubt-
ers, dear;/It's a long way to women suffrage; but it almost is
here.

A copy of the article and all other articles relating to Bessie's suffragists' activities remained in Dumaine's files until his death. The reader
may draw conclusions as to F.C.'s reaction upon reading the report.

The Boston Sunday Post of December 27, 1914, ran a feature article
covering Mrs. Dumaine's views of child rearing and the suffragist movement. Regarding the raising of children, she was quoted as saying:

Many children are killed by love. The children of the affluent
are healthy because they are not coddled. The children of the
artisan are given a "fine Time," but they die young compara-
tively speaking. The mother who worships her child is killing it
by inches through indulgence. Don't coddle!

Bessie's gave these views on the suffragist movement and the role of
women:

An argument against suffrage is that it will ruin the home. My
argument is that the men are not getting what they deserve
from the women. Women should be expected to think on serious subjects. They should discuss and vote on important issues.

When women realize these things, they will appreciate the better their duty to their children and how best serve them in
infancy so that when they are men and women they will forever rise up and call them blessed.

The January 1, 1915, Boston Record ran the following article with
the headline "Mother of Seven Children Works for Suffrage Cause."

Mother of seven children first and suffragist afterwards, Mrs.
Frederic C. Dumaine of Concord was the central figure at the
opening of the new suffrage shop on Boylston St., which at-
tracted a large number of women prominent in society and
professional circles of Greater Boston.

Mrs. Dumaine began the New Year by devoting part of her
time to selling goods for the suffrage cause. Leading suffragists
are proud to point to this woman as a refutation of the claim

SUFFRAGISTS WIN SIXTY-YEAR BATTLE

House, by Vote of 196 to 33, Sends Question to the Voters—Flag Raising Follows Debate and Parade Through Streets

PARADE OF THE VICTORIOUS SUFFRAGISTS, THEIR TRIUMPHAL MARCH FROM THE STATE HOUSE, AFTER THE LEGISLATURE HAD PASSED THE EQUAL SUFFRAGE BILL, TO THEIR HEADQUARTERS IN COPLEY SQUARE.
The front rank (left to right) are Mrs. Frederick C. Dumaine of Concord, Miss Minnie Mulry of Revere, Mrs. C. S.

From a 1914 Boston Globe

that when women enter the "vote for women" realm their homes are neglected. She has seven children, and in addition to being able to find time to help along the "cause," she is able to devote the fullest attention to her home and children.

A number of other well-known women were seen behind the counters disposing of the various wares for sale, which included suffrage novelties, literature and fancy goods.

On Sunday March 21, 1915, a full-page drawing titled "Society

Women Who are Fighting for Suffrage" was run in the Boston American. Bessie was one of eleven women depicted.

Matters between F.C. and Bessie came to an open break in 1916. Bessie took an apartment in Cambridge and a summer cottage on Cape Cod. F.C., preferring to keep the family name free of gossip and hopeful for her return, persuaded his editor friends to keep mention of it from the newspapers.

On June 6, 1919, a decree was granted to Bessie. The decree became final in December. Friends did their utmost to bring about a reconciliation. Meanwhile, Bessie became a resident of Santa Barbara, California.

The divorce was filed in Middlesex Probate Court at Lowell, Massachusetts, with alimony of $10,000 a year. Two years later Bessie petitioned the court for an increase in alimony, deposing that her husband's annual income was $150,000 and that he was worth "at least $2 million." This suit was settled out of court, with Dumaine making provision for a life income for his first wife, irrespective of her second marriage.

By 1921, following the resolution of the petition to increase the alimony, Fred Dumaine resigned himself to the knowledge that the break was final. While the two youngest children remained with Mrs. Dumaine during the separation, ultimately Dumaine was guardian of the seven children and continued to make his home with them in Concord. He kept up the customs, begun in 1897, of Sunday night suppers and of open house for family and friends at Concord on Thanksgiving Day with a suckling pig of his own raising as the main dish. It was not easy for a man, and a busy man, or his young daughters, to manage a large household of children and servants. Dumaine's mind went back wistfully to childhood memories of his mother's housekeeping.

One Monday morning, going in through the kitchen after leaving his horse at the stables, Dumaine overheard the cook complaining that the children had left the frying pan in which they had cooked scrambled eggs for Sunday night supper soaking overnight for her to wash.

"God damn it," exploded Dumaine. "My mother said that pans in which eggs had been cooked should always lie left to soak overnight. Now you clear out! Pack your trunk and be out of this house in an hour. Here's your wages! Get out!"

The oldest daughter was nineteen, the youngest boy only four when the separation began. In the years to come, with all his business correspondence and demands on his time, Dumaine would write weekly letters to the children away in boarding school. These letters show his affection for and pride in his children and his efforts "to bring them up right" and to be close to them as a parent. He particularly worried that his growing affluence might affect their disposition for study, work, and service to humanity. He chose excellent schools for them, but their pocket allowance was invariably less than that of their schoolmates.

Dumaine created one of the classic "spendthrift trusts" in which he had been tutored by such men as Richard Olney, T. Jefferson Coolidge, and Philip Dexter. From 1920, Frederic Dumaine's personal money went into the trust known as DUMAINES. It was "a Voluntary Association" under New Hampshire laws, dated July 31, 1920, "to continue for twenty-one years after the death of the last survivor of the original signers and of their children living at the time of signing." At the expiration of the trust, distribution was to be made to the legitimate descendants of the children of Frederic C. Dumaine. In establishing the trust, Dumaine wanted to ensure that the family would not fall prey to the New England saying "From shirt-sleeves to shirt-sleeves in three generations."

In the unlikely event of there being no such descendants, one-half of the trust was to be given to Harvard College, the other half to be administered for the education of the children of Manchester, New Hampshire, or the State of New Hampshire. A board of trustees administered DUMAINES, they being required to add one-half of the annual income to principal, the other half being distributed at their discretion to the Dumaine family.

At the time of its formation, the value of the trust was $1.07 million. Of this total, $773,000 was in shares of Amoskeag Company. While this amounted to 72 percent of DUMAINES trust, it represented only about 3 percent of the shares of Amoskeag stock outstanding. While Dumaine was clearly the chief executive officer of the company, by no means was he a majority stockholder.

The children's relations with their father varied with their personalities. "I was afraid of my father as a boy," recalls his son Chris, "but one day, when he had me in his library for a blistering bawling out, I happened to turn as I left at the door, and caught him smiling, a twinkle in his eye. I suddenly realized that the tongue-lashing was an act — his idea of a proper parental procedure.

"What really brought him and me to an understanding was the morning I came into the stable yard just as his horse had been acting up. Dad had the reins close-held and was punishing the horse with his whale-

58

bone crop. He was so furious he did not hear me come up behind him until I snatched the crop on its back-swing and broke it in bits over my knee. Then I grabbed the reins and led the horse away. Dad turned without a word, went into the house, took the train to his office as usual. Next day in the mail came a letter he had written at the office. Just one word. 'Thanks.'"

Dumaine taught all the youngsters to ride, on ponies at first. Every morning, all who were at home were expected to get up and ride with him before breakfast. Betty, Cordelia, Buck, and Pierre excelled in horse-manship. Dumaine never rode with the hunt, but he would ride out proudly to watch his children set out with the hunt or attend horse shows to see them win ribbons. He was a devoted and proud father.

Three portraits in oils that Dumaine commissioned illustrate the domi-nant happy memories of his life. In his bedroom hung the large can-vases of his father and mother, painted from old daguerreotypes. In his office was the fine portrait of T. Jefferson Coolidge.

The ideals of service he instilled led two daughters, Polly and Betty, to serve overseas with the Red Cross, one in World War I, the other in World War II; two (Betty and Harriet) would qualify as registered nurses; Harriet and Cordelia would serve as schoolteachers; and Harriet would work at Dr. Wilfred Grenfell's mission in Labrador. All three of his sons were sent to work for experience in a mill or factory.

In 1917, Dumaine worried constantly about his oldest daughter, Polly, whom he often addressed as Jackie. "Cable at once if all well with you. No letters for seven weeks" was a wire that expressed his anxiety when she sailed through the submarine zone to England with the Massachu-setts General Hospital unit. In 1918 he cabled:

> American newspapers the last few days have been full of head-
> lines regarding German raids upon English hospitals... anxious
> to have some word of your safety.

At the same time, his oldest son Buck, although only sixteen, was eager to leave school to enlist. Dumaine had a hard time holding him down and agreed to his going to Plattsburgh in 1918 to train with a cavalry unit. The November Armistice ended his anxiety.

It was about this time that Dumaine wrote a note to his oldest son, Buck, to be delivered in the event that F.C. met a premature death. When Buck finally received the note, he had it framed as a reminder of his role as head of the family's next generation. The note read as follows:

59

F.C.

My dear Buck ⁓ If this [note] is ever handed to you by Dr. Houghton, it will be when a great responsibility has come to you. With Polly far away, I want you to stick to Betty and Hatsie to help them to carry on the work of building up a respectable and effective family.

You must be their protection.

Do your duty, old man, to your brothers and sisters. Keep this letter to your own self and if you are ever tempted by any one to leave the girls, read this over and see what Dad had in mind.

Mold yourself into a truthful, honest, hard-working man.

When you have questions to decide, do it with thought and deliberation and never let impulses govern you.

Play the game hard and if the time ever comes when you want to select a wife, do it with the greatest care.

Remember, a good family counts in a man's life and if you are clean and decent you are entitled to any woman.

Be a credit to me Fred for the love we have for each other and remember always. ⁓ Dad

In the summer of 1918, Dumaine sent Buck to work in the Amoskeag Mills, just as Lucius Sargent had sent him to Manchester thirty years earlier. Dumaine was convinced of the importance of genuine experience on a job in the formation of young men for a career. He was not yet convinced that a college education was necessary.

In his mid fifties, Dumaine looked back on the beginnings of his own career and forward to the day when his son might be to him the right hand Dumaine was to "Grandpa Coolidge."

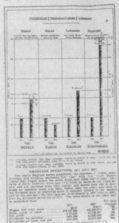

C H A P T E R   V I I

Labor Unrest at Amoskeag

In 1880, when Dumaine went to work for the Amoskeag Mills, the average American woman's dress required from eighteen to twenty yards of material; skirts swept the ground; sleeves came to the wrist and ballooned in leg o' mutton pattern. The fashion of those times kept the spindles whirling, looms thumping at Amoskeag and many other mills. As late as 1913, women's preference for the quality ginghams and cotton textiles of the Amoskeag label meant full employment for the workers and 10 percent dividends for the stockholders.

After the First World War, abbreviated skirts to knee length, the straight silhouette, and chopped-off sleeves reduced the fabric required for a dress to seven yards. Higher incomes resulted in people substituting silk stockings in place of cotton or lisle. New rayon fabrics began to compete with the tried-and-true gingham or cotton of the past.

The declining market in textiles was compounded for Northern mills by the fact that the mills in the South, with wage rates substantially lower, were not only able to compete for the declining market, but were expanding their plants to take advantage of what was to them still a profitable market. The effect of this was to add to the supply of goods, further depressing the price.

The Amoskeag directors had long been aware of the cost advantage of the South. In 1886, the company records show that when the Jefferson Mill was constructed, T. Jefferson Coolidge knew that as an alternative the mill could have been built in the Carolinas. At the time, the management of Amoskeag was praised for its concern for the laborers of Manchester. F.C. Dumaine continued this practice when he built the Coolidge Mill in 1909. Dumaine had been trained by his predecessors in the concept that Amoskeag was a Manchester firm and should remain so.

After World War I, the financial climate changed dramatically with the cessation of war orders. The national income of the United States declined sharply, from $75 billion in 1920 to $59 billion in 1921. Seven million demobilized veterans or defense workers were competing for jobs. Housewives, feeling the pinch in the pocketbook, cut down on purchases. Government experts and industrialists alike were convinced that swollen war wages must drop back to meet market conditions. The National Railroad Labor Board recommended wage cuts. Railroad employees went on strike. The steelworkers had struck in 1919. The same year the clothing workers of New York went on strike. The police of Boston went on strike. Textile workers were not exempt.

In ninety years, the Amoskeag Mills had known but one strike and that, in 1886, a wildcat walkout of a hundred men, was settled in two weeks. In 1912, during the violent strike in textile mills of Lawrence, Massachusetts, Amoskeag operatives had stayed at their machines. The welfare program pioneered by Dumaine when he became treasurer, the health services, educational and recreational opportunities, housing benefits and pensions contributed significantly to the peaceful relations between management and labor.

However, by 1920 this program was being sneered at by labor leaders as "paternalistic." The sense of the times is best illustrated by an oft repeated episode in office small talk at Amoskeag and in the homes of the various Dumaine children. One of F.C.'s grandchildren, Dudley B. Dumaine, offers this recollection on one labor leader's attitude towards Dumaine's employee benefits:

> One of Grandpa's personal friends was labor leader Horace Riviere. When one was in the other's town, they would get together. It was obvious that they talked about the plight of the working man, as well as business problems. One such conversation got in to what AMC had, and continued to do, for its people. The list was long. Apparently Grandpa was very pleased in listing it. When he was done, Riviere looked at him and said, **"Fred, just put it in the envelope."** Apparently this impressed the Old Man, or the story never would have gotten out.

Dumaine, whose own father had been a factory-hand, had no class feeling. In his management of the mills, he had strived to promote equally the interests of the workers as well as the stockholders.

In 1922, Amoskeag workers struck the mills in response to the second wage cut in two years. The trouble had begun by March of 1921 when Amoskeag had to cut the price of napped goods from 37½ cents a yard to 12½ cents to meet competition in the depressed market. Wages at the mills had been cut 22½ percent. The workers accepted this first cut, since they could see that an overall decrease in the cost of living following the war resulted in their being able to maintain their standard of living. However, another cut in the hourly rate of 20 percent was announced throughout the textile industry on February 2, 1922. The rate would be put in effect on February 12. Both wage cuts were attempts to bring Northern mill costs in line with the South. In the 1922 cut, management stated that the hours of work would be increased by 10 percent. Dumaine summarized his feelings on the matter in the following note to his eldest son, in which he also comments on the upgrading of equipment in the mills:

> Dear Buck,
>
> I spent the last couple of days at Manchester... They have 39 new spinning frames running in the Jefferson and about as many more up at the Amory. They are going. . . to put another hundred in the Jefferson... They look first rate and ought to work well....
>
> They had to post notices of a 20 percent reduction this morning and an increase in hours from 48 to 54. That is, they will have to start at quarter to seven and work until five-thirty on weekdays and twelve o'clock on Saturdays. I am sorry to have to do this, but it is one of the unpleasant things life offers up to you.
>
> With the Southern competition very much greater than I have ever known it before, and if we are to live in New England, the rates have got to be equalized, although we shall always strive to pay a better wage and work less hours, which we can probably do and still beat the mark, but with the present existing difference, it would not be possible to go on forever. [Amoskeag was paying 45 cents per hour; Southern mills were paying 28 cents per hour for the same work.]

Today's reader, whose own experience is limited to ratcheting increases in wages might well sympathize with the workers. Two points should be emphasized. First, the war years were accompanied by considerable inflation followed by deflation. The wage increases during these years exceeded inflation. After the second wage cut the weekly earnings in constant purchasing power was still greater than prior to the war. Second, the goal of this second wage cut, which was uniformly imposed by all New England mills, was to make Northern mills competitive with their Southern counterparts. Dumaine, and all other Northern textile men, would have preferred that the Southern wages had risen to equal those in the North. What was of primary importance was not the level but the parity of the wages, if New England firms were to survive and thus be able to maintain employment in a post war economy.

To better understand Dumaine's and Amoskeag's positions on the labor issue, consider the following three sets of income statements for New England and Southern textile mills. In the nineteenth century, there was little production of textiles in the South. The industry in New England could expect to have labor costs equal to about $40 for each $100 of sales. All other costs, including material, overhead and energy, amounted to an additional $55. This left a $5 profit margin, which was sufficient to justify plant investment. Whenever the increases in demand or other factors caused the profit margin to exceed the normal $5 level, competitive forces would cause new or existing firms to expand output in search of these above average returns. These forces would continue until deteriorating market prices caused the profit margin to return to the normal level. See the first set of income statements for the 1820-1880 period.

When Southern firms began to produce textiles, they did so with a labor rate some 25 percent below the Northern mills. This would amount to $30 per $100 of sales rather than the $40 in the North. While the advantage of a trained labor force in the North and the increased demand as a result of the war allowed the North some time to prepare, eventually the equalization of labor skills and the end of wartime production resulted in a situation where the Southern mill owners had the economic incentive of excess profits and were rapidly expanding output. The second set of income statements depicts the economics facing the New England and Southern mills in the 1880-1920 time period.

While Southern mills realized that their continual expansion of output would cause the price to drop, they knew they could still earn a normal profit. On the other hand, as long as the South had a labor cost

Comparison of Textile Mills
Income Statements

New England			Southern		
			1820-1880		
Sales	$100		Sale		XXX
Expenses			Expenses		
Labor	$40		Labor	XX	
Other	55	95	Other	XX	XX
Profit (Loss)		$ 5	Profit (Loss)		$ X
			1880-1920		
Sales	$100		Sales		$100
Expenses			Expenses		
Labor	$40		Labor	$30	
Other	55	95	Other	55	85
Profit (Loss)		$ 5	Profit (Loss)		$ 15
			1920 - on		
Sales	$ 90		Sales		$ 90
Expenses			Expenses		
Labor	$ 40		Labor	$30	
Other	55	95	Other	55	85
Profit (Loss)		($ 5)	Profit (Loss)		$ 5

advantage, the North would face negative returns as depicted in the third set of income statements in the 1920 and later time period.

The 10 percent increase in the hours of work was imposed for two reasons. First, it was a means to increase the Northern mill workweek to approach that found in the South. The net effect was to reduce the average overhead cost of machinery per labor hour. Second, and more important, it was to mitigate the impact of the hourly rate cut. Surprisingly, it was the increase in the workweek that caused the greatest concern for the workers and the union.

While the unions were preparing to take a strike vote, the newspapers of the city were advising caution on the part of the workers. They were urged not to resort to violence. Any such action might lead to the mills being closed permanently. The union's effort was headed by United

Textile Workers' National Vice President James Starr. On February 10, the union announced that the wage cut and increase in hours had been rejected by 99 percent of the 12,150 votes cast.

When the results of the vote were made known, Agent Straw stated that there could be no compromise. He repeated that the new schedule was essential if Amoskeag were to operate profitably. Dumaine went to Manchester on Sunday, February 12, 1922, for long conferences, hoping to avert the strike, but was unsuccessful.

On Monday morning, February 13, the mill gates were picketed, and fewer than one hundred employees crossed the union's line. In response, the mills were shut down. Agent Straw said the workers would be advised when the company should decide to reopen.

Various attempts were made to bring both sides together. Local ministers conferred with Agent Straw to hear the management's arguments as a basis for suggesting a compromise settlement. Manchester aldermen invited both parties to attend a conference that might bring the strike to an end.

When UAW President Thomas McMahon came to Manchester at the end of February, he said the workers would arbitrate on wages, but not on hours. The hours principle would not be sacrificed.

Early in March, Amoskeag addressed a letter to the people of New Hampshire that was placed in all the leading newspapers. Its purpose was to explain the company's position on the proposed change in working conditions. It pointed out that during the past twenty years, while the South's number of spindles had increased over 190 percent, the North had only experienced a 41 percent growth. The primary reason that the South was increasing its share of national production was the labor cost advantage as a result of longer hours and lower hourly wage rates. The letter emphasized that each week of idleness meant a loss of $300,000 in wages.

In conclusion, the company promised that when a sufficient number of workers desired to return, management would reopen. It was Amoskeag's desire to continue to operate in New Hampshire and pay the best wages possible to meet the prices of competitive products. The company wanted peace and prosperity for itself and for the community. To attain the objective, the cooperation of the workers and of all the citizens was necessary.

In response, a series of six statements was published in the same

Strikers at the gate.

papers by the UAW, under the direction of Vice President Starr. The first statement, titled "An Excuse, Not a Reason," said that prior to the February wage cut there had been no substantial change in the relative weekly pay between the North and the South. The union argued that if the North were successful in lowering wages in New England, then the South would respond by lowering its wages.

The union's second-published statement, "Results of Southern Competition," concentrated on Amoskeag's most recent profitability. What it failed to note was the decline in profitability following the war and the future outlook as a result of recent decreases in the selling price of Amoskeag's textiles.

"Vital to Every Citizen," the third letter, contrasted the growth in earnings and dividends relative to wages for the prior ten years. The statement demonstrated that before the proposed wage decrease, wages grew at a rate similar to profits, but that dividends grew at a much greater percentage. This statement, as well as the previous one, may be indicative of poor timing on the part of New England mills' attempt to bring wages in line with the South. If they had waited two years, during which they would have demonstrated losses, their position might have been more favorably received by the workers.

In the fourth weekly statement, "The Real Competition," the union

Samuel Gompers in Manchester

concentrated on the issue of the relatively low wages in the textile industry. They pointed out that the cost of living in the North was higher than in the South. While convincing, it would have been advantageous for the workers to pursue this argument to its ultimate conclusion. In an industry experiencing overcapacity, before there can be a permanent increase in the standard of living of the workers, some producers must be driven out of business. Since the South was willing to work for lower wages, they would be the firms to survive.

In "Life and Death," the fifth statement, the union attacked the lengthening of the work week. It highlighted the historic profit margin in excess of 5 percent. Unfortunately, this was the historic rate and not the current rate that could be expected. As the future demonstrated, without a concession in wages, the operating margin would become negative.

Published on April 1, the final statement called "The Beneficial Interest," again cited past Amoskeag profits. The statement presented the following challenge to the stockholders:

> Are the stockholders satisfied with the division... between those who invest money and those who invest labor? It is right that the stockholders should assume that question, each for himself "For onto whomsoever much is given, of him shall be much required."

The management of Stark, the one remaining Manchester mill not under Amoskeag, like most mills in New England, had adopted a similar wage reduction. The Stark employees were also on strike. International Cotton, the corporation that now owned the Stark Mill, tiring of the strike, was interested in disposing of this location to concentrate its production in its Southern mills. Amoskeag, under Dumaine, purchased the Stark property for $2.6 million.

This acquisition completed Amoskeag's attempt, begun in 1906 with the acquisitions of the Amory and Manchester mills, to bring all Manchester textile production under Amoskeag. This was the first important property addition to Amoskeag since the construction of the Coolidge Mill in 1909.

On June 5, 1922, the company reopened the Coolidge Mill. It announced that other mills would be opened when there existed both a demand for the output and a supply of workers willing to accept the wage rate and hours of work. Only 100 operators reported for work the first day. Gradually, the number increased. By Labor Day, approximately 2,500 of the 17,000 labor force, including the Stark mills, had decided to accept Amoskeag's original February wage rate and work week. Over the entire period, there was little violence, to the credit of both sides.

About this time, Pacific Mills at Lawrence, Massachusetts, offered to rescind the 20 percent wage cut that had been in effect for more than six months. Over the next two weeks, other mills in New England followed its lead. On September 10, Agent Straw announced that Amoskeag would concede on the wage rate but was holding out on the work week.

UAW Vice President Starr recommended that the strikers refuse Amoskeag's offer. He warned that if they went back to work under the current stated conditions, the company could cut wages at a later point and end up winning everything.

During all of the time, there were continual efforts on the part of city officials and Manchester clergy to end the strike. By the middle of November, approximately 50 percent of the company's looms were in operation and approximately 7,000 operators had returned to work. By the end of the month, with 9,000 workers back in the mills, the union called off the strike.

In retrospect, it might have been judicious to compromise early in the strike. The union was opposed to lengthening the work week, but it acknowledged a willingness to discuss a wage decrease. In light of the eventual loss of the hourly wage issues by the company and the fact that due to continuing cost disadvantages the company would never operate near capacity following the strike, one could ask whether a compromise resulting in a 10 percent reduction in wages and no increase in hours might not have been a viable alternative that would have left both parties better off. The workers would have been left with the same reduction in take-home pay as the original company plan without incurring the increase in working hours. The company would have been left with some economy in labor costs that did not depend on operating at capacity. An even more important issue is what would have been the response on the part of Southern manufacturers to a permanent drop in the rate of pay in the North. The fact that the cost of living was significantly lower in the South may have meant that wage decreases in the North would be met by similar decreases in the South. A review of the post strike history seems to substantiate this theory. If this is true, then the demise of textile production in the North was inevitable.

In 1923, a plan for "workers' councils" or employee representation was presented to the Amoskeag workers and, in spite of considerable opposition by the United Textile Workers of America, was adopted before the end of the year and functioned ⁓ with decreasing success ⁓ until the employees voted to end it in January 1933.

Negotiations in 1924 with Dan River Mills about a possible merger in the end came to nothing. The discussions afforded Dumaine the opportunity to make a study of the Southern mills. Although he recognized their advantages of geography, state taxation and labor costs, he remained determined in his resolution to continue operation of New Hampshire's Amoskeag Mills. In view of the depression in the textile industry, particularly the slump in the market for ginghams, New York financial interests were exploring the possibilities of a consolidation. Among those who conferred with Dumaine were Harold Stanley and Frank D. Bartow of J. P. Morgan Company; Percy Rockefeller, Samuel Pryor, and Robert L. Clarkson of the Chase Securities, A.A. Tilney of the Bankers Trust Company of New York; Mortimer Schiff of Kuhn Loeb and Company; and W. R. Fitzgerald, head of the Dan River Mills in Virginia.

Dumaine stood firm against moving Amoskeag's operations South.

CHAPTER VIII

The Second Time Around

His older children had come of age. Polly was engaged to be married; Harriet and Betty were embarking on their education to become registered nurses. Cordelia and the three boys were in boarding schools. Loneliness set in at the Concord house. As with many lonely men, a new interest entered his life. His good friend, Dr. Harry L. Houghton, introduced Dumaine to his wife's niece, Louise Gould, twenty-three years old.

Three short entries in the diary summarize the next happening in the family:

Monday, December 3, 1923: Arrived at the office 9:15 A.M. Old Colony Trust meeting at 11 A.M. Conference, Messrs. Dexter, James J. Storrow, T. J. Newbold on railroad situation. Talked with Mr. Rupprecht [on textiles] over the phone. Left the office 2:10 P.M.

December 3-8, 1923: Away from office on trip.

Monday, December 10, 1923: Arrived at office 9 A.M. Left for New York on the one o'clock.

On the afternoon of Monday, December 3, Frederic C. Dumaine was married to Louise Sylvester Gould by the Reverend Eugene R. Shippen of the Second Church, Brookline. The ceremony took place at the home of the bride's mother. Miss Eunice Davis was the bridesmaid and the best man was the bridegroom's son, Frederic C. (Buck) Du-

73

maine, Jr. The wedding trip occupied a week. Dumaine had conducted business on his wedding day up to an hour before the ceremony. He returned to his office at nine o'clock a week later.

The bride, born at Brockton, Massachusetts, on October 23, 1895, was thirty years younger than Dumaine. She had appealing beauty and thick blond hair. In addition, she lacked the independence of spirit that had characterized his first wife. Her tall and robust stepchildren had difficulty addressing a woman barely older than Polly or Harriet Dumaine as "mother." They soon adopted the nickname their father used, "Weesie."

The new Mrs. Dumaine was in love with her husband and was eager to win the approval of the seven stepchildren. She slipped pleasantly into her husband's friendships with couples older than herself, such as the Galen Stones, Robert Winsors, and Calvin Austins.

Besides the Amoskeag Mills, Dumaine's activities at this time included the takeover of Waltham Watch Company and directorships in the Atlantic, Gulf and West Indies and allied steamship lines, the Old Colony Trust Company, the First National Bank of Boston, the Conveyancers Title and Mortgage Company, the Mail Steamship Company, the Santander Navigation Company, and the Ocean Transport Company.

The task of rescuing the Waltham Watch Company from bankruptcy, which Dumaine had added to his responsibilities the year of his second marriage, encroached more and more on his home life. His weekends were given over to conferences with Waltham Watch executives beginning Saturday evening and continuing through Sunday. He often stopped at the factory in Waltham weekdays on his way home from Boston, arriving late for dinner.

He probably meant to be attentive to his young wife, but he felt his responsibilities to his children, as well. Dumaine had been married but two months when, in February 1924, invited by the Galen Stones for a cruise to the West Indies on the S.S. *San Lorenzo* of the Agwilines, he took his daughter Polly on what the bride may well have looked on as a honeymoon cruise.

One of the most difficult situations of all was the discovery that young Mrs. Louise Dumaine was allergic to horses. She had to give up riding with her husband due to asthma attacks provoked by her proximity to horses. Instead, Betty continued to be his companion in riding.

It was during this period that Dumaine saw his daughter Polly marry

74

and his youngest daughter, Cordelia, graduate from school. She received distinction in both her work and play, and it was a source of much gratification. He made the following notation in his diary:

> Saturday, June 27, 1925: Betty and King [Cordelia] sailed on the *Paris* for three months abroad.

The trip was his graduation present to Cordelia, who had passed her entrance examinations for Smith College, and he hoped a holiday for Betty would ease the tension between her and her stepmother over the running of the Concord house, which for so many years Betty had supervised. Dumaine, too, after the many years he had been alone with his youngsters, could not help taking sides with his boys when incidents arose.

In one episode, Chris and Pierre (as Dumaine had renamed him) shared a bedroom. Dumaine, always anxious to instill patterns of industry in his offspring, had arranged a job one summer for Pierre (Spike) Dumaine in a machine shop. It interfered with Spike's dates with the girls he was beginning to find interesting. The job required he carry a lunch pail from home and eat the noon meal at the shop. Weesie found it simpler to give him a quarter to buy a hamburger.

One evening, Spike was rebellious over his father's strict curfew for working boys. He had a date to go to a square dance. He made a dummy in his bed with blankets, topping it off with an improvised wig from the skin of a rabbit he had trapped in the woods. Hardly had he disappeared out of the second-story window to climb down by the porch, when Chris saw the door open softly and Weesie move toward Spike's bed, murmuring, "Sorry, I forgot your quarter. Here it is."

The figure in the bed made no response, and Chris, also, lay motionless and mum. He saw his stepmother place the coin on the table and then, with an impulse of tenderness, bend to kiss the dark "head" on the pillow.

There was a gasp, and she hurried out and downstairs. Chris, stifling his giggles, tiptoed to the head of the stairs to listen.

"Fred, that boy has sneaked out. There's a dummy in his bed! What are you going to do?"

"Hm? Well, just leave me to tend to it, Weesie."

Long after everyone else was in bed, Dumaine sat playing solitaire in the library, listening for the faint creak and thud that would indicate Spike had climbed safely back to his room. Then the old man went up.

"Damn it all, Weesie," he said cheerfully in the hall, for the boys to hear, "your imagination's playing tricks on you. Spike and Chris are both in there sound asleep."

While Dumaine's diary at this time demonstrated a reasonably pleasant home life, the same could not be said about conditions at Amoskeag. Following the unsuccessful resolution of the labor rate situation during the Amoskeag strike, the company began to experience the losses it had predicted would occur without wage rate relief. For the fiscal year following the strike, the company lost more than $2.8 million.

All his life, Dumaine fought against paying unearned dividends, be it the Amoskeag Mills, the Waltham Watch Company, or the New Haven Railroad. It made him unpopular with investors but he stuck to the principle. Prior to the 1924 annual meeting, he wrote to Dexter:

> October 10, 1924
>
> My dear Phil,
>
> The Southern gingham-makers have dropped their prices two cents a yard. I suppose we should meet them and perhaps cut their stomachs out. Our sales to date of the spring lines total only 800 cases; normally they would be 12,000 and, for the season, 18,000 to 20,000.... The New England [wage] rate is probably 41 to 43 cents an hour; in the South considerably less than 30 cents....
>
> I don't know what the board will decide to do. The really intelligent thing to do is to pass the dividend. I feel about it just as I do when I'm on a springboard before jumping into cold water — after I'm in, it doesn't feel so bad. The all-important thing is to save the [mill] property and paying dividends not earned seems too much like eating up the principal.
>
> Always sincerely,
>
> F.C. Dumaine

Ten days later at the annual meeting, Dumaine presented the treasurer's report in which he stated:

> This report is one of the poorest, if not the poorest, ever presented for your consideration, and I am sorry indeed that it falls to my lot to present it to you....
>
> During the past year there has never been a time when it was possible to purchase cotton, convert it into finished goods and dispose of them on a basis yielding the slightest profit....

F.C., circa 1915

It would seem that so extended a period of unprofitable business must sooner or later end. The management, however, sees no such possibility at present and would be satisfied if the mills could be run fairly full and pay a reasonable wage without a destructive loss.

Every known economy consistent with safety and proper care of property has been instituted and all unnecessary work discontinued.

Fortunately, in the better years gone by, a reasonable surplus had been retained for just such times as these....

The management greatly regrets the necessity of the drastic curtailment of operations, and the impossibility of continuing employment for the greater number of loyal people who for a long period have worked in the mills, but it has been impossible to dispose of the output, and curtailment has therefore been compulsory.

Following this statement, Amoskeag developed a policy of only accepting orders with which it could come close to breaking even. When the company had a potential sales contract that would not cover costs at the current wage rate, management would approach the work rooms in question offering to take the job if the workers would take a temporary wage cut. If the workers accepted, the job was taken. If the workers rejected the offer, Amoskeag would pass on the sale.

Dumaine had made his own investigations and knew he was in for a tough fight to keep the Amoskeag Mills in operation. The Massachusetts Department of Industry and Labor had just published figures showing that in Massachusetts it cost 35 cents to produce a pound of manufactured cloth, while in the Southern mills the cost was only 22.2 cents. It pointed out that some Southern mills were operating two shifts for a total of 105 hours a week, in comparison with the 48-hour week legal in Massachusetts and the 54-hour week permitted in New Hampshire.

On a gloomy autumn Saturday in 1924, Dumaine sat alone in his office analyzing matters for his diary. Stockholders were sullen at his insistence on not paying an unearned dividend. Wage concessions by the operatives had gone only halfway far enough to enable Amoskeag to meet Southern competition in the opening sales for the spring trade. The City of Manchester assessors had not granted a decrease in valuation for taxes. In the last six months of 1924, only 18,000 bales of cotton had been spun at the mills, compared with the customary 80,000 bales. The mills' working capital had shrunk by $4 million.

Dumaine was reaping in unpopularity, what the Harvard philosopher, Alfred North Whitehead, characterized as the dichotomy of men "...required to act on behalf of collective property interests in a manner which, as a man would never have entertained.... In our age economics have swollen into huge corporate enterprises which bring a new form of oppression that wants coping with." Dumaine wrote his sentiments in his diary.

> Saturday, November 15, 1924: The outlook for textiles in New England is, to my mind, most uncertain and to such an extent that, feeling as I do today, should a reasonable bonafide offer be made for the [Amoskeag] property, I am sure I would recommend its sale. Failing in securing an offer, were the property mine, I do not doubt I would cease operations and wreck the concern for what it would bring for junk, **were it not for the sentiment I have and feeling perhaps it would disappoint the men who brought me up and managed the company so many previous years.** I am sure we could liquidate, junk the mills and give the shareholders a sum of money which, if conservatively invested, would undoubtedly yield a greater amount of money than they could possibly receive on Amoskeag stock.
>
> I am writing this statement this particular day and shall be interested in ten or twenty years to know how the result compares with today's outlook.

78

Soon his mood passed and he was hard at work endeavoring to make sales of Amoskeag goods, consulting with the Dupont interests on starting a rayon division at Amoskeag, talking with engineers of Insull, General Electric, and Stone and Webster about flood control and production of power on the Merrimack River, planning consolidation to remove one New England competitor in the ginghams field, and urging, individually and collectively, with his board of trustees that sentiment for the community of Manchester, New Hampshire, required continued operation of the mills.

Dumaine realized that his work obligations made conditions very hard for his young new wife. In June 1926, Dumaine tried to divert her attention by sending her on a vaction to Europe, but he could not be away himself, and he sent his daughter Harrietalong as a companion. A few months after their return. Dumaine made up his mind that Weesie was not going to adjust to happiness in the Concord home that another woman had planned and furnished and that the seven children considered theirs by right of priority.

On May 2, 1927, he purchased for Weesie a house on Farmers Row, Groton, a hundred acres of farm land, meadow and woodland, ending along the bank of the Nashua River.

The Waltham factory in its heyday.

C H A P T E R   I X

Replacing the Mainspring at Waltham Watch

In the Fall of 1922, while the strike at Amoskeag was still in process, Dumaine was asked to assume additional responsibilities in yet another business. His friends, Robert Winsor of Kidder, Peabody and Company and Philip Stockton of the First National Bank of Boston, requested that he take over the management of the Waltham Watch Company.

Waltham Watch was originally founded in 1850 by Aaron Dennison under the name of Dennison, Howard and Davis. The company operated in Roxbury, Massachusetts, until 1854, when it moved to Waltham. The move was motivated by a desire to find a location where the dust of city life did not hamper the delicate work required in watchmaking. In 1857, Dennison found himself in financial difficulty. The plant was taken over by Royal E. Robbins, who purchased the facility at auction for $56,000. Dennison remained in the employ as factory superintendent.

After two years of difficult operations under Robbins' ownership, the company began the "Golden Age" of profits and growth. The name was changed to the American Watch Company. The success of the company can be attributed to the excellent progress that the company made in the development of intricate special purpose machinery. The success in this area allowed for the simultaneous improvement of quality through uniform production and the lowering of costs through the substitution of machinery for tedious labor.

81

Royal E. Robbins   *Aaron L. Dennison*

However, like all industries, the entry of new firms eventually had its impact. In his annual report for 1879, Robbins warned:

> In years gone by our main anxiety has been in regard to quality. In the days of inflated money, inflated prices and a partial monopoly it was easy to pay high wages, to use unperfected machinery and yet with ready sales to make money. Now that... the inevitable competition has come with depressed and exacting markets our task now... has become a very different one and much more difficult.

Six years later the name was changed to American Waltham Watch Company, after the city in which the company now operated. Then in 1906, the name was abbreviated to the Waltham Watch Company.

The Waltham, which had a national reputation for producing quality watches, experienced alternating periods of prosperity and depression. By 1921, it was in severe financial difficulty. The company was overextended with bank loans it could not repay. A forced sale of the assets would not have covered the liabilities, much less leave anything for the shareholders.

The firm's equity consisted of 50,000 shares of 6 percent, $100 par value preferred stock, and 70,000 shares of $100 par value common stock. This did not reflect the true value of the firm. The preferred stock was selling as low as $36 a share, while the common could be purchased for as little as $6 a share. Even these market prices overvalued the firm if the loans were to be called in. At this point the banks took over the company and appointed Gifford Simonds, of Simonds Saw and Steel Company, to try to reorganize the firm.

After eighteen months of wrestling with the situation, Simonds resigned, claiming he did not have the cooperation of the banks. By this time, the price of the preferred had dropped to $11, while the common could be purchased for $2.50.

Shortly thereafter, Dumaine received his first indication of his future involvement with the firm. On Tuesday, September 19, 1922, following an Old Colony Trust Directors' meeting, Dumaine met with Robert Winsor, who had designed a reorganization plan for Waltham Watch. The plan called for Kidder, Peabody and Company to issue new preferred stock with the proceeds being used to bail out the banks, provide much needed additional working capital, and, hopefully, save some of the old stockholders' investment. To entice Dumaine to take over the management with no salary, Winsor's original proposition was that Dumaine's compensation should be 25,000 shares of a new class A common stock.

On December 13, 1922, only two weeks after the end of the Amoskeag strike, Dumaine agreed to assume the position of president and treasurer. As might be expected, the new board of directors featured many of the same individuals who served on Amoskeag's board of trustees. In addition to F.C. Dumaine and Robert Winsor, the names of Charles Francis Adams, Philip Dexter, F.C. Dumaine, Jr., Allan Forbes, George P. Gardner, Jr. and James L. Richards were added to the board.

In his book, *Timing a Century, History of the Waltham Watch Company*, Charles W. Moore states "It [the reorganization] was a distinguishing achievement, and the way in which it was brought to pass is typical of financial capitalism at its highest stage of development."

When the value of the inventory was adjusted to its real worth, the liabilities, much of which were in the form of short term bank credit, exceeded the assets and the firm was effectively insolvent. The commercial banks were unwilling to renew the loans and the firm was facing forced bankruptcy. Moore wrote: "The Company was in a desperate situation, and the financial world knew it. New capital could be obtained only in case the stockholders were willing to forfeit a large part of their equity."

The refinancing plan called for the current preferred and common stockholders, wishing to maintain the maximum amount of their prior investment, to subscribe to a new issue of 7 percent prior preferred on the basis of one new share for each ten old shares owned. The common stockholders that subscribed to the new 7 percent preferred issue were then able to trade ten of their old common shares for nine new class B common shares. Preferred stockholders that subscribed to the new 7 percent issue were able to trade in ten old 6 percent preferred for eight new 6 percent preferred. Failure to subscribe to the 7 percent issue resulted in the common and preferred stockholders receiving only two and a half new shares for every ten old shares, thereby losing 75 percent of their old stocks. In this manner the firm raised $1.7 million to pay off bank loans and provide some working capital. In addition 25,000 shares of a new common stock class A at $10 par value were issued. While the original refinancing plan called for this class A stock to be given to Dumaine as an incentive to run the troubled business, it was later determined that they must be purchased, providing an additional $250,000 in working capital. Dumaine agreed to purchase slightly under half, with Kidder, Peabody purchasing a like amount.

On Monday, January 15, 1923, at the Old Colony Trust Directors' meeting, the board of directors for Waltham Watch was selected. That afternoon, Dumaine took the train to New York to confer with Jarvis, who was head of the Amoskeag Mills sales office in New York. Under Jarvis's employ in the sales office was Israel E. Boucher, who had started work in the Amoskeag Mills in 1902. Apparently Dumaine's trip to New York was to see if Jarvis could spare Boucher to free him for a position at Waltham. Following the trip to New York, Dumaine summoned Boucher to Boston. Boucher relates his involvement in the situation:

> Dumaine said nothing of the reason for calling me to Boston. Even on Monday morning he only told me briefly, "I'm tied up. Waltham Watch is bankrupt and reorganizing; they're going to vote on it this afternoon. If you have any customers to see, go out and do it. See me here around four o'clock."

> At four, I was told that the vote had been favorable, that he was going to take on Waltham and he wanted me with him. Still no details were given of the position or the salary. We were to meet for dinner at the Algonquin Club. There Mr. Dumaine introduced me to Waltham's former treasurer, Harry L. Brown. At dinner Brown brought up some question as to future policy at Waltham.

> "Don't ask me," barked Dumaine. "Ask Boucher. He's the new manager and what he says goes."

84

This was Boucher's first indication of his involvement with the reorganized firm. One month after the February 9, 1923, takeover of Waltham, Dumaine sailed for Europe. This incident was not unlike the experience that Dumaine had in 1903 when T. Jefferson Coolidge left for Europe, leaving him with the responsibility of reorganizing the Manchester Mills.

In *Timing a Century*, Moore attributes much of the success in the turnaround at Waltham to Dumaine's addressing the organization of the executive staff, the redesign of the product mix, and the elimination of excessive overhead. In reference to the executive reorganization, he states:

> Dumaine and Boucher arrived at Waltham in February 1923, and took over the management. There was nothing uncertain or tentative about that action. It was apparent to everyone who saw and talked with Dumaine and his associates that the transfer of authority was complete and final....

> Dumaine was conspicuously successful in retaining and using most of the talent in the old organization... he studiously avoided unnecessary changes in Waltham supervisory personnel and that, when changes were absolutely necessary, they were made with the least possible inconvenience to the men concerned....

> The attempt to retain the old personnel did not involve any compromise with the old top management — that was eliminated, root and branch.

On the issue of product mix, Moore states:

> One of the most serious difficulties at Waltham was the fact that the factory did not produce what the market wanted. The World War had contributed to the popularity of the wrist watch, and... Swiss manufacturers set the pace in catering to this market.... It was even questioned whether Americans could compete with Swiss skill on such fine delicate work as the new designs required. Certainly they would not do it for the wages that Swiss workers received.

Dumaine decided to respond to the challenge in the marketplace. At Waltham, more than 90 percent of production was pocket watches when Dumaine took over. He gradually altered production until 90 percent of production was manufacturing wrist watches.

Moore's observation on the reduction of overhead costs is particularly interesting:

There was need for economy at every turn, but the administration of the office needed immediate attention.... Economy began at the top. Dumaine himself received no salary: Boucher's compensation was "very moderate."...Salary reductions for top executives and for certain members of the Sales Department were in order, but... no general reduction of salaries was attempted. A large reduction in office payroll was possible... [because] Many of these jobs were abolished at once.

The Accounts Payable Department had consisted of nine clerks, a chief clerk, and more than half a million dollars worth of bills, some long overdue. Instructions were given to pay all bills. Some of the creditors were so delighted to get payment that "cash"discounts up to 10 percent were allowed. When the creditors had been paid, a single clerk could handle that phase of the accounting.

There was a department for cost accounting and production control, but the department, two years behind in their work, did not know what it cost to make a watch. Originally the department had 151 employees [cuts prior to Dumaine entering Waltham had reduced this number to 17]. Under Dumaine's direction, Boucher cut it to a single person.

Other departments experienced similar cutbacks, resulting in the elimination of 92 jobs and a savings of $1,000 a day. Lest the reader assume that these cuts might have a negative impact on the well-being of the organization in the long run, Moore points out:

He [Dumaine] had a facility for closely coordinating all the activities of the business in terms of industrial finance. The problems were intricate and complex, but the method of solution was simple.

The Dumaine management was proud of the absence of any "system" of control. There were no charts, no voluminous reports, no bulky files of forms and records. But if one wished to know any of the essential figures [since 1923] of performance or cost, he could find them in a series of some half-dozen looseleaf books, indexed for easy reference. The entire set, [eventually] covering twenty-one years of operation, would fill about the top drawer of a standard desk. The current data covered but a few sheets of paper. These were the bare essentials, the vital statistics of the business. Special reports were prepared as required, but no data were collected regularly unless they were of constant and important use. The records were simple, brief and direct.

The Dumaine family's folklore on the subject emphasizes both the success of the downsizing and one interesting aside relative to Dumaine's order to reduce the cost accounting department to one person.

Boucher cautioned, "Yes, Mr. Dumaine, but sir, I will not be able to comply with the IRS tax forms as they require an accurate inventory, and they will reject anything we will send them without one." Dumaine responded, "You let me worry about that. Simply send the agents to me when they come."

At the end of two years under Dumaine's control, Waltham showed a significant profit even after writing off a substantial amount of useless inventory. The company filed its tax return and submitted a check for the tax obligation on the profit.

As Boucher had predicted, the IRS agents made a call on him inquiring about the tax return. When Boucher informed F.C. that the agents were questioning the return, Dumaine simply said "Bring 'em down." When the agents entered Dumaine's office, he asked, "What can I do for you?" The lead agent stated, "Well, Mr. Dumaine, the tax return Waltham Watch filed doesn't comply with regulations relative to the accounting for inventory."

F.C. looked up and inquired, "Did you receive a check for taxes due?" "Yes, sir," was the response. Dumaine asked, "When was the last time you received a tax payment from Waltham?" The agents admitted that it had been several years, which prompted Dumaine to ask, "Did you bring the check with you?"

The agents answered affirmatively, handing the check over to F.C. who held it at his forehead in a ripping position. Dumaine announced, "Gentlemen, you have two choices. First, Waltham will comply with your regulations and I will rip up this check. Second, you can take the check and get the hell out of here."

They took the check.

While oral history can be subject to considerable embellishment, certain facts support the folklore. When Dumaine took over Waltham Watch, the firm was operating at a loss. Relatively soon, through the elimination of overhead, the simplification of the accounting methods and improvements in sales, Waltham was finally operating profitably and paying taxes.

However, this dilemma of turning over a check to the Treasury Department did not come about until Dumaine had first tackled stockholders who were prematurely asking for dividends, and a strike by the workers in response to the company reducing the wage rates of some operators in the factory.

Shortly after Dumaine's management started to show improvements in the operation of the factory, stockholders started calling for the resumption of dividends. In a June 4, 1923, letter to Philip Dexter, who was in Europe at the time, Dumaine summarized his thoughts:

> ...the only safe thing to do is to use surplus cash [generated through liquidating inventories] to reduce the permanent debt. ...When I agreed to take this [Waltham] thing over, it never occurred to me an outsider would undertake to dictate... as to whether money should be taken from the business or not.
>
> To fight one's friends in addition to many other disagreeable things is rather more than should be required of one person and it occurred to me that if dividends were likely to be early considered my feelings better be known before going further. The time to straighten a situation like this is in the beginning and my experience convinces me a manager should be given a free hand in regard to his trial balance, the payment of money out of the treasury, and not forced to part with funds he feels could be better kept in the business.
>
> At any rate, I was brought up in that sort of a school and I'd rather not try to learn new tricks in this late day of life.
>
> I agree with you if the earnings are big and the income more than necessary for the business there is no reason why the shareholders should not benefit.
>
> It is beyond human possibility to make big earnings out of these figures except in two ways: 1st, increased efficiency and reduction of overhead cost. A lot has been done along these lines and there is undoubtedly still an opportunity to do more, but what is needed is $1 million or a 25 percent saving in the cost of operation. Too great an amount. 2nd, to secure a dollar a movement more in the trade, [but this is not possible since] our prices must be comparable with the Elgin Company or we lose the business.
>
> [The generation of cash through the liquidation of excess inventories] is not to be called profit, for so far as it has been possible, not one order for material has been placed, except when absolutely necessary. Also, the sum of $30,000 monthly has been saved in salaries and advertising expenses. Therefore

my position is this apparent extra cash should be paid back to the bank from which it was borrowed.

...it occurred to me if the question of dividends was likely to be raised in the immediate family, it better be understood now, and before getting in deeper, just how I stood on the subject. Of course, it would be gratifying to put Waltham on its feet; but not at the cost of one's principles. Besides, it is no fun working at loggerheads with your associates, and life is too short to do it. The work already accomplished is valuable and has paved the way for further economies. For my part, I do not feel like going on if there is doubt as to whether the funds will he properly applied.... When a board doubts its manager's good faith on such matters, it is time to stop, particularly when one's as old as I am.

Dumaine put the financial policy outlined in his letter to practice that same year when he retired $1 million of the company's debentures. The source of the $1 million was the liquidation of inventories. The eventual rewards of the economies in production and marketing would not materialize until 1926. Eventually all of the $6 million in Waltham debt would be retired, eliminating the interest burden.

Once Dumaine succeeded in temporarily putting the issue of premature resumption of dividends to rest, he turned to the labor issue.

On August 11, 1924, a strike began when 200 workers walked out of the finishing department. The walkout was in response to an attempt to realign the wage rates in various departments that, in the opinion of management, suffered from excessive overpayment to a few positions as a result of poorly conducted rate studies by the prior administration. Moore described the first day of the strike:

The workers of each department left their benches in a body, like volunteers enlisting in a glorious cause. As they appeared at the factory doors, the waiting throng cheered madly and soon there were bugle calls and marching and singing. Women were marching, as many as the men, laughing and singing, "We Ain't Gonna Work No More, No More." Who could resist it? Such confidence of success, such assurance of victory. Who would want to be known as a deserter when these stalwarts returned at the request of a chastened Management? Two hundred, fifteen hundred, twenty-seven hundred, and finally all but a handful joined the marching, milling crowds or, hoping that they might return without loss of caste among their fellow, had slipped quietly away.

The workers had two complaints prior to the new rates being announced. First, wages in general were too low and had not been raised from the depression levels of 1921. Their second complaint was that as a result of the rates previously established by the industrial engineers, some workers in low skill areas were receiving higher pay than positions requiring greater experience and skill. While this second point was similar to the position taken by Dumaine, the workers felt that the resolution to this problem called for an increase in the relatively underpaid areas rather than dropping the rates in the relatively overpaid area.

As might be expected, the workers expressed their feeling of persecution with comments such as, "We think it better for Waltham to have this industry, of which we have so long been proud, perish from the earth than to have these financial pirates triumph and treat their workers like the serfs of old." Having just experienced similar incidents in the Amoskeag strike of 1922, Dumaine understood the passion of crowd psychology.

Dumaine's decision to lower the relatively higher wages was a result of the conditions in which Waltham Watch found itself. It was paying wages higher than domestic competitors and it was losing money. If jobs were to be maintained in the long run, then in addition to economies in overhead and improvement in product line, those wage rates in the factory that were above the industry average must be reduced.

As might be expected, following the August 11 walkout there was frequent discussion between the management and the newly formed union representing the workers. On October 6, in response to one compromise offer by the union, Dumaine made a counteroffer. When the counteroffer was not successful in resolving the situation, the company made the following statement which provides an excellent summary of its position:

> The factory has not operated profitably for years. The present management upon assuming control proceeded at once to try and make it profitable. Every apparent unnecessary expenditure was discontinued and every economy, short of lowering wages was instituted. The results have shown that even with these economies the Company was not able to compete profitably. Wages were the last thing the Company desired to change, but lower rates prevailing elsewhere in the industry made this adjustment compulsory.
>
> Although the Company could ill afford it, yet to show a desire to make some concession for the sake of bringing about peace

90

promptly and future harmony, a 25 percent reduction in the original cut was offered. The offer was promptly rejected by the employees. It is no longer open. The company returns to its original position which it now adheres to.

Perhaps a strike was inevitable before the workers would realize the seriousness of the situation. An October 24 editorial in the Waltham News Tribune posed the following:

For the strike the responsibility must rest upon the Company, not because it was forced to reduce wages but because of the disregard of justice and equality and the crude manner in which men and women of character and intelligence were called on to accept the cut.... For the continuation of the strike, after it has become evident that the wages paid prior to August 11 will not be restored, the responsibility rests upon the strikers.

Following the unsuccessful negotiations in early October, increasing numbers of workers reluctantly returned to work under the company's terms. By the first of the new year, 670 had returned to work. A week later the strike ended. Dumaine made the following notation in his diary:

Thursday, January 10, 1925: Left for Waltham at 3:30 P.M. Last night at a meeting of the strikers it was voted to call off the Waltham strike which has been in existence since August 11 or nearly five months. This action was recommended by the State Board of Arbitration. The strike has been conducted with the greatest amount of vigor and persistency imaginable and over a most extended period. About 10 o'clock this morning, the strikers began arriving at the factory to register for work; during the day more than 800 filed applications. Their spirit was pleasant and agreeable and it looks as if the factory will be able to start up under favorable conditions and we shall have an opportunity to find out if it is possible to profitably manufacture watches at Waltham.

However, when conditions improved at the factory, Dumaine again came under pressure from some stockholders for dividends as the following diary notation indicates:

Monday, February 16, 1925: Went over to see Winsor, Endicott and Remick; had a conference with these people in which I told them I would not be interfered with in the Waltham matter; I felt it was contrary to best interests of the concern and if they felt otherwise, it was best they get someone else to manage the business. Two years had been spent in trying to correct

An adverstisement from the collection of the Waltham Museum.

existing abuses and it was too much to expect a man to go on with that kind of work and feel all the time there was dissatisfaction with the office methods. They said they had no desire to make any change and were satisfied to leave the entire situation in my hands.

Following the successful settlement of the strike, Dumaine quickly turned Waltham into a profitable venture. Through the introduction of economies and the expansion of wrist watch production, the company

92

was able to provide continual employment for its workers.

In 1926, the firm showed its first profit since the Kidder, Peabody reorganization. In that year, the company earned almost $1.3 million. However, Dumaine felt that the resumption of dividends was still premature. Instead he continued the process of retiring the company debt and began repurchasing the company's preferred stock and Class B common stock. Over the next two years he retired approximately one third of both preferred issues and the Class B common.

The following year the company earned $872,000. With this advance the company payed out $240,000 of the 7 percent prior preferred dividends that were in arrears. In July 1 of that year, the board of directors paid Dumaine $75,000 as a bonus for the progress that Waltham Watch had made under his management. This was also in light of the fact that he had not received any compensation for the prior three and a half years. From that date on, Dumaine began drawing an annual salary of $25,000.

In 1928, a third successful year, Waltham was earning $807,000. In that same year, Waltham became current on both preferred stock issues and was able to declare the first dividend on the Class A common stock.

In 1929, the year of the stock market crash, Waltham recorded yet another profitable year. While earnings dropped to $660,000, this was more than adequate to maintain the dividend levels established in the prior years.

At the end of 1929, few people realized the severity of the downturn in the economy that was ushered in by the October stock market crash. Dumaine could look back at the progress made in the past seven years with great personal satisfaction. Jobs for 2,500 workers were secure and there was continuing improvement with the financial aspects of the corporation. This was doubly satisfying, since his oldest son, Buck, was serving as the assistant treasurer. In addition, his youngest son, Spike, had begun a career on the production side.

Stock certificates of the new and original corporations.

C H A P T E R   X

Stockholder Unrest at Amoskeag

Based on Frederic C. Dumaine's October 1924 report for the Amoskeag Manufacturing Company, the trustees announced that the common dividend normally paid the following month would not be approved. Prior to this action, Amoskeag had an uninterrupted dividend record that began in 1834.

In an effort to offset declining demand for gingham, Dumaine was experimenting with the production of rayon cloth. The new fabrics were highly endorsed by New York buyers. Boston merchants who had examined some of the "rayonized" cotton samples declared they were "the most beautiful they had ever seen." Following this fine reception of Amoskeag lines, conversion was near completion of one of the company's Manchester plants for the manufacture of its own rayon requirements. Some rayon was sold to other mills. Buyers included Royal Little and the Suncook Mills. Amoskeag wove some shirting and other men's wear fabrics from its own rayon.

At the same time that Amoskeag was experimenting with alternative product lines, Dumaine was investigating the possibility of altering the company's financial structure to ease stockholder concern. They were becoming increasingly distressed that the accumulated earnings from prior profitable years would be squandered away through continual production at a loss. On August 7, 1925, the trustees unanimously approved a plan for the formation of a new trust that would take over all of the Manchester plants, receivables, and inventory. At the same time,

95

the new trust absorbed the plants of the Parkhill Manufacturing Company of Fitchburg, Massachusetts. The new trust, which would carry the old title "Amoskeag Manufacturing Company," would also be given $6 million in cash from the original company's accumulated surplus. Approximately 93 percent of the new trust would be owned by the original company, whose name was shortened to the "Amoskeag Company." The remaining 7 percent ownership in the new trust would belong to the principals from the Fitchburg Plant.

Amoskeag Company, the original trust, was a continuation of the original 1831 corporation. In addition to all cash above $6 million, it retained all investments in securities. The total value of cash and securities amounted to $18.7 million. In this manner, Dumaine assured the stockholders that their retained earnings beyond $6 million would be protected from being used to subsidize the current unprofitable operations. At the same time, Amoskeag Company would be a holding company of the new Amoskeag Manufacturing Company, which could be to the advantage of the parent company's stockholders if the manufacturing company were to become profitable in the future. Unfortunately, conditions in the New England cotton industry never improved significantly. While some of the trustees were eager to liquidate Amoskeag in 1925, Dumaine fought to continue operation of the mills. The establishment of a separate manufacturing company was a compromise to the opposing views: liquidation of the Amoskeag Mills and salvage of the accumulated surplus of the original capital invested; and the continuing operation in Manchester regardless of future profitability. At any time in the nearly one hundred years from the beginning of the mills, it had been in the discretion of directors to distribute this surplus as extra dividends. Now, after the long strike of 1922 and a depression in the textile business which had already lasted five years, they chose to do what Dumaine in November had forecast, which was to place their money "where it could receive a greater return than from Amoskeag stock."

The confidence of the trustees in Dumaine's ability was shown by entrusting to his care the management of this capital sum of the Amoskeag Company and was justified by his carrying it through the long years of the depression, paying dividends regularly and increasing it from an initial $16.6 million in 1927 to a market value of $27.2 million at the end of 1951, the year of his death. (The low value during the depression was $5.8 million in June of 1932.)

Dumaine had won his argument that the Amoskeag Mills should

continue operation. He had to accept the loss of the nest egg he had squirreled away for bad times for the benefit of the mills. Henceforth, the treasurer of Amoskeag Manufacturing Company would have to rely on the banks for working capital to finance purchases and payrolls, paying the going rate of interest.

In his annual report for 1925 as treasurer, Dumaine pointed out a few statistics of the twenty years since he had taken the office.

> During this period of twenty years your property... has distributed $23 million in dividends, $154 million in wages besides paying more than $20 million in taxes. In the past twenty years each share of Amoskeag as it stood in 1906 has received $371 in cash dividends, and the aggregate value of the shares which now represent one share of the Amoskeag of 1906 is more than $600.

Frederic Dumaine was completely sincere when he ended his report with the words:

> I hope that the next twenty years will show as good results as the past, by the consistent applications of the principles and practice which have succeeded in improving your property, paying suitable dividends, and putting your company in a position to ride out the worst storm the textile industry has ever known in this country.

The years 1925 to 1927 brought continuing hard times in the textile industry. New England's textile mills lost three million spindles while Southern mills added nearly as many. The Amoskeag Mills had an operating loss totaling more than $3 million for 1925 and 1926 and did not pay dividends on the preferred stock in 1926.

The textile industry was again suffering from a revolution in the world of fashion. Japan, an ally in World War I, had been too far from the theater of war to suffer interruption to its textile industry and was now producing for export cotton fabrics competing with the export trade of Britain and the United States. Japan was also a major supplier of silk fabrics and synthetics, both of which were becoming increasingly popular. Men wore silk shirts and pajamas; women were wearing silken lingerie and silk or rayon dresses.

In 1926, the Amoskeag Mills operated at only 60 percent of capacity and, even so, much of the product remained in inventory for lack of sales. Agent W. Parker Straw was having his troubles with the operatives, who would not accept a temporary pay cut to secure a certain large order that would have given months of employment, and vocally resented surveys in the plant to fix responsibility for deterioration in quality of standard fabrics. Complaints came in from customers. Said Dumaine:

> We received a letter from the O.D. Baker Co., a concern which has used A.C.A. tickings for a generation or more. They complain bitterly because the salvages curled and the finish on their goods was too stiff. It was most humiliating and I told Straw so, at the end of nearly 100 years of producing cloth to have such a complaint from such a concern. I told Straw it seemed to me inexcusable.

The years 1925-26 brought Dumaine problems at Amoskeag. In addition, he was assuming increasing responsibilities in banking, railroad, and watch manufacturing. He had his sixtieth birthday in 1926; he was overworking and it showed, reflected in tensions in his domestic affairs. He was unreasonable and arbitrary about the marriage of his oldest son, Buck. In fact, at one point he declared roundly that if Buck got married, he would disown him. Dumaine's diary records his thoughts on the situation:

> Wednesday Evening Sept 1, 1926: Told Buck until he had shown by a practical exhibit his willingness to do what every man who has succeeded in life has done. That is take up and go through a period of training that will justify the feeling that he is competent and sufficiently dependable to be loaded with responsibility I could not approve his being married. That I was unwilling to load him upon any of the concern [i.e., appoint him to a position with Amoskeag Company or Amoskeag Manufacturing Company] with a salary sufficient to support him before he had demonstrated his worth. All of which gave me the greatest unhappiness and his failure to do what he knew and agreed was the right and proper thing to do was a source of the greatest disappointment to me. He gave me no hope or indication of his intention. My impression was he'd disregard my views and carry on in his own way.

The old groom Tim Splaine recalls a ride the following morning in which he heard Dumaine muttering and damning Buck. In the seven years that the Concord house had been without a mistress, Splaine, a loyal, warmhearted Irishman, had become very fond of the youngsters. Now he spoke out.

"Mr. Dumaine, sir, did that boy ever make you lie awake one night with sorrow? Are you being' fair to him, sir?"

"Damn it all, Tim! Shut up! You're fired!" barked Dumaine, putting spurs to his horse and galloping away.

However, hours later, while Tim was rubbing up tack in the stable supposing Dumaine to have taken the eight-thirty train to Boston as usual, his employer suddenly appeared in his city clothes. He had been brooding in the library. Now, with the candor that endeared him to his familiars and removed the sting of his rages, he admitted that he was wrong.

"All right, Tim," he said gruffly. "You're right. I'll go to the wedding. Now, does that satisfy you?"

Tim got through to F.C. The children were coming of age and entitled to lead their own lives. Some 70 years later following Buck's own death, the original September 1, 1926, diary notation was found safely tucked away in one of Buck's books. Whether F.C. gave it to Buck at the time he told Buck that he would bless the upcoming marriage, or Buck found it upon the death of his father, is uncertain. What is clear is that Buck saved it. While it was not matted and framed in a manner similar to the letter charging Buck with the responsibility of leading the next generation, it was preserved for posterity.

Dumaine's favorite horse was Pat Rooney, a mettlesome roan, well schooled in jumping but loving to stretch out in a fast gallop. Dumaine himself did not follow the hounds or ride in races. Once, and once only, he told Splaine to set up the hurdles in the paddock and he rode Pat Rooney at them. He did five four-foot jumps cleanly. He was satisfied. He had proved to himself he could do it. He never did it again.

Early on the morning of July 6, 1927, Splaine brought Pat Rooney around at six o'clock and he and Dumaine set out through the woods toward the river. Pat Rooney saw a clear stretch and sped up. Tim, following on Jake, heard a resounding snap and a curse.

"By God, Tim, I've broken my leg!" Dumaine called.

The broken stub of a branch had snagged his stirrup. Both bones of his leg had broken cleanly under the impetus of the horse's rush. Dumaine lifted the leg over the saddle horn and Tim led the two horses home and carried his master to a couch.

"Sure an' I knew I must get the boot off before the leg swelled," Tim would recount. "Well I knew he'd skin me alive if ever I cut one of those boots that cost him seventy-five dollars in London. So I took hold an' pulled."

Dumaine's rugged stoicism endured this first aid and the panic of the awakened household. He insisted he would not go to a hospital; they must take him to Dr. Russell MacAusland in Boston. The leg was splinted on a board. He was carried to the automobile, made the forty-mile ride to Boston. He chomped on a cigar through the x-rays, setting of the fractures, and application of a cast. The doctor then suggested again that he go to a hospital.

"No, by God! " said Dumaine. "I'm going home. My Betty's a nurse and she'll know how to look after me."

For the sake of the Amoskeag Mills he could not be hospitalized. He, better than anyone else, knew what was in the mind of speculators. For five months he had been jotting notes in his diary. He knew that all possible economies had been effected, that the market was showing an upturn, that those who set greedy eyes on some $30 million worth of Liberty Bonds in the portfolios of the holding company and operating company would move soon if they hoped to encompass liquidation. In February of 1927, there had been a considerable advance in the price of Amoskeag, based on rumors that Dupont was trying to buy Amoskeag.

The following month, Nelson News Bureau inquired concerning the speculation in Amoskeag stock and the rumors as to who was buying it. Murray Howe informed Dumaine that he had a customer who wanted to buy the plant at Amoskeag. When asked as to his feelings on the subject, Dumaine stated it depended on what his offer was and how it was made. Dumaine said, "If I did not think it right, I would not even submit it. If I did, I would." He then added, "Unless he was prepared to disclose his principals, our people felt they were not justified in supplying him with detailed information." One week later, Murray Howe reported that his principals were Hemphill-Noyes and Company.

Dumaine was scrupulous about keeping the other trustees informed about Amoskeag. Some were frankly advocating liquidation, among them the Fitchburg men who had acquired stock as a result of the merger with the Parkhill Mill. Dumaine suspected them of selling this stock, hitherto closely held by the old trustees. Robert Winsor, riding to Boston on the morning trains with Dumaine, advocated a sale if the price were right. "If you were twenty years younger, Fred," said Winsor, "we could afford to sit tight and do nothing." Dumaine and old Yankee textile men like George Wigglesworth were not ready to admit the mills could not be operated profitably and they were reluctant to see a great city plunged into the misery of unemployment.

100

The next move of the New York interests came while Dumaine was immobilized with his broken leg at Groton. When Dumaine suffered his riding accident, Amoskeag stock had been quoted from $50 to $60 on the market. In 1935, Dumaine would provide the following testimony to a Congressional Committee about the August activity of the stock speculators.

> Robert Winsor telephoned me at Groton. They got me into a machine [automobile] and I came to Boston and talked the matter over with Mr. Philip Dexter and Winsor and Allen Curtis, who claimed to represent these New York interests. Curtis said that they were going to undertake to get control of the property, liquidate it — he spoke about making $1 million himself. And we asked him what about the city of Manchester and the people who were working in the mills and his reply was that he wasn't a philanthropic institution and if he could make $1 million he was going to try to do it. I asked Winsor how we could prevent them from getting control and he said the only way was to buy the shares, partly for DUMAINES account and partly for Kidder's account.

The Wall Street maneuver was a forerunner of the epic proxy battles for stock control of corporations that would enliven the scene in the second half of the century. It was a new experience for Dumaine because for a century Amoskeag stock had been in the hands of a group of closely knit families who thought alike and acted together with real sentiment for the mills and the city around them. Now, for the first time, stock was available in the open market and outsiders with no sentiment for the mills were bent on getting control to realize personal gain on the liquid cash and Liberty Bonds.

To Dumaine and Winsor, in the finance-capitalism of their day, the simple answer to the situation appeared to be to buy in the floating stock and consolidate control again.

On August 30, 1927, Winsor's investment banking firm of Kidder, Peabody and Company wrote to all its customers, advising them not to sell Amoskeag shares at the current price of $90. On September 8, the Amoskeag trustees issued a circular, signed by Wigglesworth as president and Dumaine as treasurer, along with the other trustees, characterizing the Curtis offer in these words: "It is proposed that you give the purchasers your plant for nothing. Your trustees regard the proposal as inadequate and not for your best interests, and have declined it."

Through the DUMAINES Trust, F.C. borrowed nearly $1 million from

Kidder, Peabody to buy up shares to keep control in the hands of Amoskeag. Since these purchases were made through a loan, the securities were promptly sold following the eventual reorganization. Winsor probably invested a similar sum. In 1936, this transaction was reviewed by the referee in the bankruptcy case, as found in the records of District Court of the U.S. District of Massachusetts, Amoskeag Mfg. Co., Debtor. Referee Arthur Black summed it up succinctly:

> In the summer of 1927 an offer had been made by outside parties to purchase the assets of the Amoskeag Company.... The avowed purpose of the buyers was liquidation.... Dumaine opposed the sale. Winsor, who was also one of the trustees regarded the shares as worth more than the then market value and advised shareholders not to sell. A counter-plan was formulated by Dumaine and Winsor, Dumaine and Winsor purchasing in the open market enough shares of the Amoskeag Company to secure voting control. Their purpose was, first, to give timid stockholders a chance to get their money out of the textile business; second, to avoid control by an outside group whose sole purpose was to liquidate. They obtained all the stock they needed to secure adoption of the trustees' (counter) plan. The stock was in turn passed on by them to Consolidated Investment Trust and to DUMAINES, a similar trust.

The efforts of Dumaine and Winsor were sufficient to fend off this takeover attempt. The newspapers had indeed been having a field day with rumors and prognostications. On October 6, 1927, a Boston Globe article titled "Amoskeag Company Flouts Wall Street Offer," reported on Amoskeag's annual meeting:

> The famous $42 million offer made by Edward C. Carrington of New York on behalf of principals who have never been named got its answer. Fred Dumaine, using a crutch, sat confidently at the elbow of the chairman. Nobody knows what his salary is, said an awed whisper from a local resident. They say he turned down a $75,000 salary to manage another textile mill. He has a direct wire from the mill agent here to his office in Boston....
>
> When Attorney Glenn rises there is a tense moment while Treasurer Dumaine in a hoarse whisper inquires 'who this man is'.... What Mr. Glenn wants is for the shareholders to instruct their trustees to investigate the Carrington offer and report back at an adjourned meeting.... But between Philip Dexter and the company's chief counsel, Edward K. Woodworth, points of order are found to check him at each move.... Then Mr. Dumaine,

to a proposal that he let the meeting into his confidence, opens up on the outsiders.

Dumaine extemporaneously remarked, as he leaned upon his crutch:

It is now ninety-six years since the original charter was granted to Amoskeag. During the whole time... its bills and obligations of every sort have always been paid and its returns to the owners compare favorably with those of other New England textile companies. The owners have never been required to come forward and help from their pockets.... Your trustees have followed a conservative policy which would enable them to meet just such a period as is now being encountered.

It has never been their intention to abandon operations in Manchester and bring to the city such disasters such a move would entail... but the possibilities of existing conditions have been repeatedly pointed out to you, and if the community is as desirous as the management of maintaining the business, it will be necessary for it to do its share.... With your assistance and the community's support, we propose to stay in business if it is at all possible to do so without loss of assets. Failing to do so profitably, we will ask your authority to discontinue in an orderly manner. There is no occasion for the owners of this property to pay anyone, or make anyone presents, for liquidating their property.

Dumaine, in his blunt way, meant to assure speculators that he would give them battle, to inform shareholders that he would protect their capital, and advise citizens that their cooperation was necessary. For Dumaine to be successful in fighting off the next hostile takeover attempt, action had to be taken immediately.

Amoskeag's plan originally suggested by Philip Dexter was outlined in a circular to the common shareholders of the Amoskeag [Holding] Company dated November 21, 1927, in which they were given the choice of either continuing to hold their Amoskeag Company shares or swapping them for $52 in cash and a $40 bond of the Amoskeag Manufacturing Company. In addition, they would be given one share of the manufacturing company.

Seventy-three percent of the common stockholders accepted the offer and 27 percent left their holdings in the Amoskeag Company. While Dumaine sold most of the shares that he had bought on credit, he kept the shares that he had owned coming into 1927. His 9,300 shares which had originally represented approximately 3 percent of the total holdings of Amoskeag Company, now represented 10 percent of the shares outstanding. In the years that followed, he would add to his holdings of Amoskeag. By 1935, the year of the bankruptcy filing, he owned 20,100 shares or 22 percent of the total.

In later years Dumaine would be criticized severely for these two refinancing operations. Typical of the allegations were the statements of Arthur Black, the bankruptcy master in the eventual bankruptcy of the manufacturing company. In reference to the 1925 separation of a holding company and a manufacturing company, Black wrote:

> Whatever motive there was behind the purchase of Parkhill, I am sure it was but incidental to the "segregation" of the Amoskeag Manufacturing properties and the conservation of the cash of the Old Trust.

In a later section in his report Black addresses the 1927 refinancing:

> This plan, sometimes referred to as a recapitalization, was really devised as a hedge. It withdrew $8 million more from the risks of manufacturing. It gave the timid ones a chance to get their money and quit. It gave the bolder ones a chance to gamble with greater security. They still controlled the operating trust through its common stock. They could get the profit from any business improvement through that medium. If the worst came, they had their bonds.

In reference to the combined refinancing, Bankruptcy Master Black stated:

> When they said, after three additional years of loss, and the withdrawal of $26 million in cash ($18 million by the segregation of 1925 and $8 million for the retirement of preferred stock in 1927), that the "Manufacturing Company" still had "sufficient means to operate," they were not consistent. The truth is they were pulling out their money as fast as they could and they didn't want to acknowledge it.

An alternative interpretation of the first financial restructuring would be that the 1925 separation of the manufacturing company from the operating company was a way of satisfying stockholders that Dumaine and the other trustees would not risk all prior accumulated profits in a firm located in a geographical area with substantial cost disadvantages. At the same time if labor costs in the North approached those in the South, the firm could then make prudent investments in the operating company.

104

The 1927 refinancing was a further attempt to meet the needs of both Amoskeag's stockholders and employees through a three-pronged approach. First, it discouraged future "corporate raiders" from purchasing Amoskeag stock with the goal of making a substantial gain through the liquidation of both the holding company's and the manufacturing company's assets. Second, it provided those current Amoskeag Company shareholders that desired to liquidate their holding with a mechanism that would generate more funds than if they sold their stock to outside "corporate raiders." Third, and most important, it allowed the Manchester based manufacturing company the opportunity for survival. In reference to this third objective, the company candidly stated:

> This plan places the plant where it should be, upon its own responsibility to succeed or fail. The Manufacturing Company is provided with sufficient means to operate. Bond interest must be earned and paid, as well as a reasonable return upon money invested in the business. To accomplish this end the management must institute every possible economy and the community and employees must do whatever is necessary to enable the concern to compete in the market with other mills. Otherwise, there can be but one result.

A review of the DUMAINES trust for the years between the second refinancing and the event-filled closing of Amoskeag Manufacturing clearly indicates that F.C. could have elected to take the easy and more profitable option of simply allowing the mills to close. The trust's investments — other than Amoskeag — performed well during the 1929 crash and the Great Depression. Dumaine's actions clearly indicated an ability to be an investor for all seasons. However, the ownership ethic that he had been taught by T.J. Coolidge and the original "Boston Associates" would not allow him to take the easy option.

The situation at Amoskeag was not unique. Thousands of firms, both prior to and following the 1925-1927 time period, were faced with a similar situation: increasing competition from a section of the country or the world with substantially lower labor costs. What was unique was Dumaine's response. Amoskeag could have begun a program of relocating to the lower-cost region of the South. Instead, the option selected was to try earnestly to continue in Manchester. If the company should not be capable in the long run to earn a profit over and above the interest payments, then the company should be liquidated. This alternative allowed the manufacturing company the opportunity to try.

1913 post card of Union Station, Manchester, New Hampshire

South Station, Boston, Massachusetts

C H A P T E R   X I

Early Years in Railroads

The perennial problems of the railroads of New England captivated Dumaine's attention for fifty years. His lifetime began when railroads were the only mechanized form of ground transportation.

Dumaine's love affair with railroads dated to when he began his career with Amoskeag as an office boy in Coolidge's Boston office. At that time, he purchased his first three-month commuter ticket for $4 and commuted daily from Dedham to Boston.

Dumaine was well aware of the role of the railroads in the overall prosperity of the economy--from his position as a buyer, his later role as treasurer, along with his regular dealings with the issues of transportation of raw materials to the distribution of the finished product throughout the country, as well as the railroads' vital role to exporting.

New England railroads had a peculiar problem in that, from the beginning, the various roads had been built neither by government land grants nor by aggregations of syndicate capital, but were an unconnected network of short lines, locally owned and locally built, connecting principal cities. This produced a struggle, lasting more than a century, between two developing theories: One advocated the efficiency of a single management, the other stressed advantages of competition and the opportunity for new firms to enter the industry. Dumaine would be involved in the New England railroad question from 1908 until his death half a century later.

107

The New Haven No. 1003 passing through Canton, Massachusetts.

The 1880's and 1890's saw the theory of combining properties rise. J. Pierpont Morgan became a director of the New York, Providence and Boston Railroad in 1887; two years later, when he assembled the principal rail and banking executives of the country in his library to join in the "gentleman's agreement" to end the rate-cutting war, the New York Sun could say complacently: "It is the substitution of straightforward business principles for chicanery and corruption."

While a contemporary reader may have difficulty accepting the outlook presented, it is useful to consider the "Morganization of Railroads," the term given to J.P.'s efforts to add stability to railroads. The industry was suffering from three evils. First, the short lines often imposed unnecessary costs associated with transferring cargo from one train line with one rail width to a second and even to a third train line, each with differing track widths as cargo passed to its ultimate destination. Second, security speculators often combined or built new lines, not with the intention of meeting a growing need for traffic, but with the intention of selling overcapitalized securities to a gullible investment market. Third, main trunk lines such as the Pennsylvania and the New York Central were beginning to invade each other's geographic territory.

Morgan is often quoted as saying, "There are always two reasons why one does something, a good reason and the real reason." The real reason Morgan attempted to reorganize bankrupt railroads and to prevent the overexpansion of successful railroads was that it was in the best interest of the security holders that he served, and thus affected the profitability of his firm in the long run. His actions also served a good reason. The refinancing of bankrupt railroads provided security to bond investors while restoring dependable service to existing lines. The prevention of overexpansion of new lines ensured the financial stability of the existing lines, protecting the investments of both bond and stock holders, and at the same time ensuring that the existing lines would continue to provide service for years to come. While the customers often profited from the lower rates that price wars wrought, the history of railroads demonstrated that this was quickly offset by bad and discontinued service of bankrupt firms.

In 1892 J.P. Morgan became a director of the New York, New Haven and Hartford, often shortened to "the New Haven." At that time, cutthroat competition existed between the New York and New England Railroad and the New Haven Railroad. Morgan hired Charles S. Mellen away from the New York and New England. Under Mellen's presidency of the New Haven, Morgan began a period of expanding the territory of the New Haven through lease agreements with some lines, outright purchases of other lines, and stock control of additional lines. In 1893, the New Haven began a lease agreement with the Old Colony Railroad, thus completing a shore line to Boston.

That same year Morgan succeeded in establishing the First Corsair Agreement in which the Boston and Maine agreed not to try to enter into railroading south of Boston. By the turn of the century, there were three principal railroad systems operating in New England. The New Haven controlled approximately 2,000 miles in the three southern New England states. The Boston and Maine had slightly more milage in Northern Massachusetts and the three northern New England states. The Maine Central operated approximately 800 miles in Maine. While the New Haven controlled fewer miles than the B&M, its traffic volume was greater and it was considered the premier New England railroad.

Under Morgan and Mellen, the New Haven began extending its geographic monopoly into other transportation industries. By 1912, it had amassed 90 percent of the water transportation in New England. However, its acquisition of existing steamer lines would cause new firms to enter that industry with the hope of being bought out by the New Haven.

The New Haven also expanded into local ground transportation. By 1913, it controlled 100 percent of Rhode Island and Connecticut and 20 percent of Massachusetts electric street railroads.

In 1907, the New Haven acquired 40 percent ownership in the Boston and Maine stock, giving the firm effective control. Boston and Maine had control of the Maine Central. Morgan had all of the primary New England railroads under his direction, with the New Haven calling the tune. Morgan served on all three boards, and Mellen was the president of the three railroads.

In 1908, Dumaine was appointed to his first railroad directorship. That year he was elected to the Board and the Finance Committee of the Boston and Maine Railroad, a position he held through 1918. During a portion of this tenure, Dumaine served concurrently with J.P. Morgan.

While the public at first supported the "Morganization of Railroads," the pendulum began to swing to the other extreme of popular thinking.

Philadelphia Public Ledger, December 12, 1912

110

People looked on the New Haven as an octopus with a strangling grip on New England. Louis D. Brandeis and Joseph B. Eastman spearheaded the attack on "foreign control" soon taken up through state legislatures. The result of this effort was Massachusetts legislation that forbade the New Haven from direct control of the B&M.

The New Haven's response was the creation of the Boston Railroad Holding Company. F.C. Dumaine served as the holding company's first president. Through this separate corporation, the New Haven could circumvent legislation that would forbid direct ownership of B&M stock by another railroad. Shortly after this transaction, Dumaine left the presidency of the holding company but continued to serve on the Boston & Maine board of directors.

With the inauguration of the Democratic administration under Woodrow Wilson in March 1913 and the death of Morgan the following month, an era of New England railroad history would end. On October 17, 1914, the New Haven signed a consent decree with the U.S. Department of Justice to transfer to five trustees its ownership of the Boston Railroad Holding Company, thereby severing the New Haven's effective control over the B&M. The trustees were to exercise all of the powers of the owners of the shares of the Holding Company, except the right to sell or dispose of them until otherwise ordered.

In 1918, the government took over all of the nation's railroads in conjunction with the war effort. It was then that Dumaine resigned his position on the B&M board. In 1920, the railroads were denationalized. Dumaine did not return to the board.

In May 1922, the Federal Court gave the New Haven the right to name five directors on the Boston and Maine board in recognition of its ownership of 28 percent of the Boston and Maine stock. In June of the following year, the court dissolved the voting trust and ordered the stock of the Boston Railroad Holding Company returned to the New Haven. The effect of these two rulings was to invalidate the 1914 consent decree.

In 1923, Dumaine became a member of the New Haven board of directors. Personally, Dumaine believed that the two roads should be united, the New Haven having natural and geographic interests with New York and the South, while the Boston and Maine logically served northern New England through its gateways to northern New York and Canada.

In November of 1928, Dumaine was elected a member of the Execu-

111

tive Committee. About that time, Dumaine suggested that John J. Pelley, president of the Central Railroad of Georgia, be appointed to the New Haven presidency. His diary states:

> January 15, 1929: New Haven directors' meeting at New York. J.J. Pelley was proposed for president, with the understanding he is to report to the chairman of the board, and the committee was authorized to make an arrangement with him if on further investigation they were satisfied he would consider the position and it seemed he was entirely desirable. After the election of Pelley as New Haven president, there was still a vacant directorship on the board of directors. I proposed Homer Loring, from the Boston and Maine, for the New Haven vacancy. The suggestion was not well received by New Haven board members, despite the fact that they were adamant about having their interests represented on the B&M board.

Dumaine's tenet was that Boston was the terminal for all three main rail systems from the north, west, and south, so the railroads should be in the control of men aware of New England's needs. The experienced rail executive John J. Pelley, who served as the New Haven's president, shared this view. In 1929, Robert Winsor of Kidder, Peabody and Company, Dumaine, and other allies joined with Dumaine's friends on the Pennsylvania Railroad to secure control of the New Haven.

The diary shows the interruption to the plan caused by the stock market crash. On Black Tuesday, October 29, 1929, F.C. Dumaine and Buck hurried to New York to cope with the situation.

> Wednesday, October 30, 1929: Went with [James L.] Richards to call on [John] Country who had come on from Philadelphia to meet us specially. He told us he had purchased 100,000 shares of New Haven; was not to purchase any more at present; had no funds; and we were relieved from any action and at liberty to do whatever we might feel like doing. Offered us a share of his purchase. We told him the amount purchased was insufficient to give us a dictating position and we wouldn't therefore be interested.

> Thursday, June 26, 1930: Trumbull came in to explain as best he could their reasons for deciding to discontinue purchases of the New Haven as agreed — the position they take is embarrassing, puts me for the first time in life in a position to be unable to carry out a bona fide agreement. Nothing has ever happened in my business career to give such concern — I am hoping it will finally iron out satisfactorily.

From the collection of Keith Morse, Manchester, N.H.

The Pennsylvania Railroad had acquired 23 percent of the New Haven stock, giving it effective control. However, much had been purchased at high pre-market crash prices. It appeared that Dumaine would have to wait for a later date to attempt to gain control of the New Haven.

In 1930, with $21 million of government loans falling due, the New Haven Railroad sought permission to sell its stock in the Boston Railroad Holding Company, which in turn controlled the New Haven's B&M stock. The economic impact from the depression caused the New Haven to become unprofitable.

Buckland, as chairman of the New Haven board, had sponsored the petition to sell the holding company stock. The Massachusetts legislature, fearful of outsiders getting control, denied the request. The position of Dumaine and his friends was illustrated in the statement of Thomas Nelson Perkins at the legislative hearing: "I don't want New England railroads gobbled up by outside interests." Dumaine, at New Haven directors' meetings, was advocating utmost economy and efficiency in operation of the railroad, and conservatism in declaring dividends. In reference to the curtailment of dividends, he found himself in direct conflict with the majority on the board.

May 26, 1931: New Haven Board meeting.... Quarterly dividend of $1.50 on common stock declared, after heated discus-

113

sion — Pelley taking active part in favor. On the final vote, Milligan and I were the only people who voted against it — although, after the meeting, a majority of the board expressed themselves as agreeing with us in theory but unwilling to vote against the management.

It was the worst case of failure of men to stand on their own convictions I have had occasion to run across. Richards and Pelley were strong for the continuation, no doubt affected by the fact they own large quantities of stock pledged in banks against which they pay considerable interest charges.

In August 1931, Dumaine met with representatives of the Pennsylvania Railroad, He recommended that "the Pennsy should not dispose of their New England holdings. If a consolidation of the New Haven and Boston and Maine were made, which I had always favored way back in the Mellen days, it would seem a great advantage to the community, provide very much more economical management, and the Pennsy interest would be most helpful as to credit and other railroad problems."

The following month at the September New Haven board meeting, the directors voted to pay the fourth $1 dividend for the year, which totaled $6 million, of which only $3.5 million had been earned, reducing the prior surplus by $2.5 million. Dumaine was outvoted 13 to 3 in opposing the dividend payout.

The next fifteen years of his directorship were arduous for him because he was in the minority on the board. With the election of Franklin D. Roosevelt as president and the appointment of Joseph B. Eastman as coordinator of railroads, a new era of politics and philosophies began. However, this did not come in time to prevent New Haven's financial condition from deteriorating as a result of increased competition from non-rail transportation and the overall decline in demand that was associated with the Great Depression.

On Tuesday, October 22, 1935, the Interstate Commerce Commission refused to approve a loan of $5 million to New Haven Railroad from the Reconstruction Finance Corporation due to the railroad's inability to meet the financial requirements. The following day, at the New Haven directors' meeting, the management decided to file a petition in U.S. District Court at New Haven for permission to reorganize under Section 77 B of the Federal Bankruptcy Act.

The New Haven would be in bankruptcy for nearly twelve years with the directors mere figureheads as the management was vested with the trustees under the court. By 1935, New Haven revenues had dropped from $142 million in 1923 to $70 million. Including two government loans, the New Haven's indebtedness stood at $283.3 million.

In a letter written on December 6, 1938, to Morgan Brainerd of the Aetna Life Insurance Company, Dumaine expressed his thoughts on the situation:

> I'm not advocating any action in connection with the New England railroads (that was not true six or eight years ago), since then it's been the sideline for me, hoping, as you, for some suggestion which would make for a sound basis. Had such an arrangement been made, the two roads would have saved $16 to $18 million.... As for me, except for a very considerable stake in Maine Central common shares, I have no great direct interest in the securities of either road, too many other cracking headaches to permit time for outside things.

Dumaine's diary entries and correspondence illustrated the frustration that he felt as an outside director with a minority viewpoint. In his positions with Amoskeag, Fore River, and Waltham, not only was his view with the majority of the board, he served as the chief executive officer. The policies of these corporations reflected his judgment. Amoskeag and Waltham Watch were preserving capital by refusing to pay dividends in excess of current earnings. Dumaine was the one to make the final decision on appointments on key executive positions. This was not the situation with the New Haven.

115

Kidder, Peabody and Company's Boston office

CHAPTER XII

Kidder, Peabody – A Friend in Need

Frederic Dumaine's desire to save a dollar, or in his words, "not waste an apple core," combined with his generosity to help a friend in need, was the reason he came to lose the equivalent of an orchard of apples, in what he later ruefully referred to as "the million dollar telephone call."

The loss was the result of going to the aid of the investment banking firm of Kidder, Peabody and Company of Boston. The senior partners, Frank G. Webster, Robert Winsor, and William Endicott, had long been Dumaine's close friends.

Robert Winsor died on January 7, 1930. In his diary notation for the day, Dumaine praised his friend:

> To him and him alone is due the credit for deferring the Boston and Maine receivership... In 1923, it was Winsor who made possible the reconstruction of the Waltham Watch; the company had passed into the hands of the banks and he devised the plan and underwrote it.... In 1927, when certain New York interests undertook to purchase Amoskeag for liquidation and profit to themselves, Winsor came into the picture with his money and genius, and helped prevent the sharks from gobbling and destroying this great New England industry.

More likely than not, the actions with respect to Amoskeag and Waltham caused Dumaine to assist Kidder, Peabody in its hour of need.

117

Within two weeks of Winsor's death, Frank G. Webster died. Dumaine's diary reflected, "[Webster] had been a friend since boyhood, a kindhearted man and a great loss to the community." He had two sons, Edwin S. Webster of the firm of Stone and Webster, and Laurence J. Webster. Dumaine had never forgotten that it was Frank Webster who first extended credit to him, enabling him to lay the foundation of his personal fortune.

Kidder, Peabody & Co. was organized on April 1, 1865 when three former clerks in the Boston investment banking firm of J.E. Thayer & Brother took over that business. The Thayer business dated back to 1824. Ten years later in 1834, Thayer was one of 13 brokers who established the Boston Stock Exchange.

The three original partners of the new organization were Henry Kidder and Francis H. and Oliver W. Peabody. Frank G. Webster, who had joined the Thayer organization one month before the sale to Kidder, Peabody, became the new firm's head clerk. The firm, which operated out of Boston, was active in the reorganization of railroads, many of which were overcapitalized and in default.

While seeing itself as a Boston firm specializing in the financing of New England firms, Kidder, Peabody opened up a New York branch office in 1873. Thirteen years later, Kidder, Peabody acquired a seat on the New York Stock Exchange. From its inception, it had held a seat on the Boston Exchange. At this time in history, investment banking was not seen as a national industry. There were firms operating in all of the major cities in the country, providing investment banking services for their respective geographical areas.

In 1878, Kidder, Peabody became the American agent for the London banking firm Baring Brothers & Co. Ltd. In addition to being active in the flotation of securities, Kidder, Peabody specialized in foreign exchange and extending international letters of credit.

At the end of the nineteenth century, Kidder, Peabody participated in the flotation of industrial securities through the various syndicated distributions. It often served as the primary underwriter of American Telegraph and Telephone issues as a result of that firm's origin in the New England area.

The significance of Kidder, Peabody at that time is demonstrated by the fact that it was one of only three investment banking firms invited by J. Pierpont Morgan to the famous 1889 conference. At the historic meeting, Morgan laid down the law to the leading railroad firms that

118

Frank Webster   *Robert Winsor*

there would be no further underwriting of securities for the purpose of building railroads where the traffic did not justify expansion. The other two investment banking houses present were Drexel, Morgan and Brown Brothers. While such a move would not be looked upon favorably by today's governmental standards, Morgan, at the time, was heralded for the courage of his action, bringing stability to an industry suffering from overcapacity and cutthroat competition.

Two years later, Kidder, Peabody broke into two separate firms. The Boston group kept the original name. The four principals at this time were Francis H. and Oliver W. Peabody, two original Kidder, Peabody partners, Frank Peabody, Jr., and Frank Webster, the original clerk and the man who would later assist Dumaine in 1927 in his effort to prevent investors from acquiring control of Amoskeag with the intention of closing the mills and liquidating the business.

The group from Kidder, Peabody's New York office took the name of Baring, Magoven & Co. The loss of the New York presence came at a bad time. Investment banking was becoming a national industry centered in New York City.

After the death of the last of the original founders in 1905, Webster became the head partner. Under his leadership, the firm weathered the Panic of 1907. Later, Kidder, Peabody was active in providing financing to European countries purchasing war materials prior to the United States entering the First World War. In addition, it assisted the various munition firms in the New England area, such as Winchester Arms, with the financing that they needed to expand to meet the growing world market. Following the United States entering the conflict in 1917, Kidder, Peabody participated in the distribution of all five Liberty Loan issues of the U.S. Government.

In 1919, Robert Winsor was made senior partner. During his tenure, Kidder, Peabody was noted for its conservative management, concentrating on railroad bonds and deemphasizing the distribution of industrial stocks, which were becoming increasingly important. However, Winsor favored the issues of American Telephone and Telegraph because of the proximity of origin of the telephone industry and the gilt-edged quality of the company.

While Kidder did reestablish a New York office following the separation of the firm into two groups, the main office remained in Boston. In effect, Kidder, Peabody continued to project itself as a regional firm in an industry that increasingly was becoming national in scope. In addition, Kidder, Peabody followed the policy that worked so successfully for J.P. Morgan, waiting for the clients to come to it rather than soliciting business. Unfortunately, what worked well for the Morgan firm, with its reputation and location in the heart of Wall Street, did not work as well for Kidder, Peabody, centered in Boston's Devonshire Street. In the decade leading to the stock market crash of 1929, Kidder, Peabody's share of the underwriting business declined substantially.

Despite his generosity and the need to make critical decisions involving large sums of money, Dumaine was frugal on small matters. On the Wednesday prior to Thanksgiving 1930, Dumaine was in New York. He needed to contact his Boston office, so went to the Kidder, Peabody office on Wall Street to use the company's direct wire to Boston. While his intention was to save a dollar in toll charges, the saving on a toll call ultimately cost him almost $1 million. Following the phone call, Kidder, Peabody representatives in the office told him that the firm was in desperate need of capital. Over the previous three years, a substantial amount had been withdrawn by two retiring partners and by estates of two partners who had died the prior January. Dumaine wrote:

> They were in difficulties — a shock I never expected from that source. They said it was evident they must raise $5 million capital and the banks would arrange revolving credit of $10 million more — would I help?

Dumaine rationalized:

Mr. Webster offered me the first credit ever given me, and at a time when there was nothing to justify it except his faith in my integrity; and the extremely intimate personal relations with Winsor and Billy Endicott — the effect upon the community, country, and, perhaps, the world, an embarrassment of this old institution might cause, I told them they could depend upon every dollar I personally had to put them back into proper position.

Dumaine made several stops with Wally Trumbull and Charles Sargent, two of Kidder Peabody's remaining partners, to see if they could raise any funds. Perhaps the most important stop made that day was at the office of J.P. Morgan, where they met with George Whitney and Harold Stanley. While the Morgan firm was part of the group of banks willing to extend the $10 million line of credit, they held that the $5 million capital was properly a Boston proposition. Although this did not provide any direct funds, placing the House of Morgan seal of approval on the refinancing was vital for subsequent attempts to raise the $5 million.

Dumaine spent a major portion of Thanksgiving day and the subsequent Friday and Saturday soliciting funds from various Boston sources. Not all of this soliciting was pleasant. Among the responses that he received: "It was time these private bankers discontinued taking deposits and this was one of the greatest opportunities to break up the habit— it would be to the interest of the banks to let the concern go broke."

He cabled London. Baring Brothers responded it would contribute $600,000. Most of his appeals were successful, but the Boston engineering and contracting firm of Stone and Webster declined to participate as a firm. Edwin S. Webster did, however, participate to the extent of $750,000.

Late Saturday night Dumaine left for New York for a Sunday conference at the House of Morgan. Among those present were George Whitney and Harold Stanley of J.P. Morgan; Reed, a lawyer; Dick Whitney, president of the New York Stock Exchange; Mudge, Clarkson, and Whelpley from Chase Bank; and Sargent and Williams representing Kidder, Peabody. To that point, $3.35 million was all the money they had raised. Dumaine feared the amount was not sufficient to cover the anticipated withdrawals that could occur the next morning as a result of rumors on Kidder, Peabody's financial situation. Through continual telephone calls, the amount had risen to $4 million by 11:30 p.m. At this point, Dumaine, who had not made any personal pledge since his entire wealth was tied in securities, said, "I'll make up the last million if Morgan will lend it to me."

Dumaine caught the midnight train back to Boston, $1 million in debt and satisfied that he had assisted the firm of his friends. The $5 million subscribed was paid in to "F.C. Dumaine, Trustee." The money was to be loaned to Kidder, Peabody and Company at 6 percent interest. The four largest investors were Dumaine at $950,000, Edwin S. Webster at $750,000, William Endicott at $600,000, and Baring Brothers, Limited at $600,000. Webster's and Endicott's loans represented capital that previously had been withdrawn from Kidder, Peabody by Webster's estate at the time of his death, and Endicott himself when he retired. There was some indication that if bankruptcy did occur there might be claims for these capital withdrawals. In addition, Webster's father's contribution could be looked upon as an option. He indicated some interest in setting up his son, currently working for him at Stone and Webster, in a reorganized Kidder, Peabody. The Baring Brothers' loan seemed justified based on the fact that Kidder, Peabody was its American agent. Dumaine's contribution appears to be aimed at helping a friend in need.

The various individuals and institutions that loaned Kidder, Peabody and Company the $5 million formed the Commonwealth Corporation to oversee their investments. On December 3, an organizational meeting was held where the various creditors received stocks for the amount of their loans. Five directors were elected: F.C. Dumaine, William Endicott, James L. Richards, F.E. Snow, and Edwin S. Webster. Dumaine served as president.

Dumaine spent the major portion of December assisting the drugstore magnate Lewis Liggett straighten out his personal investments. Liggett was one of Kidder, Peabody's major accounts. Like many investors at the time, he found himself overextended following the market crash.

Dumaine spent Christmas Eve with his accountants, going over the figures of the Kidder, Peabody, and Liggett involvements. The days after Christmas were occupied completing arrangements for the $10 million revolving credit from the New York banks. The banks made it a condition of the loans that Dumaine serve on the Executive Committee, which required frequent board meetings in New York for several years to come.

On January 6, Dumaine met with Edwin Webster, Sr., to discuss his plans relative to Kidder, Peabody. Webster indicated his intention to place his son in the business along with Chandler Hovey, Webster's son in law, and Albert Gordon, who had been a classmate of the younger Webster at Harvard Business School. Dumaine spent the next two days interviewing Hovey and Gordon.

On January 14, Dumaine called on his friend, Charles Hayden of Hayden, Stone, in New York, with a view to working out an acquisition of Kidder, Peabody. Hayden indicated great interest in the Kidder situation, saying he would be glad to consolidate the two firms doing business in Boston under the name of Kidder and in New York as Hayden, Stone. Hayden indicated his willingness to add all the Kidder firm members to his firm. Their compensation would be regulated in proportion to their work. Hayden, Stone would want no profit from liquidation of the Kidder assets. Whatever excess there might be over liabilities should be used first to pay back the $5 million to the Commonwealth Corporation, and the residue would be passed on to Kidder partners. In addition, Hayden indicated a willingness to add Edwin Webster, Jr., to the organization if that would be agreeable to the Webster interests.

Mr. Villiers, Baring's representative, said his firm would be glad to continue its relations, whatever arrangements were made, as long as Morgan and Dumaine approved. While the Morgan partners agreed that Hayden was perfectly competent and financially strong enough to undertake this job, they felt obliged to attain a definite decision from Webster as to his final intention in connection with furnishing the capital. If Webster were to decide not to do so, the Morgan group would immediately start negotiations with Hayden. As might be expected, the Kidder partners were perfectly agreeable to the merger with Hayden, Stone.

Dumaine spent January 18 with the elder Webster, Chandler Hovey, and Albert Gordon discussing the options for Kidder, Peabody. During this entire period of time, the younger Webster was ill and the primary negotiator was his father. Dumaine preferred the merger with Hayden, Stone. He believed that this would have protected the $22 million capital invested in Kidder, Peabody brokerage accounts by hundreds of Bostonians. Further, it would have provided a greater probability that the $5 million loans, much of which were anted up in response to Dumaine's requests, would be paid back. At one point, perhaps partly in jest, J. P. Morgan, Jr., suggested, "You'd do better to hire their old office and put F.C. Dumaine on the door!" Despite the high regard that the Morgan group held for Dumaine and his plan, they felt obliged to proceed with Webster's proposal, if Webster so elected.

Webster elected to reorganize Kidder, Peabody along the following lines. The business, which would be centered in New York City, would have three partners. His son Edwin S. Webster, Jr., then in his father's employ at Stone and Webster, would contribute $4.8 million of his family's money to the reorganized Kidder, Peabody, with $1.3 million in cash, with the remainder in securities, of which the vast majority was Stone and Webster capital stock. Chandler Hovey contributed an additional $425,000. Hovey would head the Boston office. The third partner was Albert Gordon, then employed with Goldman, Sachs and Company in New York City. Gordon did not have the family money that his two partners possessed. He did, however, bring forth $100,000. More important, it was his drive and ability that resulted in his being selected to head the New York office. Under the plan, the $5 million raised by Dumaine to bail out Kidder, Peabody appeared at risk. Any residual value to the old Kidder, Peabody partners seemed all but lost.

Dumaine's feeling on Webster's involvement:

> February 8, 1931: Meeting in Webster's house; all members of Commonwealth Corporation present. The Webster plan or offer to take over the KP business was accepted on general principles.... My own impression, gathered from the many interviews and observations held and made during the past couple of months, is Webster is simply making a trade, the best he thinks possible, without consideration of anyone, except his own family.

Dumaine was so thoroughly disgusted at the liquidation of the firm he had fought so hard to save that he left Boston that night for Jacksonville, Florida, where Weesie was vacationing. While ironing out the arrangements, some of the young men of the old firm appealed to Dumaine and he responded, cutting short his vacation. On February 26, he heard from son Buck indicating his prompt return would be appreciated. The following morning Dumaine boarded the train for Boston. Dumaine devised a plan to submit to Webster for carrying on the Kidder business. To make sure others would agree, he took the plan to Eugene van Renssalaer Thayer, president of Merchants National Bank, Boston, and Bobbie Stone, of Hayden, Stone. It was their opinion that the plan was practical and very likely to be much more successful than any so far set up. With Snow, Dumaine submitted the plan to Phil Dexter at his house and he agreed completely. At this point, Dumaine took the five o'clock train to New York to submit his revised plan to Wiggin and the Morgan partners.

The essence of the plan called for Dumaine to be the unsalaried manager of the new Kidder, Peabody until the $10 million revolving credit and the $5 million contributions had been repaid out of earnings. Dumaine was to have the final say on salaries paid. After deducting salaries and expenses from gross receipts, 6 percent would be allotted to the $4 million new capital put up under the Webster plan. Any remaining earnings would be divided 20 percent to the new capital, and 80 percent to pay off the revolving credit and $5 million contributions.

On March 2, 1931, Dumaine submitted the proposition to Wiggin, who approved. Later, at Morgan's, he discussed the situation at length with Whitney, who agreed this proposal was more workable and likely to give better results than Webster's current plan. However, the House of Morgan felt that a definite agreement had been made with Webster and the question of ethics was to be considered. They could not adopt the new plan without Webster's approval.

The next day Dumaine was invited to Morgan's office for a luncheon. Dumaine's diary relates the meeting:

> All the senior partners were present and all were of the same opinion.... Mr. Morgan went out of his way to express himself to the effect he felt if my plan was put through, everyone who helped in the Kidder, Peabody situation would eventually be reimbursed. Only one thing more to do, namely, to submit the proposition to Webster, who would be in New York Wednesday.

> March 4, 1931: By appointment, met Webster at Morgan's with Whitney at 2:15. Explained my feeling of responsibility in having induced a number of friends to put money into the business on the theory if the $5 million was subscribed it would enable the business to continue.... I had never asked people before to subscribe to any scheme where there was not at least an opportunity of recovering. If I had the money, so strong was my feeling, I should at once indemnify all subscribers and trust to luck for reimbursement. Unfortunately, I was not able to do this. I tried to use as an argument to convince Webster my feeling was for a plan which would bring harmony, goodwill, and perfect cooperation to him and his new firm of young men.... Pointed out the fact all to whom I had submitted it approved, including all Morgan partners.

125

He quite promptly said he did not see how it could be seriously considered because he thought it impracticable to make any changes at this time — his son was a young man of much determination....

Two weeks later the diary notation relative to Kidder, Peabody read:

March 16, 1931: Signed KP papers necessary to transfer the business to Webster, thus ending a most unsatisfactory experience.

Following the death of Frederick E. Snow in 1935, Snow's estate brought suit against the J.P. Morgan firm for the $250,000 Snow had subscribed to the Kidder, Peabody bailout. The estate asked Dumaine to be a co-plaintiff for his $950,000. Dumaine responded that he did not care to be a party to the suit, which eventually was dismissed on the finding of the Federal District Court that J. P. Morgan and Company had guaranteed nothing at the time of the subscriptions.

The children of Robert Winsor appreciated Dumaine's motives and deplored the losses suffered by him and other friends. Dumaine's reply showed that they had rightly understood him:

I had the greatest affection for your father which, naturally, was the compelling motive that all possible be done to protect him and save the concern he built up and was proud of. It is a great disappointment not to have been able to accomplish the end desired and save to you all a business justly yours. Generosity is not the word impelling the people who subscribed; they had in mind to save a situation and the family of a friend. That it might take time to make a recovery was inevitable, but a total loss seemed incredible. While my personal loss is much beyond what I had any right, for my family's sake, to make, I went into the thing voluntarily and must abide the result. My great regret is to have induced lifelong friends to go into a venture bringing them a loss they could ill afford, and which, at my age, there is little chance of my making good.

The early years of the Great Depression were difficult enough for soundly organized investment banking concerns. The new Kidder, Peabody firm found it nearly impossible to pay off the $10 million revolving credit from the banks much less liquidate the $5 million owed to Commonwealth Corporation. Through this time, Dumaine was paying principal and interest on his personal $1 million loan from J.P. Morgan and Company. He had gained the respect of all of the Morgan partners. They affectionately called him "Grandpa" and later offered to sell him J.P. "Jack" Morgan, Jr.'s, partnership upon Morgan's death. As collateral for his loan, Dumaine had pledged his Waltham Watch Company stock, 500 shares of Pennsylvania Railroad, plus all his shares of Commonwealth Corporation.

In 1936 when he had paid back some $450,000 of the principal and the collateral's market value had shrunk to $125,000, Morgan squared it off for $150,000 cash. Dumaine also had an interest charge of more than $20,000 a year for the five years, bringing Dumaine's personal loss in the bailout to $700,000.

In 1940, when the banks settled their claims with Kidder, Peabody, Dumaine made the following notation in his diary:

> Paid to revolving credit to complete liquidation, $8.5 million. Kidder's debacle closed, remaining stocks to be distributed to creditors. Equals to payment about 85 percent of principal to revolving credit; nothing for the junior money, $5 millions Commonwealth Corporation.

As the United States moved out of the depression into wartime production, Kidder, Peabody reestablished itself as one of the leading investment banking houses. To a great extent this was a result of Albert Gordon, the young man who Dumaine had interviewed in his office on January 4, 1930.

Gordon's success in revitalizing Kidder, Peabody was based on several policies. First, he developed an efficient nationwide distribution by opening branches in key cities. The new Kidder, Peabody no longer viewed itself as a regional operation.

It established a policy of only distributing high grade securities. Since past history prevented it from access to refunding of bond issues that were tied up by the original issuing investment banking firms, the company concentrated on small firms with growth potential.

Gordon emphasized the need to solicit new business. In addition, he developed close ties with major banking houses, thereby obtaining a portion of syndicated issues. Finally, Kidder, Peabody got involved with direct placement, which was becoming a growing portion of the underwriting business. All of these policies indicated a positive revitalization of a firm that would no longer be missing significant trends in its industry.

However, this was little comfort to Dumaine and the other contributors of the $5 million loan. A letter to Francis D. Bartow of the Morgan firm on January 1, 1935, summarizes Dumaine's personal feelings on his involvement with the Kidder, Peabody reorganization:

> Looking back on this and many other things, it does not seem possible a human could make so many mistakes. Thanking you for your courteous consideration....

In a 1998 interview, 97-year-old Albert Gordon commented on the role of Dumaine prior to the completion of the Kidder, Peabody reorganization. Gordon preceded his comments with a statement praising Dumaine for his actions involving Amoskeag.

In reference to his meeting with Dumaine prior to the reorganization, Gordon recalled:

> Mr. Dumaine had a rather conspicuous spittoon in his office. He demonstrated the ability to accurately hit it from a considerable distance.

Gordon gave candid observations as to the apparent conflict between F.C. Dumaine and Edwin Webster, Sr., the role of the Morgan bank in the reorganization, the reason why Dumaine's plan could not be accepted, and a probable explanation as to how Dumaine found himself supporting a plan which caused all participants to lose the funds invested to assist Kidder, Peabody. Gordon's words were as follows:

> Mr. Webster was a graduate of M.I.T., trained in engineering. This gave him the ability to evaluate the situation and determine what had to be done. He realized that the bankruptcy was inevitable. Dumaine, with his background in textiles, did not have the education that Webster had. Dumaine could not look upon the situation objectively.

> The people at J.P. Morgan were extremely helpful both at the time of the refinancing and following the reorganization. They were very professional in their relations with us. They knew and respected Dumaine.

> Since the accounting records of Kidder, Peabody were so poorly kept, we did not know the extent of potential claims from actions prior to our involvement with the firm. For this reason, a complete new start had to be made in which we eliminated all existing claims, including the $5 million raised by Dumaine.

> Perhaps the reason that Dumaine found himself in the position of supporting a plan that could not work was that he was out of chips when the next round of investments had to be raised.

While Mr. Gordon's comments deserve serious consideration, it does not seem likely that Dumaine would have been as naive as suggested. When he first served on the B&M Railroad with the elder J.P. Morgan, he may have been in awe. By 1930, however, he was a seasoned executive. He had successfully negotiated the sale of Fore River Shipyard to Charles Schwab's Bethlehem Steel. He had dealt with three U.S. presidents and two U.S. Supreme Court justices. Most important, he was respected by the group at J.P. Morgan.

If Dumaine did not elect to ante additional chips, it was not because he was out of capital. At the end of 1930, the DUMAINES Trust was worth more than $3 million. More likely, he would not be part of a refinancing that resulted in the original $5 million being wiped out. Most of these funds were contributed at his request.

If Dumaine could not look upon the situation as objectively as Webster, it was because his desire was to assist the firm that had been so helpful in forestalling the takeover attempt at Amoskeag and in preventing Waltham Watch from closing. Dumaine was acting according to the principles instilled by the "Boston Associates." As was the case with Waltham Watch, Dumaine fully expected to see the reorganized firm operating profitably and retiring existing obligations out of future profits. If necessary, he was willing to oversee the process while receiving no compensation.

At the time of the incident, John R. Macomber of Harris, Forbes and the First Boston Corporation, considered "the dean of investment counselors," expressed his feeling in the following note:

> I called up to see you but found you were away. I just wanted to say ⁔ and I would rather have said it than write it ⁔ that I think you are the best sport I have ever known. One does not have to race or prize fight to be one. There are other things in life that come to a man that show the stuff he is made of.

Dumaine carefully preserved Macomber's letter to the end of his life, and it was found among his "assets," as he had written to Macomber:

> My dear John,
>
> When my executors examine the assets, if there are any left, one of the most valuable, to my mind, will be this nice letter of yours.

The once vibrant millyard area lay eerie as the demise of Amoskeag became inevitable.

C H A P T E R   X I I I

The Depression Hits Amoskeag

The depression that crippled the nation from the stock market crash in 1929 until the country's entry into World War II arrived early in New England textile towns. Continual expansion of Southern mills with their labor cost advantage supplied the nation's demand for textiles. The New England and Mid-Atlantic States' firms could not match the Southern prices and operate at a break-even point, much less earn a profit. The obvious alternatives of cut backs in production or total curtailment of operations followed.

Dumaine attempted to explain to the employees the problems of the industry. On Saturday, April 21, 1928, he spoke at the Amoskeag employees' dinner at the Carpenter Hotel, in Manchester, New Hampshire. His diary notations of the event summarize his view of the meeting:

> Gave them a little formal talk. Afterward they propounded questions for an hour and a half. It was altogether an amicable meeting, a success and beneficial. I enjoyed going there. I tried to point out to them without equivocation that the whole situation depended upon their being able to produce cloths in competition with other sections of the country....

Dumaine had authorized an experimental rayon plant and for several years trials were made, finally attaining a production of 10,000 pounds of yarn a week. An explosion in the mixing room of the rayon plant called Dumaine out of bed for a hurried trip to Manchester to find costly damage to building and machinery. Dumaine found it impossible to work out manufacturing agreements with either the silk-producers of France or with the DuPont people of Delaware on synthetics. Furthermore, labor had demanded two shifts, six days a week, but the manufacturing of the product required a continuous operation. Therefore, in 1933 the rayon plant was discontinued.

Dumaine's own project for diversification, that of renting some of the unused mills and the water power, seemed hopeful at first. In July of 1928, he called on Arthur Vining Davis, president of the Aluminum Company of America, and pointed out the waterpower situation at Manchester. Davis seemed interested and agreed to make a survey of the situation. The following month, Dumaine was informed that the Aluminum Company would require 15,000 or 16,000 continuous horsepower units to operate an aluminum smelting furnace. Even with all the water power in Manchester, it was not possible. If, by chance, one of these units was interrupted for any cause, it would cost many thousands of dollars before it could be started again. While Manchester was a desirable place to locate, there was not a chance of considering the city as a point of production in view of the limited amount of power available and the fluctuations of the river.

Dumaine was making every effort to increase efficiency and to effect economies at the mills. There were certain economies, however, that he would not consider. In January, 1928, a meeting was held in Dumaine's Boston office. At the meeting were Treasurer Dumaine, Agent Straw, and President Lowe. To preserve capital, Lowe suggested the elimination of company pensions. Because the pensions were not prefunded and the company had no legal obligation to continue the payment it would only require a board decision to stop all future payments. Straw argued to maintain the pensions. When Dumaine offered to pay the lower grade pensions out of his own pocket as a contribution toward the welfare of the company, the issue was dropped and the pensions continued until the Amoskeag bankruptcy.

Dumaine did not feel that labor alone should bear the responsibility for reducing costs. He decreased his own $100,000 salary to $65,000 in January 1929. As the depression extended, Dumaine cut his salary to $60,000 in 1931, and, by June 1932, to $40,000.

Friction mounted between the trustees and agent W. Parker Straw. Dumaine, out of regard for father and son, tried to persuade Parker Straw to transfer to the New York sales office, without success. On January 17, 1929, the Executive Committee of Trustees – Philip Dexter, Arthur Lowe, and George Wigglesworth, with Dumaine, dismissed

Parker Straw. The committee hoped that a change in management of the mills would help to bring about the economies in production necessary for survival. Dumaine once again offered him a position in the New York office in vain. As a final gesture, Dumaine sold Straw the Amoskeag Manufacturing Company house that he occupied as agent for $50,000, although it had cost $90,000 to build. Dumaine recorded the event in his diary:

> January 17, 1929: The interview was embarrassing, particularly so. Twenty-five years ago I induced his father [H. F. Straw] to take him [W. Parker Straw] on as superintendent, with the expectation he'd gather sufficient information and experience to be valuable in the days when I would naturally be considering retiring. It's a great disappointment to change at a vital time like this.

The Amoskeag Mills for the year 1928 had shown an operating loss and reduction in net working capital of more than $1 million. Dumaine, sixty-three years old, confronted with extremely adverse conditions in the textile industry, had to give up thoughts of retiring. He picked three men who would work closely with him: Arthur Roberts, already a superintendent at Amoskeag; Henry E. Rauch, expert accountant and seasoned in textiles through experience at the Hamilton Mill; and his own eldest son, Buck. Naturally, a faction in Manchester, accustomed to three generations of the Straw family as agents, resented outsiders and hinted at nepotism, seeing the treasurer's son in the saddle, even though Dumaine conscientiously had insisted on Buck going in at $5,000 a year. The three, beginning January 20, 1929, were to give up Sundays and evenings from then on for long conferences at Groton with Dumaine.

During the years 1929-1931, more reliance was placed on individual wage adjustments than on general reductions. A plan of "reservation prices" went into effect in the summer of 1929. It provided that those employees working on certain types of cloth would be paid at a reduced rate when it was necessary for Amoskeag to compete effectively for a given order.

The Old Man himself went to Manchester on February 4, 1929, to talk frankly at a banquet of city officials and businessmen. The New Hampshire Labor Review reported:

> When the city fathers of Manchester invited F.C. Dumaine to break bread with them... much of the reputed aloofness and sarcastic qualities erroneously attributed to the Treasurer of

the Amoskeag through the years was dissipated as he stood up and talked man to man... they beheld a human being sincerely motivated by a desire to advance the interests of the stockholders, yet a man who harbors in his heart a deep concern for the economic wellbeing of the community.

At the end of the first year of the new management, glowing praises appeared in the press as, after seven years of red ink, the annual report showed a profit, interest was paid on the bonds, and a dividend declared on the common stock for the first time since 1924.

In the March 19, 1930, issue of The Business Week, a rather lengthy article reported on the accomplishment. Observations included:

New England's textile industry, depressed by years of reverses, gloomy from the advance of Southern competition, has been heartened by an unexpected ray of sunlight. Amoskeag Manufacturing Company, once ready to liquidate, announces a dividend of $1 on stock and a 5 percent bonus for employees from 1929 earnings! As if a corpse had leaped!

It wasn't magic. Amoskeag's return to fruitfulness is a result of courage and economy. This economy was applied grimly to management as well as labor. While the man in overalls was asked to do more work for less money, holders of soft jobs with fat salaries were mercilessly divorced from the payroll. In cutting items of plant costs not a useless penny was spared. These Spartan measures were accepted philosophically. Liquidation was the only alternative.

Frederic Christopher Dumaine, treasurer of the company, accomplished the feat. It is the peak achievement of a past master in old-fashioned New England economy.... Early in 1929 the outlook was so black that there was a powerful sentiment for liquidation. The treasurer shut his teeth and declared that he intended to carry on.... Mr. Dumaine had the courage to declare:

"Liquidation – the last thing those of us with a personal regard for this city and the property want – means the most terrible sacrifice of money values imaginable.... I am ready to do all possible, institute every economy, shoulder every responsibility and stand every criticism, to carry on."

The article closed with an assessment of Amoskeag's long-run potential:

Factors in favor of Amoskeag's continuance are rock-bottom costs, modernized fabrics, general promise of more goods for

134

women's dresses because of longer skirts. Factors against, are the lower costs of Southern manufacture, overproduction everywhere.... Also there is a possibility of recurring labor troubles.

What the article failed to predict was the length and depth of the Great Depression in which the entire United States was falling. This both worked against the favorable factors and contributed to the negative factors summarized above.

Since Amoskeag's profit in 1929 was partially a result of wage concessions that allowed the firm to accept production contracts otherwise unprofitable at the general wage rate, the company declared a 5 percent bonus in 1930 to all employees "in good standing" during all of 1929. On March 13, the company announced that it would pay the bonus in the form of bank deposits during the first week of May. Notices were placed in all departments of the mills stating the banks that would accept the deposits. The bonus to Amoskeag mill hands had amounted to $433,000.

The significance of having the money placed in savings accounts rather then distributing the bonuses in cash was indicative of Dumaine's frugal instincts. He was attempting to foster savings on the part of the employees. On the other hand, the employees could simply withdraw the funds and have the same effect as a cash payment.

The bonuses were distributed the first three days of May, and by the end of the third day of distribution more than 75 percent of the money had been withdrawn.

Some six weeks later, the Merrimack River Savings Bank, one of the banks authorized to receive the employees' bonuses was closed by the State Bank Commissioner due to problem loans in the western part of the country. Upon hearing this information, Dumaine at once took the train to Manchester and, in the words of his diary, "made good $60,000 in the closed bank."

> Interviewed Operatives Labor Committee — agreed to take operatives' bankbooks in the failed Merrimack River Savings Bank and guarantee those leaving their deposits in the bank or supply them with a bankbook in any other bank of their choice for the face amount of their bonus deposit.

Developments in the wage situation at Amoskeag continued on the same basis in 1930. Wage reductions were put into effect in various mills to make it possible to obtain more orders on certain goods. It was made clear that if the reduction was refused, the particular mill would be closed. In August, the bag mill would not accept a 10 percent wage cut. It was closed. The point was made. Shortly afterward, the drawing-in department in No. 11 Mill took a reduction that averaged 12.5 percent to remain in effect for only three months until the specified order had been filled, but it was prolonged by the acceptance of a repeat order at the same reduced wage rate.

On November 29, 1930, a program was introduced in which each week between 8,000 and 9,000 of the operators still employed at Amoskeag could elect to have 10 cents deducted from their pay envelopes to aid those laid off. The company agreed to match the employee contributions and the proceeds were distributed.

A six-month general wage reduction of 10 percent was put into effect in the fall of 1931. At the same time, Dumaine reduced rents on Amoskeag-owned tenements by the same 10 percent to offset the reduction. In addition, he promised:

> If during any year while wage adjustments are in operation, the company shows a net profit, on a third of such profit it will be divided among the employees in direct proportion to their earnings for the year.

Amoskeag was establishing as a formal policy what was practiced in the 1930 bonuses. However, the company cautioned the employees that such a distribution would be impossible in 1931 due to losses sustained in the first eight months of the current year.

When Dumaine, on April 15, 1931, presented his report for the year 1930 to shareholders of the operating company, he noted that July 1931 would mark the 100th anniversary of the granting of a charter to the Amoskeag Manufacturing Company. He told how manufacturing had been tried at the falls for twenty years, but without success, until five men of vision, Ira Gray, Willard Sayles, Oliver Dean, Leonard Pitcher, and Lyman Tiffany formed the Amoskeag Manufacturing Company. He summarized the history, emphasizing how over that 100 years the company had paid out more than $300 million in wages and $15 million in city taxes. Dumaine closed his presentation with a warning:

> During the past ten years we have been sailing on a troubled sea which has grown constantly more threatening, and during the past five years has almost wrecked the textile industry in the United States. If the pioneers had been in charge of Amoskeag in that period, they would have needed all the courage and skill that they brought to the solution of the problems

136

in their own day. In these difficult times, without the contin-ued cooperation of the employees, Amoskeag might have been forced to close its doors. Our troubles are not over. There are more spindles in the United States than are required to supply the needs of the people, and law forbids any getting together to eliminate wasteful and destructive competition. Reasonable and orderly limitations of production, without raising prices of goods higher than is needed to pay a fair return to labor and capital producing them, could be arranged, if it were not for our rigid antitrust laws. But so long as Congress refuses to modify them, the necessary limitation of production can be attained only by the ruin of the mills and of the communities of which they form a part. Neither the textile workers nor the textile mill owners are receiving justice from our elected representatives.

When I look back and consider what difficulties the founders of the company 100 years ago must have met and overcome, and the trouble that came upon the mills after the Civil War, I find courage to go on, to try to surmount the present difficul-ties. I find faith to believe that the day will come, if not in my time, then in that of my successor, when your treasurer will stand before you and tell you of success.

As the economy worsened, the public was looking for a scapegoat. When the Amoskeag Company, the holding company, held its October 1931 annual meeting it was met with the following critical editorial of the Manchester, New Hampshire, Democrat:

The old cat is gradually creeping out of the bag which has for years kept the Amoskeag secrets. The Liberty Bonds of the company has [sic] been sold and stock purchased that has shrunk in value over $5 million dollars. What a story, what a story. Even the great Amoskeag Corporation [sic] with Dumaine at the helm has been dragged into the vortex of the Wall Street stock crash.... What does Dumaine care? He draws a big salary and besides there is more money in the company's treasury with which he can play the stock market. To make up a $5 million loss will require a lot of sweating and backbreaking and slave-driving among the already underpaid and overworked employees. The Amoskeag workers can prepare to keep their backs bent for the beggarly wages now being paid for a long time to come, and pray that Dumaine will not buy any more stock, because if he does buy more bum stock, he probably will be back telling the workers another 10 per cent cut in wages will be necessary. So watch out and keep one eye on the stock

137

market and the other eye on Dumaine because he may open up a new box of tricks if he buys more bum stock.

While the holding company was doing as well as could be expected during the Great Depression, the same could not be said of the manufacturing company. Both stock and bondholder were becoming increasingly concerned with the outlook for textiles. The market price of the Amoskeag Manufacturing Company $100 bonds had dropped to $56. Dumaine retired some $1.5 million worth of bonds through market purchases at slightly over half-price, producing a savings of better than $90,000 a year in interest payments. He urged the stockholders to be patient, saying: "As sure as daylight follows darkness, conditions will change for the better and a measure of happiness and prosperity will return if we employ fortitude and patience."

About this time, Dumaine received a report on Southern textile wages showing that the Amoskeag pay averaged about $2 a week higher. This was not news. The fact was well known. What troubled Dumaine was that the large Dan River gingham mills had recently instituted a 10 percent cut in the Southern wages. About the same time, the Amoskeag management had taken an order for 700,000 yards of fancy worsteds at a loss to keep the mills running in anticipation of the operators taking a 10 percent pay cut. They refused to cooperate, even though promised that one-third of any profits earned would be distributed as a bonus. Amoskeag had no alternative but to lay off the workers. After a month, the employees reconsidered and, by a vote of about 60 percent in favor, readjustment of wages was accepted.

In spite of the bitterness of some of the operatives and the pessimism of investors frankly urging liquidation, Dumaine was determined to keep the Amoskeag Mills operating if it was humanly possible.

In December of 1932, Dumaine drafted a letter to be sent out by Amoskeag Manufacturing Company's trustees to the current bondholders of Amoskeag's 20 year 6 percent bonds, due in 1948. Further payment of interest while the company continued to operate at a loss, said the advisory, would reduce the corporation's capital to the point that the bondholder's principal would be at risk. If the net working capital assets fell below 50 percent of the face value of the bonds still outstanding, the bonds would be in default and the company could be forced to liquidate. A forced sale might then result in the assets not generating adequate funds to pay the bondholders their principal. It was recommended that the $100 bonds be exchanged for $100 in 7 percent noncumulative preferred stock.

If the bondholders preferred, they could elect an alternative strategy to exchange the $100 bonds for $35 in cash and $50 in 7 percent preferred shares. The Amoskeag Company, the holding company, was willing to exchange its bonds if the majority of the other bondholders would do likewise.

The proposal kindled the beginning of a rift in Dumaine's long acquaintance with Frederick H. Prince, a Massachusetts-born magnate of the Chicago stockyards and railroads. In the Coolidge and Hoover administrations, Dumaine tried to assist Prince in securing the ambassadorship to France. Dumaine had done his best, but opposition from the West was too powerful. With the rise to power of the Democrats and Dumaine's support of Roosevelt in 1932, Prince was disappointed to find that Dumaine had no political influence with the new administration. As he frankly wrote Prince:

November 10, 1932

My dear Fred,

The Democrats swept the country from stem to stern, carrying [Senators] George [Moses], Jim Watson and Smoot. If not the greatest political turnover, at least nearly so. George tells me he did everything possible to make the grade.

Who can tell the result; at any rate something is wrong when a great national party is repudiated in such a general way. Although knowing some of the workers, I have no intimate connection with the new government and therefore unable to tell you what the real policies are likely to be.

Enclosed is a suggestion we have in mind for Amoskeag Manufacturing Company bondholders, you will remember the company covenants to keep its quick [working capital] equal to 50 percent of the face of the bonds. This proposes to give them 35 percent now and 50 per cent in preferred stock, the two equalizing the existing quick. With cotton and wool at going prices, this makes the cash payment possible and leaves enough probably for present-time operations without debt. I'm hoping you'll agree paying one's debts is the best use money can be put to in uncertain times. The bonds should never have been issued; it should have been noncumulative preferred or income bonds.

I'm sorry not to have had a look at you before you sailed. It seems a long time since we had a chat. The best of luck and kindest regards.

Dumaine, while speaking with five years' hindsight in saying that the

139

bonds should never have been issued, was being overly critical of himself. In 1927, when Robert Winsor, Philip Dexter, and Charles F. Choate had favored issuance of Amoskeag Manufacturing Company bonds, the offer of cash and preferred stock as opposed to cash and bonds would not have been successful in combating the future potential takeover activity. If the preferred stock paid dividends, there would be greater cash drain from the company. If it failed to pay dividends, there would be stockholder unrest and a new wave of stock raiding.

In 1927, Prince bought $300,000 worth of the bonds. Since then had come the stock market crash, the Depression, and hard times all over the world. When Dumaine made a personal appeal to Prince to turn in his bonds and stop the drain of 6 percent interest on the Amoskeag Mills, Prince declined. Neither Prince nor most other bondholders showed any interest in the Amoskeag's proposal. On February 10, 1933, it was withdrawn.

The financial situation of the country was at its darkest. Franklin D. Roosevelt was elected in November 1932, but would not take office until March of 1933. He declined to confer with Herbert Hoover on interim measures. By February 14, 1933, Dumaine was noting in his diary that "All banks in Michigan closed today."

> Wednesday, March 1, 1933: Bank closings throughout the country have started general hoarding ― $400 odd millions of currency has been withdrawn from New York banks in the past few days. One corporation is reputed to have withdrawn $7 million in gold. Hoarding adds to the already serious situation and, except to provide temporary relief for payrolls, there seems nothing to do but select the best banks (supposedly) for the cash and await results. Bank deposits generally falling. Having in mind the difficulty of securing payroll currency in 1907, I decided to place $300,000 in small bills in the Guaranty vault at 524 Fifth Avenue against an emergency.

> To provide temporarily for Waltham payroll I drew $100,000 in 5's and 10's, depositing them in a box in the Old Colony Trust vaults.

> Saturday, March 4, 1933: Out of a clear sky, very early in the morning (4 A.M.), orders from Federal Reserve Bank were issued to all banks in the country to declare a holiday for two days. It seems withdrawals at New York during the week (probably $1 billion) reduced their reserve to 26 percent, and there seemed no other way out of it for the moment. The striking feature is the patient spirit of the public.

That same month Amoskeag lowered wages in one additional attempt to bring costs in line with Southern mills. The rate was maintained until Friday, May 19, when 8,000 employees protested the wage and went on strike. In response Amoskeag announced that it would close the mills until August 1 when a 15 percent raise would become effective. Apparently the company planned to use the shutdown to dispose of excess inventories, since continued production at the proposed wage rate could not be justified.

The following Tuesday a riot broke out among 4,000 strikers at the company's main gate. In response, four companies of the national guard were mobilized. A serious riot ensued upon the arrival of the guard at the armory. Some 2,000 strikers and supporters began throwing rocks. Tear gas had to be used to disperse the crowd. When it was over, there were 70 injuries and 39 arrests.

U.S. Labor Commissioner William Lawler and Manchester's Roman Catholic Bishop Peterson served as intermediaries trying to settle the dispute. The following Wednesday Bishop Peterson announced that the trustees of Amoskeag acceded to his request to immediately grant the disputed 15 percent increase. On Friday of the same week, employees voted 3,633 in favor, 1,184 against the proposal to return to work. While this strike was much briefer than the nine month strike in 1922, it was also much bloodier and more bitter.

Throughout this time period Dumaine actively was seeking cooperation from Washington. In June 1933, he appeared as a witness in front of Congress on Roosevelt's proposed Industrial Control Act. While supporting the President's plan, Dumaine argued for a national policy supporting one 48-hour shift instead of two 40-hour shifts. This position was often favored by Northern mills where the one shift was prevalent as opposed to the two shifts often found in the South. Traditionally, Northern firms found it difficult to recruit labor for the second shift. Dumaine also argued for a uniform labor rate throughout the country, hopeful that legislation would succeed in gaining the rate parity he had sought since the strike of 1922. Dumaine received a note from President Roosevelt thanking him for his support of the legislation. Dumaine met with President Roosevelt at the fiftieth anniversary of the Groton School, which Roosevelt and his sons had attended. The Dumaine property abutted the school. His diary notation for the day summarizes his appeal to Roosevelt:

Saturday, June 2, 1934: Groton School celebrated 50th Anniversary. President Roosevelt present for two days. Had short, informal conversation with him on textile situation, pointing out machine capacity exceeds country's needs ⁓ that one reasonable shift was all it was practical to operate. This would employ less hands but enable higher earnings and provide steady work. Cotton textile strike averted ⁓ 25 percent machine hour curtailment order remains unchanged and will go into effect Monday. Wage rise demand to be studied by NRA and reported on within 14 days.

When the National Recovery Act went into operation, Dumaine went to Manchester to address the operatives personally: "The New Deal is the reason for this meeting. The New Deal has given new hope to weary hearts. The workers have chosen a union of the American Federation of Labor as their medium. We are resolved to work with them graciously and harmoniously. We are trail-makers in a new approach to the labor problem," he said.

On September 4, 1934, the Amoskeag workers joined the United Textile Workers national strike call, closing down the mills for three weeks after which "the strike was called off and the workers returned without any change in working conditions."

In February of the following year, Dumaine went to Washington to speak in front of the Cotton Textile Code Authority, an organization authorized under the National Recovery Act to address the issue of wage rate differences between the North and the South. Of course, Dumaine spoke in favor of wage equalization. His diary notations of this event are below:

> Tuesday, February 26, 1935: Code Authority meeting. Colonel Buxton submitted a proposition to put the industry on a double shift of 35 hours each, continuing the present pay for 48 hours, equal to 14 1/4 per cent wage advance.... Anderson and other members of the Code Authority representing the Southern states emphatically declared they would not agree to equalization of wage rates. Called upon Miss Perkins [Secretary of Labor].

He returned to Washington the following month on the same issue.

> Tuesday, March 26,1935. Washington. Breakfast with Senator [David I.] Walsh. He assures us he intends to place the New England textile situation squarely before the administration as soon as it is possible to make an appointment at the White House which he has failed to do the last week or so. Mr.

President Roosevelt at the Groton School, Groton, Massachusetts

[Louis McHenry] Howe's illness has apparently upset the daily schedule.

For the four prior years the company lost over $3.5 million. At the April 1935 annual meeting of the Amoskeag Manufacturing Company, Dumaine reaffirmed the continuing difficulty of manufacturing in the North. He cited higher taxes and wages paid in New England, the periodic labor strikes, and an overall depressed demand for textiles. Of particular significance were the following comments concerning the lower NRA wage scales allowed for Southern mill employees:

> We should pay a living wage, sufficient to provide a comfortable and happy existence. We have no desire to reduce our people to lower standards, but what can our future be if we are unable to bring others up to ours?

For a while it appeared that legislation might produce the equalization of wages that Amoskeag had been seeking since the strike of 1922. However, the South won this political battle and was granted the right to provide employment at a rate below that set in the North. One positive outcome for the North was that the Cotton Textile Code Authority secured permission from the National Industrial Recovery Administration for a 25 percent production curtailment. But even this victory was short-lived when this curtailment, together with all other NIRA policies on regulating output, wages and prices, were declared unconstitutional by the United States Supreme Court the following May.

In summarizing the history of Amoskeag following the reorganizations of 1925 and 1927, the reader should appreciate the following facts:

The early years demonstrated cooperation between management and the employees in the program of "reservation prices," whereby the workers would be willing to take temporary pay cuts to enable management to accept contracts that otherwise would be unprofitable. In return, the workers would receive year-end bonuses equal to one third of any profit the company might make. One 5 percent wage bonus was paid in 1930 to the employees of record in 1929.

Unfortunately, wage concessions at Amoskeag enabling it to compete more effectively with the South were met with subsequent cuts by the South. In turn, this led to increased frustration on the part of both management and labor. This was demonstrated by deteriorating labor relations.

It was during one of the brief but violent strikes that occurred during this time period that a different side of Dumaine emerges from the family oral history. During his youth, Dudley B. Dumaine had heard this story told by family members. Later, Phil Coburn, the primary principal involved in the incident, confirmed the story.

During the strike, plant managers would travel to Groton to report first hand the conditions in Manchester. Topics included the number of employees still working, data on production, and reports on costs. The reports could last several hours. They were held in the library of the Groton house where Dumaine would stand on the fireplace hearth with his elbow on the mantel.

In response to a question as to the feeling of the strikers, Coburn stated, "Mr. Dumaine, I regret to tell you sir, but the men hate you."

Tears uncontrollably flowed from this supposedly tough, gruff leader. Not a further word was said. The men left without formalities for fear of further embarrassing Dumaine.

Left in this soul-searching situation, perhaps Dumaine wished for the wisdom of Solomon. For years, Dumaine was fighting those stockholders who simply wanted to liquidate the mills. Despite his efforts, he was becoming the enemy of labor.

F.C., about 1933

Dumaine fully accepted his ultimate responsibility to the investors. Throughout this time, he demonstrated candor in stating that the company could not be expected to continue to run losses in an effort to provide employment. Ultimately, Amoskeag had an obligation to provide stockholders with a return on their investment.

The question yet to be resolved: Did the combination of lower cost of living and the lower expectations on the part of Southern labor make it inevitable that the South would ultimately cause Amoskeag to cease operations?

145

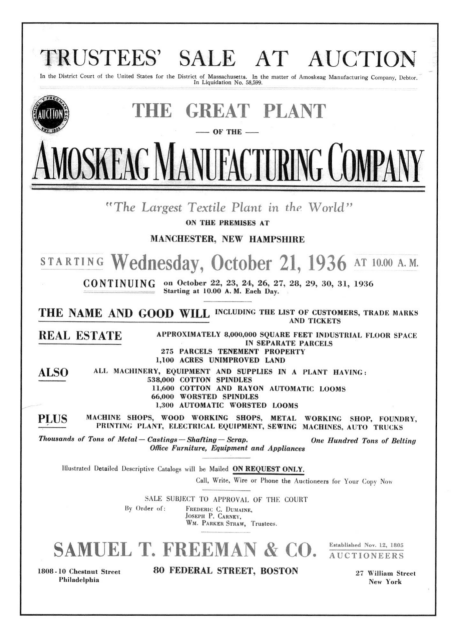

Auction notice following the closing of the mills.

C H A P T E R   X I V

Closing of the Amoskeag Mills

In the spring of 1935, Amoskeag began a process of curtailing operations. By September, most production rooms were closed and fewer than 1,000 operators remained in the corporation's employ. Despite the massive layoffs, Dumaine's diary shows that he refused to consider liquidation.

> September 3, 1935: Meeting at First National Bank with [Charles Francis] Adams and [Philip] Stockton. Amoskeag Manufacturing Company situation in great detail. It was agreed to liquidate might be a grave mistake if the community and workers want otherwise.

Earlier that same year, Amoskeag began divesting some of its excess property. In March of 1935, it razed Langdon Mill No. 1 and two other smaller mills in an attempt to lower property taxes. On June 6, Amoskeag sold Mill No. 12 on North Main St. The mill, which cost $164,000 to construct in 1902, was sold for only $17,500, providing testimony to the depressed conditions. On July 12, the local newspaper carried an article telling how the corporation sold one of its tenement buildings to the Manchester Building and Loan Association, which intended to raze the apartment house for a new bank on the site. The article noted that it was the first sale of tenement property in the company's history and demonstrated Amoskeag's desire to dispose of some real estate.

Following the September shutdown of the Amoskeag Mills, the

147

general public became increasingly concerned with the situation. New Hampshire Governor Styles Bridges appointed a Textile Advisory Board to look into the situation. The committee, headed by Bishop John Peterson, met with local bankers and merchants, labor leaders, union officials, and Dumaine. When Dumaine met with the board, he provided a written statement that financial reorganization would be undertaken if:

(1) Employees would accept the principle of competitive cost basis, and operations would be conducted in an orderly and peaceful manner;

(2) Tasks, rates, and speeds could be determined by management to maintain competitive costs; and

(3) The company could gain relief from local property taxes.

On November 12, the Governor's Textile Advisory Board submitted its report, which called for greater production efficiency, further relief from local taxes, and a new spirit of cooperation between management and employees. The committee opposed wage cuts, one issue considered essential by Dumaine. The rationale for the board's position was:

To make any general reduction in rates of pay in order to place Amoskeag mill in a better position to compete with low-wage textile centers would be hazardous. Such action would encourage a further lowering of wages in other centers; and the result would be still lower wages in this industry, already underpaid.

However the committee added the following qualification:

At all events it [a wage cut] should be considered only if necessary to make a decision as between a temporary sacrifice and the total closing of the mill.

The Textile Advisory Board stated that the condition at Amoskeag was part of a national problem of overcapacity and argued for national limitations on machine hours and the destruction of less efficient capacity. Moreover, it called for federal action to curb foreign imports.

As for local issues, the board opposed the destruction of mill property to save taxes and suggested that Manchester adopt the "Fall River Plan" in which buildings temporarily not being used for manufacturing were given tax relief. The report also called upon security holders to make sacrifices so the mills could reopen.

In September of 1935, following the closing of the mills, Dumaine again traveled by rail to Washington. This time he met with Colonel

Westbrook to discuss the possibility of the government leasing part of Amoskeag to fill orders that might be allocated to New Hampshire on a noncompetitive basis. After hearing of Manchester's plight, Westbrook set up an appointment between Dumaine and Jesse Jones of the Reconstruction Financing Committee. Jones suggested that the government would consider a loan to Amoskeag with the proviso that Amoskeag rid itself of the current bond obligations that would allow the government to be in a first mortgage position. Because the issue of the bonds was never resolved, Amoskeag was never seriously considered to receive funding from Washington.

Details of Dumaine's attempts to obtain refinancing from the government are found in his diary notations on the subject:

> Monday, September 9, 1935: With Buck and Peary called on Jesse Jones at 11:30 with balance sheet and all data concerning the company's financial affairs. He brought in Ben Johnson, head of Industrial Loan Department, who in turn called in Claude E. Hamilton, Jr., a department attorney. After an examination of balance sheet, insurance, and Manchester tax valuations, they inquired what plan we might have; explained we were there at request of Hopkins' department with no worked-out plan. My offhand thought would be the creation of a new company, the R.F.C. loaning it $5 million to buy the plant, $12 to $15 million more to operate, with $5 million additional for renewals. This would pay the bonds in full and leave something for the common. Full operations in Manchester would be assured and work for the operatives if local costs permitted competitive sales — 6,000 already on welfare.
>
> Johnson would not subscribe, on the theory they could not loan money to pay security holders. Hamilton was of the opinion it would be legal under the Act as it would provide work for the unemployed. Jones and Johnson would not agree to such a loan unless the bond situation was eliminated and they could secure an underlying mortgage on the whole property which, if done, would place them in position to make a very substantial loan for rehabilitation and operating expenses. The question of the new company buying assets of the old was talked over — it seemed there was plenty of authority in the Trust Indenture provided no fraud could be alleged. As stated, if a new company was formed, the R.F.C. would loan the added money to operate, etc.
>
> Asked Jones to go with me to Hyde Park to see the president from whom had come the suggestion of the Hopkins contact

to find out how far he, the president, would like to go. Jones said that, although he was always glad to go to the president, he did not feel he should unless invited ⏤ the President had never intimated how or to whom loans should be made. Johnson is to be in Boston Wednesday and glad to cooperate with us in any way possible. Will try for an evening meeting with [John L.] Hall, [Charles P.] Curtis, [Charles Francis] Adams, [Philip] Stockton, and [William] Dexter if it seems wise.

With Buck on four o'clock to New York ⏤ Jesse Jones aboard ⏤ pleasant conversation with him. Reiterated he would loan large sums for operations and replacements if the new setup was accomplished.

Tuesday, September 10, 1935: Breakfast [in New York] with Bob Stone, Hull [of the Agwilines], Buck. Jesse Jones breakfasting with three others, passed time of day with him, said he would telephone Hyde Park during the day, have heard no more. Senator Huey P. Long of Louisiana died by bullet fired by Dr. Carl A. Weiss, who was killed by Long's guards.

Wednesday, September 11, 1935: Adams and Hull on one o'clock to Boston ⏤ told them result of Washington meeting and talked over possibility of reorganization under indenture ⏤ ethics the question.

Dumaine had waited over Monday night and all day Tuesday in New York, hopeful that Jesse Jones would secure an appointment for them to go to Hyde Park for an interview with the president. The Roosevelt Papers at Hyde Park, New York, contain a typed memorandum of a telephone conversation made by Dumaine on that Wednesday before he left New York. The memorandum read as follows:

I am head of the Amoskeag Mills in New Hampshire. They are shut down. I was called for by Colonel Westbrook to come down there to see what could be done to put these 10,000 people back to work. Well, I have been to Washington and I don't get very far there.... I have done all I can in Washington and I am just as anxious to put them back to work. I wanted to get this story to the Chief and if he wanted me to, I would come up and see him but don't want to bother him unless he is anxious to know my side of the story.

They sent me from one place to another and I had a long talk with Jesse Jones on the only way I can see out of this thing is for those people to lend me enough money to put that thing in shape.

There are some complications about a lot of bonds and Jesse Jones, while he knows he has a right to do it because his lawyer said so, has the notion he can't do a thing unless I buy them off or go through receivership or something of the sort—77-B—and you know that takes, ordinarily, several months to do and what they want to do is to get these 9 or 10,000 people back to work. I'm not trying to bother anybody but I would like to have the Chief know what I've done.

It is apparent that Dumaine did not succeed in talking by telephone to the president personally. The typed memorandum at Hyde Park bears a note reading: "Mac, will you get hold of Jesse Jones and see what we can do about it. F.D.R."

The administration at Washington, in spite of Dumaine's support of Roosevelt and his cooperation with the N.I.R.A., had not one cent for Amoskeag. With a campaign for reelection due in 1936, politicians might have found it more useful to pay workers directly through the Work Projects Administration. Dumaine was requesting a $5 million loan from the R.F.C. He did not get it. In September, 1935, when Dumaine had to close the mills for lack of cash, there were exactly nine persons in Manchester on WPA. In October 1936, the month before the presidential election, the figure stood at 4,007. In total, the WPA paid out $6.3 million in three years in Manchester, New Hampshire.

When the 1927 bonds were issued, they carried a proviso that the net working capital of the Amoskeag Manufacturing Company should not fall below 50 percent of the face of the bonds. Accumulated losses since 1928 amounted to $9 million. Only $2 million was the bond interest. Another $2.5 million was "processing taxes." The Supreme Court ultimately would rule that this tax on the manufacturing process as opposed to profits was unconstitutional. Since this decision did not occur until January 1936, it was too late to prevent Amoskeag from having to file for bankruptcy.

For the first six months of 1935, sales of Amoskeag goods were one-third of normal. Dumaine tried unsuccessfully to get help from many sources, including the government.

The first suggestion of reorganizing the Amoskeag Manufacturing Company had come from Jesse Jones, with an implied thought that R.F.C. funds would be forthcoming if this were done and "the bonds out of the picture." Dumaine now discussed this, reporting on his Washington conferences with the trustees. He reported that the company showed a loss of more than $668,000 for the six months ending June

30, 1935. Following this meeting, the trustees published the following statement on September 30:

> The mills are closed to prevent further losses. When the Trustees are convinced production can be carried on at Manchester peaceably and profitably and that the public favors it with their support, the Trustees will undoubtedly give the question serious consideration.

Dumaine, still hopeful of reopening the mills with R.F.C. funds, had the whole production staff of the mills at his house in Groton all day the next Sunday, and on Monday went to Providence for a long conference on costs and wages with labor leaders Thomas McMahon and Horace Riviere of the UTW, and Kingman of the law firm Edwards and Angell. The gist of their talk, Dumaine recorded, was, "McMahon wants forty-hours, two shifts, competitive rates. We stand for one shift and larger [pay] envelope. To run two shifts and pay Southern wages, the pay envelopes would be so small, averaging $13.50, that it would not be fair to labor, would not command the best class, and would invite future dissatisfaction and labor troubles."

On October 3, in a meeting with employees and union officials in Manchester, Dumaine expressed his hope to avoid liquidation, stating; "I will never consent to liquidation until I am confident that further operations of the mills are impossible." He went on to point out that it was Amoskeag that purchased the Manchester Mills in 1903 and the Stark Mills in 1922, when both were facing permanent closing, and thereby provided continuing employment to their Manchester employees. However, he cautioned:

> Is Amoskeag next in line to follow them? I hope not. I lived in Manchester, and I have loved it. I love Amoskeag and I will stay with it until the ship goes down.

At the same time that Amoskeag was negotiating with the union, it was conferring with city officials about property taxes. While Mayor Damase Caron had chastised the corporation for asking for a tax assessment cut in September of 1935, by November, following the publication of the Governor's Textile Advisory Board's report, it became increasingly obvious that, if Amoskeag were to close permanently, the city would generate little tax revenue from mill property. Amoskeag representatives met with city officials, local businessmen, Bishop Peterson representing the Governor's Textile Advisory Board, and New Hampshire Chief Justice Robert Peaslee on the tax issue. On December 4, the city announced that it agreed to tax Amoskeag property on a par with their competitors' tax rates in the South. The first major obstacle to reopening the mills appeared to be resolved.

On December 16, Dumaine met with Thomas McMahon, president of the United Textile Employees of America, at the Parker House in Boston. At this meeting the two signed an agreement to operate at a competitive cost basis. Two days later a follow-up meeting was held to establish the basis for calculating the competitive wage.

Following the first of the two meetings, Dumaine was so optimistic by the cooperation of labor officials, stockholders, and the R.F.C., that on December 17 he entered a bid for the Amoskeag Mills for 1.25 million yards of ginghams for government requirements and, on December 18, held a staff meeting of mill executives and supervisors. Since September he had been conferring with trustees, bankers and attorneys on a plan for reorganization that would "get the bonds out of the picture" as Jesse Jones wished before lending R.F.C. funds, invoking also, as Jones had originally suggested, Section 77-B. The Executive Committee of Amoskeag Manufacturing Company voted for the plan on December 20, 1935.

The full board of trustees met on December 24, 1935, and confirmed the recommendation, authorizing a letter to be sent to security holders. The letter to the bondholders and stockholders stated that to avoid forced liquidation, the Amoskeag Manufacturing Company had filed for bankruptcy and proposed reorganization. Dumaine was determined to reopen the Amoskeag mills. The letter to the security holders was dated December 24, 1935, and it began with the sentence, "The mills are now closed." Historians and the general public point to this correspondence as illustrative of Dumaine's cruelty. "Scrooge Dumaine" closed the mills on Christmas Eve. In reality, the mills had been closed since the beginning of September. The letter was to inform the stockholders that Amoskeag was attempting to voluntarily reorganize in order to reopen the mills. But why ruin a good story with the truth?

Three days later, Dumaine held yet another meeting with union officials about calculating the competitive wage. Dumaine informed the union that he must have a decision by January 20, the date of the next scheduled court hearing on bankruptcy. On January 13, one week prior to the deadline, a final meeting was held and the issue was resolved with the union. While the matter still had to be voted on by the Amoskeag employees, it appeared that a second major obstacle to reopening the mills had been overcome. All that remained was to get the approval of the security holders and the bankruptcy court on the reorganization.

On January 6, 1936, Amoskeag had received good news on another front. The Supreme Court declared in United States v. Butler, the processing tax collected under the Agricultural Adjustment Act to be unconstitutional. Amoskeag might recover $2.5 million paid in processing taxes, which would produce a much needed cash injection to the working capital.

The success in the areas of taxes and wages resulted in Amoskeag trustees feeling confident that it would be able to recommend a formal reorganization plan to the bond- and stockholders. At the January 20 bankruptcy hearing, in front of Judge Sweeney, Amoskeag's attorney expressed the opinion that the reopening of the mill "was not far distant." At the hearing, the judge set March 9 as the date for submission of a plan for reorganization.

A meeting was held on February 28 to map out the details of the labor agreement to be voted upon by the employees. In addition to management, union, and employees, also attending were Governor Bridges, Bishop Peterson, and former Mayor Arthur Moreau, who represented the Citizen Committee, a group of local civic leaders. The agreement reaffirmed competitive labor rates and barred lockouts and strikes. Moreover, violations of the agreement would be justification for discharge; management would not discriminate because of union membership; and local unions would give the international officials the authority to negotiate with management.

Following three days of voting, on March 4, the results were 3,669 in favor and 3,133 against the agreement. Since the strike of 1922, Amoskeag had attempted to establish wage parity with the South. At last it appeared to be resolved. While all those associated with Amoskeag — the city, the employees and the management — would have preferred to see Southern wages rise to the level in New England, at least a common wage, low as it might be, could provide the mechanism for sustained employment in Manchester.

At the March 9 court date, Amoskeag submitted its reorganization plan. Key points were:

1. General creditors would be paid in full in cash.

2. Bondholders could exchange each $100 bond for either:

    a. One share of first preferred 5 percent stock and 15 shares of common, or

    b. $50 in cash and one half share of second preferred 5 percent stock.

3. Holders of common stock would retain their current holdings.

The notice went on to say that the preferred shares were noncumulative and, as such, would only pay dividends when earned. In addition, if more than half of the bondholders elected alternative B, to take half of their bonds in cash, then the corporation would be left without adequate working capital and would have to withdraw the reorganization plan. In effect, the reorganization plan would not proceed if either:

A majority of the bondholders voted against the plan in its entirety, or a majority of the bondholders voted in favor of the plan but elected to turn in their bonds under option B, thus depleting the company of necessary working capital.

That same day Amoskeag Paper Company owner Frank Carpenter, who had served as an Amoskeag trustee from 1906 through 1928, was reappointed. In addition to being one of Manchester's most prominent businessmen, Carpenter was also one of the city's most generous benefactors. Carpenter's acceptance of the post at this time (he was 90 years old) appears to have been motivated by a desire to serve as an intermediary between Amoskeag and many New Hampshire investors who had mixed feelings about whether they wanted to see the mills reopen under Boston-based management.

On March 17, the Amoskeag Company, the holding company, announced its willingness to accept the plan and choose alternative A, provided sufficient other bondholders also accepted the alternative. Since Amoskeag Company owned approximately 32 percent of all the outstanding bonds of Amoskeag Manufacturing Company, the reorganization plan appeared to be well on its way.

However, the optimism generated by the March 17 announcement received a substantial setback the following day when the combination of a severe rain storm and the seasonal snow melt caused the Merrimack River to overflow the Amoskeag Dam. Substantial flood damage occurred in the mill yard. The city's McGregor Bridge, together with four of the Amoskeag's pedestrian and utility bridges, were washed away. Severe structural damage to the company's mill buildings was limited to its wooden storage sheds. Despite the fact that all of the mill buildings

The 1936 flood ravages the Amoskeag mills.

between the lower canal and the river experienced considerable flooding, they all weathered the storm, a tribute to the quality of the construction over the previous century. Unfortunately, the machinery inside the mills did not fare as well. The flood waters carried silt that clogged much of the machinery on the first two floors of the mills in the lower section of the yard. The timing of this natural disaster could not have been worse. More than 50 percent of the bondholders would be required to leave their cash in the corporation.

Dumaine had spent Wednesday, March 18, in New York for a board meeting of the New Haven Railroad. His normal practice was to take the evening train back to Boston. On this occasion, however, he remained overnight in New York. Some speculate that he was expecting to be summoned to Washington to confer with Roosevelt about the possibility of a loan for Amoskeag. The meeting never took place. Buck Dumaine called him on Thursday morning, March 19, explaining the severity of the flood. Dumaine took the ten o'clock train to Boston where he was met at the South Station by his family to take him directly to Manchester. In his diary Dumaine wrote:

> Worst ice jam in years. Found 16 feet of water on the dam — 5 feet more than in '96 and '97 freshet. All the company's bridges gone, as was the Bridge Street bridge. At Granite Street, water was over the roadway. For the next 9 hours, the water rose

156

Amoskeag workers try to sandbag the oncoming water.

about 1/10 of a foot an hour, reaching the peak at 3 a.m.—17 feet, 2 inches; where it held for about 5 hours. At 1:15 a.m. our lights went off although the power company continued to operate, probably from their Portsmouth power.

When Buck telephoned me at the Biltmore Thursday morning, I instructed him and Chris [Dumaine's second son] to secure all bags in and about Boston and arrange to have them transported by truck without a moment's delay. I forget just how many were used, about 100,000 according to the number of trucks required to land them in Manchester. Detours, roundabout routes, road difficulties, and high water caused the last truckload of bags to arrive after two in the morning and the Manchester supply was nearly exhausted.

Nothing but these bags of sand could have held the flood at both ends of the dam. When the water first started to cover the railroad bed, there was not time enough to remove the tracks and the sleepers. More or less water found its way between the sleepers, causing some trouble and anxiety. This is important to remember. Buck and I passed the night with the men, he on the west side, I on the east. Chris was in the sand pit this side of Hooksett. Too much credit cannot be given to Hagan, Ranch, Wheeler, Ahern, Worthern, Peterson, Captain Dunlap of the National Guard, and many others who at great personal risk worked and led the crews. It was a gallant fight and victorious...

157

The flood takes its toll on the Granite Street bridge.

In all probability, [without this effort] every city and town in the valley from Manchester to Newburyport would have been destroyed. When the water finally dropped to normal, there were spots on the Jefferson [Mill] and Bag Mill floors where sand and silt were 6 feet deep.

During Thursday afternoon, the authorities closed all bridges and it was necessary to haul sand from Hooksett, four miles. Thirty-odd trucks and 600 to 700 men filled 100,000 bags with sand (the only thing which seems to combat water) and piled them near the gate house and across the railroad tracks until the rise ceased. It was nip and tuck which would win. As the crews tired, recruits from militia, CCC, and WPA took their places. The same went on at the other end of the dam near the Hydro Station which was saved. Buck was over at that end.

Members of the [Amoskeag Manufacturing Company] staff and many others were on duty 36 to 40 hours without rest. The city government, citizens, and all organizations volunteered and there was the greatest cooperation, unity, and cheerful helpfulness. They deserve credit for preventing what threatened to be a most appalling disaster. It was thrilling to see houses and the Hooksett bridge come down and bound over the dam.

The damage is terrible — mostly to machinery, bridges, steam pipes, and power. Just at the moment the effect upon the fu-

The devastating destruction of the flood of 1936 was hard to imagine.

> ture is hard to determine. My feeling is the bondholders will prefer cash by all odds and with the expense all this damage has caused, it seems hopeless to think sufficient funds will be available. Fate seems to have taken an important part in the situation.

The pessimism expressed in Dumaine's final paragraph did not last long. One week later, on March 24, Dumaine went to Manchester to plead personally with New Hampshire bondholders to approve the reorganization plan and elect alternative A. He reminded those in attendance that Amoskeag Company had already selected that option. Catholic Bishop Peterson and Episcopal Bishop Dallas urged the cooperation of the local investors. Several of the bondholders stated their need for additional time to consider their options.

On April 3, Dumaine received a letter from a group of Manchester bondholders stating that unless Amoskeag met certain demands relative to management of the organization, trustee representation and security holder's rights, they would vote against the reorganization and select alternative B if the reorganization was approved by the court.

At the scheduled April 6 court hearing, there were four groups that registered opposition to the plan through their attorneys. Frederick Prince, the internationally known financier who held $300,000 of the bonds, opposed the plan, serving notice that he intended to challenge the constitutionality of the bankruptcy laws. Mrs. Eliza Leland, who held $20,000 in bonds, opposed the plan and presented the argument that Amoskeag Company's bondholders in the manufacturing company should be subordinate to all other bonds. Charles M. Green, a holder of $2,000 of the bonds, objected to the plan stating that it was unfair. The United States Trust Co. also opposed the plan with the argument that many of the estates under trusteeship would suffer losses if the plan were accepted by the court. Obviously, these groups felt that an immediate liquidation would provide sufficient cash to make the option superior to either alternatives A or B. If the court were to decide, as it eventually did, that Amoskeag Company's bondholdings should be subordinated to all others, the probability of receiving 100 percent of the bond's face value by all other bondholders was even more likely.

John Hall, Amoskeag's attorney, reported that 70 percent of the bonds outstanding accepted the plan. While this was over the two thirds majority, the results on the selection of alternative A or B were less than satisfactory. With only 41 percent electing alternative A, the company was short of the 50 percent deemed necessary prior to the flood damage. This was particularly disappointing when it is remembered that 32 percent accepting that alternative were owned by Amoskeag Company.

Attorney Allen Wilson, representing more then $1.1 million of bonds owned by the Manchester group, requested an extension of time for his bondholders to consider the proposed plan. This group was now in an extremely strategic position. If they voted for the reorganization and elected alternative A, the mills would probably reopen. If they voted against or even elected alternative B, the mills would be liquidated. At Attorney Wilson's request, Judge Sweeney granted a postponement until April 20.

In an April 11 letter, the Amoskeag Manufacturing Company responded to the Manchester bondholders' demand letter, meeting some of the requests and explaining why certain other requests could not be met at that time. The mood of some of the New Hampshire interests may best be represented by the anonymous quote that was floating about then: "It's time to have Dumaine do what we want him to do."

Dumaine returned to Manchester on April 16 to meet with the local bankers. He pointed out that while the floods caused $2.5 million in damage, not all of the equipment needed to be replaced at once. Since the company planned to operate at a lower capacity if it reopened the mills, the cost of the repairs and replacement could be spread over the next three years. In effect, the trustees of both the holding company and the manufacturing company would continue to favor the reorganization plan if sufficient other bondholders selected alternative A. When Dumaine returned home, he found a letter dated April 15 charging that Amoskeag's concessions, as outlined in the April 11 response, were not sufficient to satisfy the Manchester group. However, no one at the April 16 meeting saw fit to inform Dumaine of the decision.

It appears that the arguments presented by Dumaine and Frank Carpenter at the April 16 session were sufficient to sway the Manchester group. By the end of April, both the Boston and the Manchester papers reported that approximately $1 million worth of bonds held by the New Hampshire group were prepared to favor the reorganization.

The following month, Amoskeag was faced with two additional setbacks. On May 1, financier Freddy Prince demanded a hearing on subordinating Amoskeag Company's holdings of Amoskeag Manufacturing Co. bonds, if the company were to be liquidated. In effect, he was supporting the position previously taken by Mrs. Leland that the holding company's bonds should not receive any payment until all other bondholders were paid in full. For any bondholder uncertain whether to select reorganization or liquidation, the potential for such a ruling would tend to tip the balance toward selecting liquidation, since the likelihood of receiving 100 percent of the bond's face value would be greatly increased. The fact that an internationally known financier supported this alternative gave it increased credibility and attention.

Friday night, May 22, Dumaine went to Washington to see Jesse Jones. Accompanying Dumaine was John P. Maguire of New York, who recounted the experience to Dorothy Wayman when she was gathering material for "Dumaine of New England":

> Jones was busy that Saturday morning, sent word that he had to go to the Hill, but Dumaine might ride to the Capitol with him. "I didn't come all the way to Washington for a conference in the back seat of an automobile," snapped Dumaine, and took Maguire off for lunch. They returned to the RFC office at two-thirty and waited forty-five minutes to see Jones.
>
> "I need a lot of money to keep a lot of people employed," was Dumaine's abrupt beginning. "I hear you are handing out a lot of money. Now, I'm not going back to my trustees to tell 'em you said something. I want a commitment in writing to show them."

161

Jones protested this was not the usual office procedure, but Dumaine had his way. At the end of the interview, walking down the hall, Dumaine stopped short.

"God, I'm glad I thought of that," he muttered. "I never flew in my life but, by God, I feel like flying tonight," he said to Maguire, who was flying to Newark. "You get me a reservation to Boston."

The memorandum, dated at Washington, Reconstruction Finance Corporation office, May 23, 1936, was signed by Jesse Jones, Chairman. It read:

Mr. F. C. Dumaine, representing the Amoskeag Manufacturing Company, Manchester, New Hampshire, has been in discussing the proposed loan to the Amoskeag Manufacturing Company of $2.5 million, the proceeds to be used in rehabilitation of the plant with suggested repayment plan of 3, 4 or 5 years. I have stated to Mr. Dumaine that if upon investigation the facts are found to be approximately as indicated by the papers submitted, with proper provision for limitation of dividends, etc., and maintenance of a proper margin of working capital during the period of the loan, I saw no reason why we should not make the loan.

Dumaine flew home to Boston truly optimistic that the Amoskeag Mills would soon reopen. Two days later, at a May 25 meeting with the mayor and assessor, Dumaine was informed that Amoskeag's property tax obligation for the year would be double the amount that Dumaine believed had been agreed upon at a meeting the previous December, when it was decided to tax the plants at a rate comparable with Southern mills.

When the trustees met on June 1, it was reported that 49 percent of the total bond outstanding elected alternative A. This included the Manchester group's bonds. While 49 percent is quite close to the 50 percent designated as necessary by Amoskeag when it first proposed the reorganization plan, that proposal was prior to the increased expenditures required by the floods; the partial reversal of the tax concession by the city of Manchester; the lack of full support by the community's business leaders; and the movement to subordinate Amoskeag Company's bonds, to all other bonds in case of liquidation.

According to his son Buck, there was a subsequent meeting between Dumaine and Manchester investors two or three days prior to the opening of the final bankruptcy hearing. According to Buck:

162

He had driven his father to Manchester from Boston so F.C. could meet with the Manchester bondholders. Parking on Hanover Street, F.C., Jr., remained in the car while F.C. went into a legal office in the Amoskeag Bank building. When Dumaine returned to the car not a word was spoken for the first half of the trip back to Massachusetts. Finally, F.C., Jr., broke the silence. F.C. was furious. The majority of Manchester's bondholders had decided not to support the reorganization plan, he told his son. When Dumaine reminded them of their commitment to the reorganization, their response was that they had only said that they "might" go along with the refinancing.

Whether Buck was confusing this date with the April 15 meeting is unclear. Amoskeag records prove that many Manchester bondholders who opposed the refinancing at the April meeting reversed themselves and later agreed to go along with the refinancing. Whether there was an additional reversal cannot be determined. However, a significant number of the local bondholders opposed the refinancing.

The intent of the Manchester investors unwilling to accept Dumaine's plan is unclear. Their decision could have been based on a strict fiduciary obligation for the funds entrusted to their care. Many might have expected to receive 100 percent of their face value since Amoskeag's bonds were likely to be placed subordinate to all other bondholders. Alternatively, they could have seen this as an opportunity for Manchester to rid itself of the control of Dumaine and Boston interests. They might have anticipated that local citizens would be able to purchase the mills at bankruptcy prices, as eventually happened. Regardless of their reasoning, Amoskeag was left with an insufficient number of bondholders willing to support the plan to make the proposed reorganization feasible.

On June 9, the day prior to the opening of the final bankruptcy hearing, the minutes of the special meeting of the trustees of the Amoskeag Manufacturing Company and the Amoskeag Company reflected that they voted to withdraw their support for the reorganization. The votes cited as a primary reason "the failure of more than one half in amount of the New Hampshire bondholders to leave their money in the business."

Following Amoskeag's decision to withdraw its plan for reorganization, the company was declared legally insolvent in the Federal District Court on July 21, 1936. In a subsequent decision, the bonds of the Amoskeag Manufacturing Company held by Amoskeag Company were placed subordinate to all other bonds. In effect, the court agreed with the petition of Mrs. Leland that all other bondholders should be paid in full prior to the holding company receiving one cent.

Dumaine was named one of three co-trustees of the bankruptcy along with W. Parker Straw, Amoskeag's former agent, and Joseph E. Carney, the former head of the New Deal's Reconstruction Finance Committee for New England.

Shortly thereafter, a group of Manchester men organized Amoskeag Industries, a company that wished to purchase the mills prior to a scheduled bankruptcy auction. Five hundred thousand dollars was raised in cash. The local utility company offered $2 million for the power plants and water rights. An additional $2.5 million was loaned by the various Manchester Banks. While the Manchester group hoped to attract potential textile firms with bargain basement purchase prices, they also hoped to attract a diversified group of non-textile investors wishing to take advantage of Manchester's empty factories and abundant labor force.

While the $5 million probably was less than what would have been raised by the auction, Dumaine and the other trustees agreed to the purchase price. Their primary reason was to prevent the equipment that would have been auctioned off from finding its way to Southern mills. The sale to Manchester interests that intended to lease or sell the various mill buildings with their equipment intact provided the greatest oppotunity for maximum reemployment of the labor force.

Shortly after the takeover of the mills, the principals of Amoskeag Industries approached Dumaine to run the textile operations. He refused. Three possible reasons emerge: One, he may have felt that at age 70 he was too old to start over; two, he was warned by a government hearing that it would not be looked on favorably if he were to regain control of the mills; or, three, he may have felt betrayed by Manchester interests. Many of the parties involved with the financing of Amoskeag Industries were among the Manchester bondholders who were reluctant to support Dumaine's refinancing plan.

While Amoskeag Industries eventually was successful in finding firms willing to take advantage of low cost mill sites, it is questionable whether employment grew as fast as it would have under Dumaine's proposed refinancing.

Based on the proceeds from the sale of the mills, the subsequent

F.C. and son Buck in Manchester, New Hampshire, in 1936.

liquidation of current assets and the receiving of the $2.5 million back from the U.S. Government as a result of the Supreme Court's decision on the legality of the processing tax, Amoskeag was able to pay all bondholders including Amoskeag Company. Bankruptcy Referee Arthur Black commented: "Our difficulty comes from the fact that we never before had a case which paid creditors in full." The remaining surplus was distributed to the Amoskeag Manufacturing Company stockholders.

Following the liquidation of Amoskeag Manufacturing Company, the operating company, Dumaine remained the chief executive officer of Amoskeag Company, the holding company. At this point Amoskeag Company operated primarily as an investment company, purchasing the securities of various other corporations. F.C.'s ability to invest wisely in these various securities allowed him to pay dividends on both the preferred and common stock throughout the depression.

165

F.C. in Groton, Massachusetts

C H A P T E R   X V

The Woodchucks

The woodchuck, or groundhog, is a familiar figure of the New England landscape, sitting erect, head tilted a bit to one side, alert, vigilant, unafraid. It has a thick body, short legs, compact head with dark eyes, and bristling whiskers. Its short fur is brown, grizzly-gray at the tips. Neither vicious nor predatory, the woodchuck adapts to human civilization, building its burrows close to farm or suburban garden.

One day, prior to a luncheon at the Parker House, Paul Draper, a Boston wool merchant, spied Dumaine coming into the lobby and said to Al Sharp, president of Eastern Steamship lines, "Here comes the old woodchuck." The name stuck. From that day on, the luncheon group called themselves the Woodchuck Club. Eventually they made it formal, with the Parker House as the home of their Thursday luncheon.

The charter members were an example of Dumaine's broad interests. They included the wool men, brothers Paul and Joseph Draper; a Democratic ex-Governor of Massachusetts, Joseph B. Ely; a Republican ex-Governor, Robert F. Bradford; a governor of the Federal Reserve Bank, Roy A. Young; a Boston and Maine railroad president, Edward S. French; Alton B. Sharp, the steamship man; and Clarence A. Barnes, a Republican ex-attorney-general. Guests were cosmopolitan, unpredictable, but invariably interesting. One day there might be a Roman Catholic Chinese prelate, Archbishop Paul Yupin. The next week, perhaps, Supreme Court Justice Felix Frankfurter, who once, in a letter to Francis W. Buxton, summed up the qualities which endeared Dumaine to so many of his friends.

Fred Dumaine is an unceasing delight: the trenchancy of his mind and the saltiness of his spirit and the caustic penetration of his judgment — how rare they are, these qualities of his, and what a warmhearted and loyal friend.

While Dumaine's credibility with the "Woodchucks" and similar public and private officials was beyond reproach, his "press relations" were bad. He never bothered to contradict unfavorable articles about himself; he never was affable to reporters; he never sued anyone for libel. He liked men with the type of mind newspaper executives, judges, and bankers had — widely versed in national and international happenings and seasoned in understanding human nature. Among his close personal friends were newspapermen Robert Lincoln O'Brien of the Boston Herald; Frank Knox of the Chicago Daily News; Robert Norton of the Boston Post, with whom he talked politics; William O. Taylor of the Boston Globe, with whom he hunted the Maine woods; and Frank W. Buxton, Pulitzer Prize editorial writer of the Boston Herald, with whom he discussed philosophy for thirty years or more.

Dumaine's personal pleasures or recreations were on the Spartan side. He loved his horses and his dogs; the worst weather could not make him forgo his early morning ride. Nevertheless, the animals to him were not for show. His horses went to school to learn their paces, but it was his youngsters who rode them to the hunt or a horse show. His dogs, too, had their training for the field.

> Sunday, December 9, 1928: Got up at 3 o'clock in the morning and went to Sandwich, New Hampshire, with Buck and Pierre to spend the day with Chapman and give the boys a chance to look around for a deer. Chapman hitched up his dogs and gave me a 12 or 15 mile sled ride and it was quite amusing. He had 6 mask-faces, 2 setters, a pair of pointers, and his Chesapeake dog Drake for a leader. Chapman seems to have an unusual way with the dogs, and they are all very fond of him. Bad day bad driving home, reaching Groton at 6:15.

Organized sports, such as baseball or football, rarely had his patronage except for school or college games when his own boys were participating. His enthusiasm for prize fighting, however, was enormous, and he never missed a championship fight, usually taking a party of friends with him. His principal use for the radio, when it became a routine installation in homes after World War I, was to listen to the fight broadcasts. As his deafness grew, he appreciated being able to turn up the volume.

One February day in 1932, Dumaine reported in his diary that he had lunch in Northampton with Calvin Coolidge and found him "cordial and apparently receptive." He dined that evening in Boston with Roy Young, governor of the Federal Reserve Bank, and then ended his entry with "Farmers in Groton selling eggs for 25 cents the dozen." Dorothy Wayman considered this indicative that Fred Dumaine held the fact that a neighbor farmer could not sell his eggs for enough to buy feed for his hens just as important as the fact that he had lunch with an ex-president of the United States and had spoken to a banker who could affect the credit of the country.

Once at his Groton home, F.C. interrupted a Sunday conference with some of the most important figures of New England industry to help a young man who called to ask his support as a candidate for judgeship in the little country court. "Drew a petition to Governor Ely in his behalf. Secured Dr. Peabody's signature and the schoolteachers' [at Groton]," he recorded. The candidate was of Irish descent, a Democrat, and a Roman Catholic. Dumaine would leave his own important affairs to help the young fellow and take him across the road to Groton School just as naturally as he would have done a favor for young James Roosevelt, the son of the president.

Once a friend was recommending for a position in the Amoskeag Mills a man who had shown marked ability in a small mill, but he qualified his endorsement with the words, "Of course, he's a Pollock, but very smart."

"Is he a voter, a citizen of the United States? " asked Dumaine.

"Oh yes; born here, I believe."

"Then what the hell do you mean, calling him a Pollock?" barked Dumaine. "He's a citizen, a family man, a good worker. That makes him just the same as you – an American."

Unitarians, Episcopalians, Catholics, Jews – men of all beliefs were equally counted among Dumaine's friendships. Louis Kirstein, department store magnate and philanthropist, Justice Felix Frankfurter, Dr. Hermann Blumgart of Beth Israel Hospital, Father Jeremiah Ahern, O.S.B., of Saint Anselm Abbey, and Federal Judge Charles Wyzanski were Dumaine's close friends.

When someone would meet Dumaine for the first time, the person often had a preconceived impression of the textile magnate based on Dumain's poor press. Usually this impression would be subject to a 180 degree turn in a relatively short period of time. Such was the case with

Father Jeremiah Ahern, O.S.B., one of the Benedictine monks associated with Saint Anselm College. The Catholic college was established in Manchester, New Hampshire, in 1889 to educate young men in theology, philosophy and commerce. Because of the college's proximity to the mills and the fact that the majority of the mill workers were of the Catholic faith, Saint Anselm College became the primary source of higher education for the children of Amoskeag.

Father Ahern's first contact with Dumaine was in response to the brief 1933 Amoskeag strike in the depths of the Great Depression. While it could be assumed that the original encounter had been under stressful conditions, the following portions of a letter written by the monk expressed a growing mutual respect:

> Indeed, I thank you for changing your New York trip to see me.
>
> If agreeable to you, the third 'skirmish' [our third meeting] will take place at St. Anselm on the hilltop.... There will be no meeting of officials. We two will just walk and talk and sit and talk.
>
> I found you a different 'Mr. Dumaine' than the Mr. Dumaine when I first met you. You were, this last time, somewhat Aristotelian in your outlook on life's problems.
>
> I would suggest that you await a 'spring-fever' day and when you are rather nonplus. Just get in touch with me by telephone in the morning. I will be on the job looking for you in the afternoon.
>
> The special intention of my High Mass next Sunday will be one for the country's leaders and the problems facing us.

Subsequent letters to and from the monk illustrated a continuing friendship and a mutual concern for the welfare of society.

The first meeting between Justice Frankfurter and Dumaine also took place in 1933, just before the Harvard law professor went to lecture at Oxford University. Neither had sought the acquaintance.

"All I had heard about Dumaine gave me the impression of a dyed-in-the-wool reactionary, and I don't doubt he thought of me as a Harvard pedant and possibly a Red to boot," the justice recalled.

Frank Buxton, the Boston Herald editor, kept insisting that Frankfurter and Dumaine should know each other as the two men in Boston who sensed alike — though independently — the portent of Hitler's coming to power in 1933. Finally, he arranged a luncheon at the Parker House. Dumaine was there first. As Frankfurter entered, Dumaine, brusquely eschewing introductions, thrust out a large-sized menu card

170

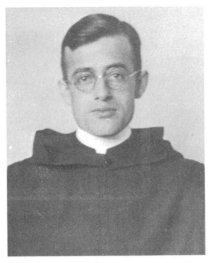

Father Jeremiah Ahern, O.S.B.

with the curt inquiry, "See anything you like there?"

"I know what I want without looking," replied Frankfurter, equally terse. "Some broiled tripe with mustard sauce."

"By God! So you like tripe, too!" exclaimed Dumaine warmly.

From that moment, the ice was thawed. Upon Frankfurter's return from London next year, the friendship quickly ripened. When Roosevelt nominated Frankfurter to the Supreme Court on January 5, 1939, Dumaine, aware of the opposition in some quarters, reached for the telephone. He enlisted the support, on the Senate floor, of Senator Styles Bridges of New Hampshire. Previously, Dumaine had supported Bridges in his candidacies for governor of the Granite State and for the U.S. Senate. In addition, Dumaine contacted Massachusetts Senators Lodge and Walsh, seeking their endorsement for Frankfurter.

Dumaine first knew Louis Dembitz Brandeis as a young Boston lawyer, pioneering in public service and social legislation. In 1938, Frank Buxton accompanied Dumaine on his last visit with Brandeis, then a retired justice of the Supreme Court of the United States, and wrote about it to Justice Frankfurter.

> I wanted to pick Fred up at the office but he thought Forest Hills [elevated station] would be preferable as we could avoid downtown traffic. We were at Forest Hills at about 11:05 but Fred was there ahead of us. I discovered him sitting on a post at

the ground level, looking as if he had been in swimming with his clothes on. His hat and coat were off, he appeared flushed and very hot, and his shirt was wringing wet, but he was blithe as the dealer in a big jackpot.

The date was August 16, 1938. The day before, Dumaine had noted in his diary "all Boston heat records shattered when temperatures climbed to 94 degrees in the second torrid wave of the month." Dumaine was worth a good many million dollars. He was president of Waltham Watch Company. His Groton garage held a small fleet of automobiles and a salaried chauffeur. To him, however, the frugal way to meet his friend was to drop a dime into the turnstile at the State Street station of the El and hang on to a strap for twenty minutes like the poorest laborer. So that was what he did. They were bound for Chatham on Cape Cod, a three-hour drive, with Buxton's son Francis at the wheel. Later on in his letter to Frankfurter, Buxton noted this interesting interchange between Dumaine and Justice Brandeis:

> ....Fred asked the Justice how long ago he had estimated that the railroads could properly save $1 million a day.... The Justice replied that the year of his startling assertion was about 1910. We all multiplied roughly and found that the accumulated waste to date is about $10 billion, plus interest. What condition would the roads be in now, if they had not spent all that money, asked Fred. He and the Justice agreed that, naturally, there would be some distress, but that a great many disasters would have been avoided.
>
> The Justice said again that the explanation of the long continuance of extravagant practices by the road was the absence of the do-or-die spirit. Fred said to the Justice that, although he had never run a railroad, he would like to have the management of a system for a year, without fixed salary but with the understanding that his sole remuneration would be half of what he could save. With his half, he said, he could retire for life. He referred incidentally to the waste in a company with which he is associated [the New Haven Railroad].

Frederic Dumaine's life illustrates the truth in the remark of the British essayist Samuel Johnson (1709-84) that "If a man does not make new acquaintances as he advances through life, he will soon find himself left alone." In the space of seven years, death robbed Dumaine of lifelong companions and confidantes; before ten years were out, he had made new friends of younger men who would be his intimates until death.

Galen Stone, Charles F. Choate, Jr., Guy Currier, and Robert Winsor were gone. "It seems sometimes as if these intimate associates were passing away most rapidly," wrote Dumaine.

Dumaine's attention was first drawn to young William B. Snow in the hectic days of trying to salvage Kidder, Peabody. When the House of Morgan and the New York banks wanted a dependable man to look after details, Dumaine recommended Snow and was pleased with his work. He used Snow again in his brief tenure at Atlantic National Bank in 1933 and watched approvingly Snow's work with the Greyhound Bus Company when the New Haven Railroad was getting the Springfield Street Railway off its hands. In 1939, there was question of a new president for the Suffolk Savings Bank for Seamen and Others — an old Boston institution whose quaint title testifies to its long standing. Dumaine went all out to see that Snow was chosen.

His diary records a long conversation in which Dumaine first overcame all the objections advanced by Stockton and finally secured Stockton's promise to speak in favor of Snow as the new savings bank president. "I think this is one of the best jobs I ever did," was Dumaine's final entry for the day. There was nothing in the Brahmins' blue book or Dun and Bradstreet to give William Brackett Snow, Jr., artificial luster. He came of sterling old New England stock, his father onetime headmaster of English High School, Boston, later assistant superintendent of the Boston schools. On graduating from Harvard in 1918, Snow had become a junior at Kidder, Peabody. He was only forty-two years old when Dumaine, almost single-handedly, made him a bank president, sheerly in recognition of his merit. There was nothing in it for Dumaine except the satisfaction of seeing a good man in an important post in the New England economy.

Even more dramatic was Dumaine's action in the case of a young New York man, John P. Maguire, not personally known to Dumaine except through his business associates as a promising youngster who was about to have a raw deal. Maguire, like Dumaine himself, had gone to work at an early age. At fifteen he had his first job as a stenographer in the old Liberty National Bank of New York, working up to specialize in textile mill credits. Eventually, he was made manager of the new Textile Banking Company, backed by the Guaranty Trust Company and the Liberty National. Both institutions were linked with the J. P. Morgan and George F. Baker interests of Wall Street, with whom Dumaine was on friendly terms. In 1933, the Commercial Credit Company of Baltimore gained control of Textile Banking. As is the case in today's mergers, a shakeup was in the offing.

"It came to a crisis on January 8, 1936. I was fired," Maguire said succinctly.

Fifteen minutes after the board meeting of the Textile Banking Company ended that afternoon, Maguire's telephone rang.

"This is F.C. Dumaine," said a hoarse voice bluntly. "Will you have dinner with me tonight here at the Biltmore?"

Ever close-mouthed as to his sources and plans, Dumaine never revealed the source from which he had such inside information. At dinner that evening he suggested that Maguire form his own factoring firm in textiles.

"Mr. Dumaine, I just got fired this afternoon," said Maguire honestly. "That doesn't look as though I were so hot."

"I know," answered Dumaine cryptically. "The fellow who fired you will be around trying to hire you back. I aim at getting you sewed up first."

Before the evening ended, Dumaine had sketched out the organization of the proposed new firm and promised the capital. Maguire was shocked by the unexpected offer. He went to Boston to confer with Philip Stockton at the First National Bank as to whether Dumaine could really have meant it all.

"He's tough," Stockton said, "but he's the best partner you could ever have. He can use your ability, and you can use his backing and brains."

A formal interview ensued between Maguire and the executive committee of the Amoskeag Company that was furnishing the capital. Maguire was a bit chilled by the ironic Yankee wit and frosty Yankee reserve of Charles Francis Adams; he never forgot the way in which Dumaine imbued him with courage and confidence when the question came up about a name for the new firm.

"Put your own name on the door, Maguire!" barked Dumaine. "You've got no skeletons in your closet, have you? I'll be over to see you in three weeks with the check."

On February 5, 1936, Dumaine called at the office Maguire had rented and handed him a check for $2.75 million. That initiated a profitable investment for the Amoskeag Company and a warm relationship between the old man and his young partner. Every Wednesday Dumaine would be in New York, spending hours at Maguire's office, exploring possibilities and studying problems. Other days there would be telephone calls. It was Maguire who accompanied Dumaine to Washington and booked his first airplane trip when F.C. was looking for financial assistance from the government.

In more leisurely times, they went together to the Kentucky Derby, to the prize fights in New York, to Miami in winter. Once, when Maguire tried to express gratitude, Dumaine put his own philosophy in one short letter:

December 27, 1940

Dear Jack,

Your Christmas remembrances are greatly appreciated, your gracious letter the most.

In five years you have accomplished more than your most loyal supporter could have predicted. It has been a gratification to watch your advance and to be in a small way helpful and a humble part of it. You have constructed an impregnable foundation and the future is secured, if good fortune favors you with health. A happy family, the respect and good wishes of all and every associate are about all one must expect in these troublesome times. They are the rewards for decent living and proper ethics.

A third young man whose career Dumaine took an interest in advancing was Charles P. Curtis, Jr. From 1932, as a partner in the law firm of Choate, Hall and Stewart, Curtis was closely associated with Dumaine in the many legal affairs of Amoskeag Manufacturing Company and other Dumaine interests. The custom of Curtis dropping by Dumaine's office was cultivated. The old man would get the bottle of whiskey and two cups from his bottom desk drawer, pour a libation, and chat. Apparently, he spoke more intimately about his early life to Curtis than to any other surviving friend. Curtis was a favorite companion for trips to Washington after Felix Frankfurter became a United States Supreme Court justice in 1939.

John P. Maguire and Father Jeremiah Ahern were Roman Catholics; Charles P. Curtis, Jr. and William Snow were Yankee Protestants; Felix Frankfurter and Louis Brandeis were Jewish. Dumaine respected them all equally. Even more diverse were the political philosophies of these individuals. Dumaine could tolerate a difference in individual beliefs as long as there existed a core of honesty and devotion to work. Perhaps in the cases of the younger men, Dumaine could see his former youthful self and wished to return the generosity that he had experienced from Coolidge and Sargent.

175

War production parade outside Waltham plant. Photo courtesy of Leslie Nesky.

C H A P T E R   X V I

Waltham Watch Goes to War

Waltham Watch was not immune from the economic havoc wrought by the Great Depression. The company did manage a profit of $177,000 in 1930, which was 20 percent of the $908,000 averaged in the prior four years. While Waltham maintained the hourly wage rate that year, the employment level was down by 35 percent.

Waltham Watch purchased additional shares of both of its preferred stock issues at the lower stock market prices that reflected the economic times. This would reduce preferred dividend requirements in subsequent years. The company elected to continue the payment of dividends on the outstanding preferred, which amounted to $273,000. An additional $132,000 was paid to Class A common.

Nineteen thirty-one was a particularly bad year. The company experienced a loss of $580,000. However, in anticipation of a relatively short downturn, the board declared dividends on the preferred issues and the Class A common. A total of $160,000 was paid out of prior years' earnings. One reason the company may have decided to continue the dividend was the rather lucrative contract that was signed with Ford Motor Company for the production of speedometers. Grandson Dudley Dumaine says his father, Buck, and other family members love to tell this story of F.C.'s negotiations with Henry Ford:

> Grandfather and Mr. Ford were good friends. [For years Amoskeag was the supplier of canvas used for automobile tops on

Ford automobiles.] Whenever Mr. Ford was in the East, he would visit grandfather. If it was at the Waltham plant, Mr. Ford would enter the building directly into Dumaine's office on the second floor by the fire escape. A bottle of brandy was kept in the desk drawer. After a toast or two, the gentlemen would fire shotguns at the ceiling. While the ceilings were structurally reinforced and did not pose a threat to the bookkeepers on the next floor, it was a way for the two to vent their displeasure for accountants in general.

On one such visit Dumaine had Ford's automobile equipped with a simplified version of the speedometer. Waltham people reasoned that it was of little significance to the driver, while in first or second gears, what speed was registered on the dial. What was important was the speed in third gear. With this concept, both the quality of performance and the cost of manufacturing improved substantially, since the mechanism did not have to be calibrated for different gear ratios.

Following the return trip to Detroit, Henry Ford called grandfather. The conversation went along these lines:

"Fred, that speedometer seems to work fine. We would like to have them in our Model A's."

"Sounds good, Henry. We would like to see the Waltham name in your cars."

"Oh, no Fred. You don't seem to understand. The only name in Ford cars is Ford." To which grandfather promptly replied, "Gee, that's funny, General Motors doesn't have that rule."

Shortly after hearing this story, this writer came across a Model A. The urge to look was too compelling. On the dashboard was a speedometer bearing the proud name of WALTHAM. As to verification of birdshot in Dumaine's office ceiling, there is none. However, that portion of the oral history dealing with the Waltham name in Ford automobiles has passed the litmus test. Ford automobile historians offer that while the 1929 and early Model A's did not have the Waltham imprint, 1930 Model A's and all subsequent years were equipped with the Waltham name.

In 1932, wages were reduced 30 percent in an attempt to restore profitability as the country moved deeper into the Great Depression. The action, combined with the speedometer contract, cut losses to $259,000. To protect the capital of the firm, the dividend was curtailed.

The following year, the National Industrial Recovery Act was passed.

The company increased wages 28 percent in support of Roosevelt's program. Employment was back to 2,500, or full operation. Dumaine would travel often to Washington to speak in support of Roosevelt's economic policies. Losses amounted to $69,000 as Waltham enacted all possible economies. Again no dividend was paid.

Dumaine's professional integrity and genuine interest in the welfare of his employees is best reflected by the following incident in which one of his Waltham employees was fatally burned:

> Thursday, July 22, 1937: *** of the *** Insurance Company called to discuss the John Kempton case. I explained to him unless he was willing to pay the family $3,000, with $150 toward funeral expenses and the nurse's bill, $256, in view of the great suffering and unusual circumstances, I could recommend a settlement on no other basis and should insist the case be put up to the Industrial Accident Board.
>
> He pointed out the question of willful negligence on the company's part might be raised if the question went before the Board and the watch company might be held for half the damages. I told him I cared nothing about that. If it could be shown willful negligence existed, the watch company should be penalized. I could see no other solution and did not care to horse-trade.

The year of 1937 had seen dividends paid on all classes of Waltham Watch stocks and a bonus of $125,000 was distributed to workers in July when the factory closed for the annual two-week vacation. The $125,000 represented a 5 percent bonus to employees. Dumaine was following the practice established at Amoskeag of sharing profit distribution to stockholders with the employees.

One incident related to Dumaine's promotional mix at Waltham may be amusing to the reader but was not at all amusing to Dumaine. For years the company produced decal stickers with the name Waltham, intended for jewelers' show windows. Dumaine decided to mass produce and distribute the sticker to be attached to automobile rear windows. Waltham paid 10 cents each to dealers or gasoline station attendants who turned in the name and registration of cars displaying a sticker. More than one million were in circulation by 1939.

While originally successful, the marketing campaign backfired when the following gossip spread across the country:

> Did you know the president of Waltham Watch Company is a Fascist? If you don't believe it, look at the signs identifying his

Fascist sympathizers. The initials are a secret slogan: We Are Loyal To Hitler And Mussolini. W-A-L-T-H-A-M!

Dumaine was furious. He had been encouraged and pressured to build a watch factory in Russia. He absolutely refused for fear it could have potential for some future military use. Now he was being criticized for supporting Fascism. After consultation with lawyers and the FBI, it was decided the best recourse would be to ignore the rumor, since the denial would both add to the notoriety and lead some to believe the accusation.

Debt was also on Dumaine's mind. To accomplish the objective of paying off all of Waltham's bonds in spite of problems with European competition and the Depression years, Dumaine had exercised the power he had wrought from the directors to determine, by his own judgment, when dividends should be declared. There had been years when, in the interests of the community, he had used company surplus to lend money to the City of Waltham, while commercial banks were refusing credit to the municipalities. In 1939, cash was so tight that no dividends were paid; in 1940, only the dividends of the prior preference, 7 percent stock were paid. Although this meant that Dumaine was forgoing dividends on his own Class A common, his policy aroused resentment among stockholders.

At the Waltham annual meeting in March 1940, minority stockholders asked Dumaine, as president-treasurer, to explain how much money must be earned before dividends would be again declared. Dumaine answered point blank that it was his policy to retire all of the $1.1 million in company bonds due in 1943 without weakening working capital. Dumaine also had reported to the Waltham directors that Walter W. Cenerazzo had organized a union at Waltham. The directors voted unanimously: "All present opposed to closed or union shop." The stockholders' meeting was further enlivened by an attack on the salaries of Dumaine and his son Buck.

Dumaine had received no salary from Waltham until dividends were earned. In addition, he had invested $125,000 of his own cash, although the Class A common stock was originally supposed to be allotted him as a bonus for taking over the management without a salary until the firm returned to profitability. Following the personal attack on his compensation at the stockholders' annual meeting, he prepared a statement for the directors.

May 19, 1941: Explained in full to board at today's meeting

the matter of my compensation... From my original election as president and treasurer of Waltham Watch Company, to July 1, 1927, I received no recompense for my services. On that date I received $75,000 for all services prior to that date. Since July 1, 1927. . . Buck's [annual] salary and mine have been,

	F.C.D	F.C.D., Jr.	Total
July '27-Oct. '31	$50,000	$ 3,600	$53,600
Oct. '31-June '32	45,000	3,200	48,200
June '32-Dec. '37	25,000	23,240	48,240
Dec. '37-Jan. '39	16,667	15,493	32,160
Jan. '39 to date	25,000	23,240	48,240

Board approved salaries to be continued as is.

Dumaine's yearly salary was a pittance compared to the 1940 salaries of Eugene G. Grace of Bethlehem Steel ($298,000), T. M. Girdler of Republic Steel ($176,000), and T.A. Morgan of the Sperry Corporation ($147,000).

Waltham was considered to have advanced technology for an American company. Dudley Dumaine's following account of the technology also points out the advances made by foreign competition:

New England in the 1930's was a leader in medical advances, just as it is today. Apparently one of our best known surgeons had come up with an idea to save a certain kind of brain injury patient through a revolutionary surgical procedure. It required the sewing of a very small severed nerve in the brain. The doctor needed a very small gold needle that would allow the nerve to be sewn together in much the same way as a seamstress would work on a hem. Massachusetts General Hospital contacted F.C. on the theory that if such a needle could be made, Waltham Watch could do it. It took three months and the only way that the eye of the needle could be constructed was to taper the "fat end" and bend it around into a loop. The needle worked, the operation was successful and the patient lived a normal life. Everyone involved with the project was proud of Waltham's accomplishment.

The "Old Man'" had a needle packaged and sent to one of the

heads of the watch making industry in Switzerland, together with a newspaper account of its creation and success. Also included was a note offering the following challenge: "Match this if you can." About 90 days later a package from Switzerland arrived. It contained Waltham's needle split laterally three ways, drilled and threaded. No note accompanied it.

As the country entered World War II, Waltham Watch played a major part in providing fuses and timing devices for the military campaign. This resulted in a shift from the production of civilian goods to government contracts, just as it did for most American industries. In time, Waltham Watch and its employees would be honored by receiving the Army-Navy production award for excellence in war production. Ultimately, the company would receive a letter from Robert Patterson, under secretary of war, stating:

To the Men and Women of the Waltham Watch Company
Crescent Street Waltham, Massachusetts

This is to inform you that the Army and Navy are conferring upon you the Army-Navy Production Award for high achievement in producing materiel needed for war.

The award consists of a flag to be flown above your plant and a lapel pin which every man and woman in the plant may wear as a symbol of your great contribution to victory in this war for human liberty.

Your record of practical patriotism is high, your production effort outstanding, and you have good reason for pride in both.

For the recipient unfamiliar with the significance of the award, the government provided the following history:

In 1906 the Navy instituted in the Fleet an award for excellence which has been known ever since as the Navy "E." First awarded for excellence in gunnery, this has been extended to include outstanding performance in engineering and communications. An honor not easily won nor lightly bestowed, it became and has remained a matter of deep pride to the men of the Service who receive it.

When the rising tide of war in Europe placed a premium on the production of war equipment, the Navy "E" Award was extended to embrace those plants and organizations which showed excellence in producing ships, weapons, and equipment for the Navy.

182

Then came Pearl Harbor and the high resolve on the part of all Americans to work and fight together until victory in that struggle is final and complete.

From that high resolve was born the Army-Navy Production Award which stands today as our fighting forces' joint recognition of exceptional performance on the production front . . . of the determined, persevering, unbeatable American spirit which can be satisfied only by achieving the "impossible."

The year 1942 was full of headaches. In addition to the problems associated with the shift to military production, the management had to contend with minority stockholders who had filed a suit to have dividends paid. That same year a federal indictment was handed down, charging Waltham Watch Company, Hamilton Watch Company, and the Elgin National Watch Company with restricting sale of their products and boycotting or blacklisting certain dealers. Ultimately this antitrust indictment was dismissed and never came to trial. Unfortunately, the stockholders' suit did not end as satisfactorily.

The following year Dumaine had the particular pleasure of writing in his diary the completion of one of his major objectives in the Waltham takeover. He had rid the company of the burden of debt, thereby greatly insuring the future prosperity of the company and the security of the employees' jobs.

May 26, 1943: Handed Old Colony Trust Company check for $1.1 million to pay last outstanding of Waltham bonds. In 20 years, the company has bought in and canceled $3 million in 6 per cent bonds and 57,512 shares of various stocks, all costing $8.5 million.

In a 1998 interview, Bill Petree, then 101 years old, reflected on Dumaine's management. Petree immigrated to the United States in 1905, when his father, a watchmaker in Coverntry, England, was recruited by Waltham Watch. In 1913, at the age of 16, William began his career at Waltham in the assembly department. His employment was interrupted for two years while he served in the medical corps in France during World War I. Following his discharge he returned to the watch factory. Petree went on to become a union official, a position he gave up when he entered management. His first foremanship was in the assembly department and later in 1943 was transferred to foreman in the escape department. In response to an inquiry on Dumaine's management Petree responded:

183

A Navy inspector presents a watchful eye. Photo courtesy of Leslie Nesky.

Dumaine's management was OK. He paid off the debt. That is what he was supposed to do. Wages were up to par. He paid the going wages. When you met him, he was just like you and me. Just an ordinary man. His sons Buck and Spike were the same way. They were all right.

During the war years, the pressure of the armed services led to an unhappy incident. Dumaine was attacked in the press as an exploiter of child labor. The military insisted on early delivery of certain war materiel essential for an upcoming invasion. At a conference in Washington, Waltham officials were assured they would receive a dispensation to employ the extra help which, Waltham told the authorities, would have to be recruited from individuals under the age of 18, since the labor pool had been exhausted. Unfortunately, the official exemption, authorized orally, was not recorded in the files at Washington. Later, the Department of Labor assessed Waltham damages for employing 102 underage girls on government contracts.

The press had a grand time with headlines like "$33,860 Child Labor Fine." Dumaine must have either chuckled or steamed that the failure to record the exemption to allow a 17-year-old girl to sit at a bench eight hours a day, at a wage seven times what he had received at the age of fourteen had caused him such unfavorable publicity. He hardly would have considered this cruel child labor. He paid the fine and said nothing.

The Supreme Judicial Court of Massachusetts handed down its decision on the stockholders' suit in February of 1944. It sometimes has been said that the decision, ruling against Dumaine, motivated him to sell the Waltham Watch Company. His diary shows that he had been willing to sell for his price to Bulova in 1941 if John W. Davis had not advised him of possible prosecution which would follow under the antitrust laws. There is no denying, however, that the Supreme Court decision pointed out to Dumaine the great change in social, economic, and financial thinking that had come over the country since 1923. Dumaine had won from the directors the one-man responsibility of moving Waltham from red ink to black. The 1944 decision was a blueprint for the swing in favor of minority investors, possibly at the cost of future job security for labor. In the process, it forced Dumaine to pay to himself some $100,000 in dividends that he had chosen to forgo to build up the watch factory's reserve.

The court reversed the decision of Judge Goldberg and upheld the ruling in favor of the stockholders in their demand for dividends on the 6 percent preferred and the Class A common stock for the years 1939, 1940, and 1941 "to the extent that they may be declared without impairing the contributed capital of the company." The decision required Dumaine to distribute $582,000 to the preferred stockholders and $210,000 to the Class A common, of which he owned nearly half.

Announcement of the court ruling caused the market price of the preferred to advance from 45 1/4 to 54, while the Class A common went from 8 3/4 to 10.

The decision, written by Justice Arthur Dolan, dwelt on the bankrupt condition of the Waltham Watch Company in 1923, resulting in its inability to secure further credit from the banks at the time.

> In view of the risky nature of the investment, it seems most probable that purchasers of the shares put all of their hope in a share of the net earnings that might result...Since the date of its re-organization, the financial position of the company has steadily improved. ... The parties are agreed that the sole issue is whether under the agreement of association and articles of

185

organization, it is within the discretion of the directors to declare no dividends on the Common Class A stock and on the 6 percent Preferred stock in years in which there are an earned surplus and net earnings of the prior year available; or whether, as the plaintiff contends, the agreement of association makes declaration mandatory in such circumstances.

This, of course, was exactly the same issue argued by Dumaine in his correspondence with Dexter in 1923. It was the issue he had argued with Liggett, which led to the latter withdrawing from the board of directors. Dumaine had won his argument then. Now his stand was reversed by the high court. Justice Dolan had put his finger on the clause that, from Dumaine's point of view, was "a mistake" in the 1923 agreement. The decision went on to state:

It is agreed by the defendants and conceded by the plaintiff that the declaration and payment of dividends on the 7 percent Prior Preference stock are expressly made subject to the directors' discretion. Yet both accrued and current dividends on that stock must be paid before any dividend may be declared on any other class of stock.

In our opinion, the language of Clause Four of the agreement of association is so direct and express that we cannot escape the conclusion that it requires the directors to declare dividends out of net earnings of the preceding year in the amount and under the terms stipulated on the Common Class A stock and on the 6 per cent Preferred stock.

Dumaine had interpreted the proviso "the company's capital will not be impaired by such payment" as permission to exercise his best judgment on the "working capital" necessary for the long run health of the business. The Massachusetts Supreme Judicial Court decision did not share this view, and ruled against it.

With the Supreme Judicial Court decision handed down, Dumaine was ready to go ahead with retiring from the watch business. He was 78 years old. He had retired Waltham's debt and substantially reduced the amount of preferred stocks through repurchases. He had brought the bankrupt business to a profitable endeavor with 2,500 employees turning out war orders at top speed. But before he could retire, he had one other burning ambition left unfulfilled. He wanted to reorganize the New Haven, which would require cash along with the services of his sons, Buck and Spike, as lieutenants.

At the meeting of the Waltham Watch directors on April 14, 1944,

Dumaine presented offers from Benjamin Katz of the Gruen Watch Company to purchase Waltham's net assets for $6 million, and from the Union Securities Company of New York, on behalf of Ira Guilden, to purchase 51 per cent of the outstanding stock.

The Executive Committee of directors discussed the question at a luncheon at the Parker House on April 17. The Gruen offer had to be dismissed because it had been found impossible to secure the necessary two-thirds of each class of stock. In addition, it appeared improbable that Gruen would secure government approval for the merger.

While the negotiations with Guilden and Union Securities went on, Dumaine secured approval from the directors and would-be purchasers for the distribution of the preferred and common Class B stock, which he had reacquired for the treasury, to the long-term employees of the company.

On May 22, 1944, the Waltham News-Tribune printed a tribute to Dumaine and his record of achievement and also printed a long list of the names of Waltham employees of twenty years' service or more who had received unspecified bonuses. The public supposed these to have been paid by the company, as originally authorized by vote of the directors and mentioned in Dumaine's diary. Actually, because government consent could not be procured, Dumaine footed the entire bill from his own pocket. He insisted there be no public mention of his benefaction.

Walter W. Cenerazzo, president of the watchmakers' union, recalled that Dumaine sent for him in April 1944. Dumaine discussed the Supreme Judicial Court decision requiring the distribution of dividends at the expense of working capital. Dumaine expressed his concern for the company in a postwar period. Cenerazzo stated:

> He [Dumaine] said he had taken care of all the stockholders; now he wanted to take care of the people who had worked with him. He wanted me to sit down and allot it [the stock] on the basis of a bonus for each year of service, only I was not to tell the money came from him.

On June 15, 1944, Dumaine held a dinner at the Weston Golf Club to honor executives of Waltham Watch. Among the 32 men honored were 12 individuals whose original tenure at Walthan preceded Dumaine's. Others honored included I. E. Boucher, the manager; F.C. (Buck) Dumaine, Jr., the assistant treasurer; Pierre (Spike) Dumaine, the assistant manager; and William A. Kilbourn, one of the superintendents and the company's first college graduate.

A mid-July entry in his diary summarizes Dumaine's final actions at Waltham:

> Monday, July 17, 1944: Today's Waltham Stockholders' meeting ended all my connection with the company. Buck resigned as assistant treasurer and director. Upon the reorganization 20 years ago, Winsor and I bought the 25,000 "A" shares at $10 each. Winsor divided some of his with F. S. Moseley & Co. Later the three of us allocated 1,500 shares to. . . employees, salesmen, clerks, etc., at the issue price.
>
> Some three years or so ago I bought with company money 1,500 each 6 per cent and "B" common . . . to be allocated to workers other than officers. With approval of the War Labor Board and Salary Stabilization Unit, the difference between the cost and the offer price. . . was allocated to 482 workers who had been employed 20 years or more, 1 share for each 20 years; 2 for 35 years; 3 for 50 years.

Over the years, F.C. had bought Waltham Watch Company stocks through the DUMAINES Trust to maintain voting control, but never did he put Waltham stocks in the portfolio of the Amoskeag Company of which he was also treasurer and a beneficiary.

Only five years after Dumaine sold his interest in the company, the Waltham Watch Company was in receivership. The Boston Herald, February 9, 1949, noted that "Trustees of Waltham Watch Company reported to Federal District Court that the company had a net loss of $1.6 million for the year ended Dec. 31, 1948." Dumaine, like the old warhorse he was–even though he was 83 years old by then–offered his resources to reorganize and rebuild again. He even persuaded the House of Morgan to endorse his concept of restructuring, with 51 percent of the ownership going to the employees and the remaining 49 percent to the merchants who sold the product.

> March 17,1949: Having been requested to take an interest in the Waltham situation, I agreed if the banks would secure the property clear, turn it over to any kind of an organization they might choose, around $3 million carrying a low rate, say 3 percent, (it has been stated they would accept $3 million for their claim of $4.6 million), I would undertake, if they wanted me, to find some method of factoring the product and supervising the operation, giving them representation on the board with the privilege of paying off the capital at par, when and when if paid, was to be distributed 51 percent to the employees and 49 per cent for the jobbers. I to have no compensation for services.

George Whitney [of J.P. Morgan and Company] intimated to Buck he would undertake to factor the operation. I had no fundamental written plan; in a general way this was along the lines pursued in 1923.

At a conference in his suite at the Lincolnshire Hotel, Boston, he elaborated on his plan to Waltham city officials. He then recorded the event:

April 3, 1950: Witnessed the signing of the Dumaine proposal of the reorganization of Waltham Watch Company; seemed in complete accord. Theme of proposal is a plan to restore Waltham Watch Company in New England industry, leave it in the hands of the workers and sales force.

The Boston Herald on April 5, 1950, wrote a sprightly editorial which reflected much of the general contemporary public opinion about Dumaine. It was captioned "Jet-Propelled at 84."

... You can think what you will about Mr. Dumaine and those around here are apt to think rather strongly, but you can't deny that the man has got what it takes to want to assume at once two of the greatest headaches hereabouts, the New Haven and the Waltham Watch Company . . . .

He's an inscrutable fellow, that Dumaine. If he takes his rugged individualism to Waltham again, it will be a kind of marriage to that hussy (to conservative business men), the Reconstruction Finance Corporation. Do you, Frederic, with your old-fashioned philosophy, that outgo of money, corporate or individual, should never exceed income, take this woman RFC who just loves to see a Lustron or a Kaiser spread the dough around?. . . There are those who say unkindly that Mr. Dumaine did better by Mr. Dumaine than by the watch company and that much of the troubles since stem from those days. But he did pull the company through the depression.... Maybe this is Mr. Dumaine's bid to confound his critics. Maybe, having restored the New Haven to Massachusetts control, he now seeks to preserve a Massachusetts industry that once was held in worldwide honor. But, speculator or patriot, he gives a magnificent refutation to the belief that at 65, a man goes on pension.

In the end, the R.F.C. was reluctant to support the proposal and the Dumaine plan was not accepted by the court. Dumaine did his own autopsy on Waltham Watch.

September 7, 1950 . . . The bankers said they would prefer not to continue in the watch business and resulted in their losing $1.1 million in the reorganization in 1948. They recapitalized and issued ten shares of common stock for every share of "A" stock. They made a Wall Street market on that stock of $26.50 (10 shares for one—$265; we got $75 [for our class A common] . . . [Later] stock was selling for 50 cents a share. Our plan was to have the RFC extend their loan until we could pay it off from earnings. Our plan was not accepted by the court.

Following the closing of Waltham Watch, the public wanted a scapegoat. Some selected Dumaine despite the fact that he had withdrawn from the business five years earlier.

In the April 1949 edition of its magazine, *Fortune* ran a short article titled "The Waltham Mess." While the primary goal of the article was to argue against tariff controls as a means of aiding Waltham Watch, it used the opportunity to question Dumaine's management. The irony of the article is that the same edition of the magazine ran a feature on Dumaine's "Capture of the New Haven." The quotations below summarize the magazine's view of Dumaine's stewardship of the watch company:

Financial troubles are an old story at Waltham. Since its founding in 1850 and its first bankruptcy seven years later, the company has been on the ropes half a dozen times. . . In 1923. . . it was saved from bankruptcy by . . . Kidder, Peabody & Co. which. . . provided Waltham with $7 million in new capital and an autocratic President, Frederic C. Dumaine.

Mr. Dumaine. . . lifted Waltham out of the red and kept it operating more or less profitably for twenty years. Whether his policies were "enlightened" or not is another matter. He cut wages, abolished jobs, canceled advertising contracts. . . He spent little on new machinery, research, and new watch design. He skinned through the depression in the thirties on shutdowns, wage cuts, and price cutting, plus the sale of electric clocks and speedometers. Then during the war his sales doubled to $11.6 million. And at the peak of Waltham's prosperity in 1944, Mr. Dumaine sold out.

The article went on to criticize Dumaine for paying off the debt and not paying dividends until he was forced to do so by the court decision. In some ways, this could be expected based on the pro stockholders view of the magazine. However, it seems somewhat hypocritical to blame Dumaine for the declining competitiveness five years after his departure, if the magazine is arguing against the retaining of earnings for subsequent plant investments.

190

Walthan Watch was eventually reorganized and the factory continued to operate under several different names. However, it never reached the volume and the stability of employment that it had experienced under Dumaine.

Criticisms of Dumaine's role in Waltham did not stop. In his 1984 book, *Revolution in Time: Clocks and the Making of the Modern World*, Harvard Professor David Landes attacks Dumaine's management:

> In the two decades that he ran Waltham, he turned red ink into black, earned substantial profits, paid off just about all that debt, made a tidy sum for Kidder, Peabody, and a fortune for himself. He did this by cutting wages and holding fresh investment to a minimum, by squeezing the last turn out of machines that had been running for decades and the last die out of toolmakers who had been working even longer.

> With exquisite timing, Dumaine sold his stock in 1944, just before the end of wartime orders.

Fortunately, not all held the professor's opinion. An editorial in Waltham's The News-Tribune criticized Landes's conclusions:

> Professor Landes doesn't equivocate about his belief of what caused the Waltham Watch demise.... He points a gun at Frederic C. Dumaine Sr. and riddles him with bullets. He charges mismanagement and greed did the pioneer firm in.

> The decision by DUMAINES to sell in 1944 is called "exquisite timing." It certainly was. Yet it is fair to bring in other facts. There was left a hefty cash and inventory reserve of $5 million. If there was faulty management, the charge could be laid at the doors of those who followed.

> Tariffs had strangled the industry to a point of extinction, with Waltham as one of a few survivors. Dumaine saw a no-win situation. Tariffs, not the Dumaine involvement, killed off the Waltham Watch Company.

Perhaps the best summary of Dumaine's stewardship with Waltham was made by two former employees of Waltham.

In a 1974 interview with Harvey Wang of Brandies University, William Kilbourn gave his assessment of Dumaine. Kilbourn, a 1932 graduate of MIT, procured his job at Waltham in the depths of the Great Depression, not only on the basis of his degree but also by the fact that he had been a driver for Dumaine in prior summer employment. Kilbourn eventually advanced to a superintendent or division manager under Dumaine. Excerpts from Kilbourn's interview are presented below:

One of the greatest things I had to live down was the fact that I had gone to college. In a factory of 2,000 odd people, none of whom had been to college, it was felt that I had wasted four years . . . a lot of theory, but no practical experience.

I started work in 1932 with a salary of 25 cents an hour, which, for 40 hours, meant I would get $10. In the first week, on the way to the factory, I stopped and helped a man who had an automobile accident, and I was an hour late. So I got $9.75 for the first week's pay. When I finally reached $28 a week, I got married.

Mr. Dumaine was of the old school. If you did a good job, he would do anything for you. But, if you were not interested in your work or were doing your work in a slip-shod manner, he would be looking for someone else to take your place. Because he was more positive in his ways, he was sometimes resented, but it probably was a good thing that he acted as he did.

Prior to Dumaine heading the watch factory, the foreman of each department made his own rules and ran his section as he wanted. There was a great lack of communication with the outside world. The foremen were not aware of simplified and improved watchmaking that could have been done to manufacturer the watches more economically.

Mr. Dumaine's greatest problem was to get people to accept new ideas to bring the price of the watch in competition with Swiss and other foreign production. In the 1930's the employees were asked to take cuts in pay in order to keep their jobs. It seems to me that if Mr. Dumaine had not taken over, the factory would have folded.

When I first went to the factory, the floors were rough, having been walked on for 75 years. The Waltham Watch Company was a complex of five buildings with a tower between each. All of the production rooms were powered by a single, large electric motor, which ran a series of shafts. Individual machines were belted to the main shaft, creating a maze of belts, noise and lost power.

Mr. Dumaine was instrumental in putting individual motors on each machine which eliminated all the overhead line shafts, belts and so forth. This was one of the great improvements. He put down new floors, modernized and painted the rooms, making the area a nice place in which to work. He wanted to save the business and make it prosperous by making a quality product, as well as making it more pleasant for the workers. I was very fortunate and very happy to be a part of that organization at that time.

A second former Waltham Watch employee who was familiar with Dumaine's management was Pasquale Caruso. In 1927, he began his career in watchmaking at the age of 17. Starting out as an errand boy, Caruso became knowledgeable in all areas of watchmaking. He went on to assume the head of the local union. In a 1992 interview with John Cox, a Waltham historian, Pat Caruso made the following observations about Dumaine's stewardship:

> Dumaine was disliked because of the reputation he acquired at the Amoskeag Mills. When he took over, there was a strike at Waltham because he cut wages. There was no organized union, the workers just walked out. After they were on strike for a while, they got hungry and started to come back a little at a time. The strike caused awful hard feelings among the help because the people who went back were looked down upon. For years they held grudges against each other. They would say, "He was a scab." That feeling stayed for a long time but it eventually disappeared.

> Dumaine held off and the workers came back. He treated them pretty well. He gave them a small cut. They could afford it. Those finishers and matchers were making big money.

> All in all, Dumaine was a good man for the watch factory and I don't understand why we disliked him so much (laughter). But we did dislike him even though we did business with him.

> He was a tough guy. You couldn't get close to him. Dumaine ran the place with an iron hand but he maintained work and kept the company going. His sons were more sociable-Spike and Buck. They helped run the place. Dumaine had a general manager named Boucher. Dumaine had a lot of respect for Boucher.

> He got along fine with the union. When the union negotiated a contract, it was just a matter of days. After Dumaine left, the union had trouble.

> Later on, Professor Landes wrote a book and attacked Dumaine. I called Landes and told him I didn't agree with him. I worked there under Dumaine. He took over the factory when it was

F.C. Dumaine

*William
Kilbourn*

Spike Dumaine

Waltham Watch outing, circa 1943. Photo courtesy of Waltham Historical Society.

$11 million in the hole. Kidder, Peabody held the paper on the company. When it was $11 million in debt they couldn't find anyone to take over the factory. That was a lot of money in the '20's.

He took it over and went in there with a surgical knife and cut out all of the dead wood and ran the place business-like. He paid off the debts and maintained the company. All through the depression he kept the place running. There was not much employment, of course, because there weren't many sales.

We worked all during the war and the company made some money. We were busy. We made wrist watches, stop watches, Chelsea escapements, and time fuses for the government.

194

Around '44-'45, Dumaine went to the stockholders and said the war is coming to an end and we've made some money. I want to refurbish this place and buy new tools so we can compete with Switzerland. But I can't pay you dividends. I want to put that money into the company. But the stockholders said no. Dumaine started to do it anyway and the stockholders took him to court and the court ruled he should pay a dividend. Dumaine said to the stockholders, "If you want to run the place, you run it." So he sold his stock to Ira Guilden.

Dumaine was a good manager. He took the place when it was $11 million in the hole and when he left there was $5 million in cash. Also, he gave everyone who was there when he came and who was there when he left a bonus.

To this day, some critics still claim Dumaine failed to adequately prepare the company for a shift back to civilian watches following the end of war related production. More likely, the failure could be attributed to the attitude promoted by the court decision in favor of dividend distribution to stockholders. In retrospect, Dumaine's measure of only paying dividends when "the company's capital will not be impaired by such payment" may have been the correct one. The court was looking at past earnings. Dumaine was looking toward the future.

President Franklin Delano Roosevelt in the White House Oval Office. Photo courtesy of Roosevelt Library.

CHAPTER XVII

The Odd Couple — F.C.D. and F.D.R.

Frederic C. Dumaine was tutored at a young age on the potential relationships between business and government. In 1889, Dumaine witnessed how T. Jefferson Coolidge was appointed a delegate in the Pan-American Congress by President Benjamin Harrison. In August of the following year, Dumaine met his first U.S. president when Coolidge was giving Harrison a tour of the Amoskeag mill yard. Likely Coolidge used this opportunity to introduce the 24-year-old Dumaine to the president. Two years later, in 1892, Dumaine was impressed that Coolidge was appointed minister to France.

Dumaine contributed to and was active in the campaigns that elected Theodore Roosevelt in 1904 and William Howard Taft in 1908. Dumaine gained a genuine respect for President Taft. He remained loyal to Taft even after the president rejected Dumaine's 1910 interpretation of the activities of certain individuals in the State Department to divert Argentine contracts away from Fore River to the New York Shipbuilding Company. Dumaine and his first wife, Bessie, visited the White House the following year. Subsequently, Dumaine campaigned for Taft in 1912 and in 1916 in his unsuccessful attempts to hold on to and regain the presidency. The Dumaine files have several letters to and from Taft after he left the Oval Office. Several were written while Taft was serving as chief justice of the United States.

Dumaine was friendly with Vice President Calvin Coolidge, who was a former governor of Massachusetts. In 1923, Dumaine missed by one day being present when Calvin Coolidge took the oath as president of the United States. Along with the vice president, Dumaine had been invited for the weekend of August 3 to Guy Currier's country home in Peterborough, New Hampshire. President Harding's sudden death on August 2 found Coolidge still at his father's home in Plymouth, Vermont, where he was sworn in as the thirtieth president of the United States.

One notation in his diary, some six years later, illustrates the degree to which Dumaine's world was becoming interwoven with national politics:

> Saturday, December 14, 1929: Ten o'clock train to Springfield and drove to Northampton. Called upon Mr. Coolidge at his house. Mrs. Coolidge said he was at his office; [went] there and had an interesting half-hour's conversation. He seems very well and interested in things generally. Inquired for Winsor and a number of other people. It was a coincidence this week that I met the President [Hoover] and called on the only two living ex-presidents [Taft and Coolidge.]

In her unpublished manuscript, "Dumaine of New England," Dorothy Wayman notes a shift in Dumaine's political thinking as the country moved into the Great Depression. She wrote:

> Dumaine's evolution toward a more eclectic approach to social problems was progressing and although he did not cross the party lines, he was strongly and favorably impressed by Governor Alfred Emmanuel Smith of New York. Dumaine was a realist. He understood very thoroughly politics from the inside, and, nevertheless, he retained a somewhat idealistic view that there should be just as much efficiency and honesty in government as in business.

> Dumaine, viewing the chaos in business and politics, evolved the idea of a Union ticket as the only way to insure political stability in the land. He proposed that a coalition be arranged to unite the two parties, with Coolidge, the Republican, as candidate for president, and Alfred E. Smith, Democrat, for vice president. To him it seemed just plain common sense, in a time when the country was threatened with bankruptcy or revolution or both, to combine the administrative and political experience and leadership of the two nationally known men, each respected and trusted by millions of voters in the two parties.

Dumaine had written his friend, Robert Norton, editor of the Boston Post, with his plan. Norton planted a "trial balloon" in the form of a feature article in the St. Paul Pioneer Press. However, Dumaine's hopes were dashed by the conservative stand-pat Republicans of Massachusetts.

It is interesting to think what might have happened in history had Dumaine's idea gathered support and his coalition ticket been successful in November 1932. Calvin Coolidge died suddenly, at noon on January 5, 1933. Had Dumaine's idea succeeded, Alfred E. Smith would have been inducted on March 4, 1933, as the thirty-second president of the United States.

Subsequent entries in Dumaine's 1932 diary relate the well known historical facts. What the notations fail to indicate is the friendship and mutual respect that would evolve between Roosevelt and Dumaine.

July 1, 1932: Franklin D. Roosevelt was nominated for President at the Democratic Convention in Chicago. The country is sadly in need of a strong character for its national head and it seems a pity the Democratic party could not have named its ablest man [Al Smith.] It's a strange anomaly when the average man you meet would prefer almost any man to the nominee of either party. I am inclined to think Roosevelt will be elected.

November 8, 1932: Roosevelt elected President and the whole country swept into the Democratic column. Three reasons, apparently: Depression, 18th Amendment [Prohibition], the claim that Hoover [and not Coolidge] was the only man who could save the country, and the demand for a change. Roosevelt did not carry his own home, Hyde Park.

Dumaine, a lifelong Republican, had contributed to the Democratic campaign fund in 1932 and had voted for F.D.R. When he first met Roosevelt is uncertain. According to Dumaine family legend, the first contact between the Dumaines and the Roosevelts occurred one day when F.C. was taking one of his early morning horseback rides. Grandson Dudley recalls it this way:

Apparently one foggy morning on F.C.'s normal early morning horseback ride through his apple orchard on his 2,000-acre estate abutting the Groton School property, he caught a young boy stealing apples off one of his trees. He grabbed the boy by the ear and marched him to the headmaster's home. Shortly thereafter, F.C. received a telephone call from the lad's father, Franklin Delano Roosevelt, apologizing for the son's behavior.

From that date on, each year Grandfather would send a box of apples to the Roosevelt family.

Dumaine was with Roosevelt on October 29, 1932, when the candidate visited Groton School and broadcast a campaign speech favoring federal aid for the unemployed thirteen million persons in America. He recalled that occasion in writing to Roosevelt nine years later.

September 12, 1941

Dear Mr. President,

This household on Farmers Row near where you spent happy days [Groton School], was thrilled with your last night's speech. It was sound in principle, and like the Presidents of old, there was no fear or retreat.

Since the night in '32 when you were good enough to let us join you at Parents House on your way to Portland and dear old Mack [Maurice McIntyre, presidential secretary] tried to imitate Cotty [Dr. Endicott Peabody of Groton School], I have heard your every talk. Beginning at Chicago when courageously and alone you told the American people of their great peril, you have handled the foreign situation with skill and the foresight of a statesman.

"T.R." told me at Oyster Bay how he warned the Kaiser (when the German fleet was anchored off the coast of Venezuela) unless he withdrew, Sampson at Key West had sealed orders to sail at midnight, and the Germans departed. Let us hope they heed your warning; if they don't your record is clear and cannot be misunderstood. May I be so bold as to say the world is depending upon your guiding hand in these present and desperate days to come; for God's sake, spare yourself needless burdens no human is able to sustain.

Whatever the attraction of Roosevelt's personality and Dumaine's admiration for some of his accomplishments, the industrialist was not slavishly infatuated. In 1936 Dumaine recorded in his diary:

Voted against him and for no reason except his reckless expenditure of public money. I have great sympathy for many of his ideals, although, as you must realize, he never earned money himself and I fear is susceptible to surroundings.

Perhaps the fact that Dumaine was unsuccessful in contacting F.D.R. in the days prior to Amoskeag's final bankruptcy also was a factor in the decision. However, as subsequent incidents will illustrate, Dumaine was not one to hold a grudge if he believed the other person's actions were made in good faith.

In 1934, when Roosevelt came again to Groton, for the school's fiftieth anniversary, he paid Dumaine the compliment of calling personally at the Dumaine home for an hour's chat. Dumaine felt the President's great personal charm but was a little disillusioned with the New Deal, as he wrote to his friend Sir George Roberts in London on January 1, 1934:

> America has had a hell of a time since '29. All property has shrunk to little or no value—banks, insurance companies, railroads, industries. Fortunes have been swept away and people with generations of comfort behind them are forced to contract and in many cases there is real hardship.

> Roosevelt is not by any means the cause of all this. I voted for him because the country was bound to have a change, regardless of what it might be. He's an attractive man, most agreeable, and would, without doubt, do all possible to end this terrible Depression if he knew the remedy, which he doesn't, no more than the rest of us....

Justice Felix Frankfurter recalls that of three men with minds keenly aware of implications of world events — Franklin D. Roosevelt, Winston Churchill, and Frederic C. Dumaine — Dumaine was possibly the earliest to express the imminence of World War II. As early as January 1938, he was consulting with United States War Department officials on pilot plans for converting the Waltham watch factory to the manufacture of fuses.

Dudley B. Dumaine, recalls being present at a telephone conversation between his grandfather and Roosevelt about the likelihood of war and the role of Waltham Watch:

> For some reason, Dad [Buck Dumaine] took me into the Grandfather's Boston office at 199 Washington Street. Just outside F.C.'s office door was a small area, foyer, you might call it, with a big old roll-top desk. Under the roll- top portion was an old Bell Telephone switchboard. The rest of the roll-top desk had an old Royal typewriter, plus all the other stuff a secretary would have. The secretary's name was Johansen. Grandfather would address her as Miss Jo. She had a desk chair on wheels so she could slide around on the hardwood floor without having to get up.

Dad took me into F.C.'s office and sat me down on the end of a black leather couch. Dad and grandfather were talking. On grandpa's desk was an old "candlestick" telephone. Because of grandpa's hearing difficulty, there was some type of sound magnifier attached to the earpiece. F.C. would hold the hearing device at almost 90 degrees from his ear when using the phone. Because the sound was magnified, anyone in the room could hear both sides of the conversation.

Dad and F.C. were talking, I haven't the foggiest idea about what, when F.C., in a loud voice yelled, "Miss Jo!" I still can hear the sound of the wheels of the chair searing across the floor as she pushed herself out from her desk to be in view of the "Old Man."

"Yes, Mr. Dumaine."

He replied, "Get me the president."

About 20 minutes went by. I saw the old man look up several times within the period with an aggravated expression, but he never said a thing. Then I became aware that there were several people standing in the doorway just to my right. I could see that Grandfather was aware of them. After about five minutes he looked up and said, "What is it?"

In response one of the group responded, "Mr. Dumaine, we have had a meeting to determine which president you want to speak with, the president of Middlesex and Boston, Eastern Steam Ships, Shawmut Banks . . ."

"Of the United States, you damn fools!"

The staff disappeared.

The next thing I heard was Miss Jo in an argument with, it soon became obvious, the secretary to President Franklin Delano Roosevelt. The argument was over who was going to pick up the telephone first. F.C. would never waste time waiting for someone else to pick up the phone. He wouldn't waste his time saying hello or good-by either. Needless to say it was tradition that the President of the United States was not expected to wait for someone on the other end of the line, either. I was surprised to hear the argument end with a self-satisfied tone in Miss Jo's voice, "Mr. Dumaine, the president is on the line."

Grandfather opened the conversation: "Franklin, we're going to war. Waltham Watch Company is the only jeweled time manufacturer that the country can count on. We don't have the machinery to produce timing mechanisms for all the planes, tanks, warships, trucks, and bombs we're going to need. Now, I want you to go to the Congress and get a $5 million loan for Waltham Watch."

The president's response, perhaps to maintain secrecy, was "Fred, we're not going to war. And, by the way, thanks [with this I saw the ear piece going down to the candlestick] for the apples. They...."

Click! By this time grandfather was already talking with dad on another subject.

America did go to war, and Waltham played a major role in providing the government with military timing devices. Prior to the outbreak in Europe and up through the United States' entry into the conflict, Dumaine constantly reverted to the theme in his letters to Sir George Roberts, his friend in England.

January 4, 1936: America has been agog with gossip upon the great question in your country [the abdication of Edward VIII]... The whole thing is a great misfortune. Many of us think the stability of Britain will help preserve world civilization. In the meantime, I am hoping a European war will be avoided, for what is the good? Distress and heartaches are no compensation.

September 30, 1938: We have spent the past weeks listening to words from all over the world and now comes yesterday's Munich agreement. Many of my friends feel, and I must agree, Britain was sold out to the German paperhanger. You may be richer today on paper; I'm wondering if the price was too cheap.

September 19, 1939: What's it all about and where will it end? It's most concerning to an old man. I try to be neutral, yet my instincts rebel against our fiddling while our best neighbors are in trouble and the civilization you and I have known seems to be in jeopardy. I'm hoping the embargo will be promptly lifted and that American industry will, of its own volition, refrain from excessive profits. Profits paid for in blood won't be wholesome.

October 4, 1939: My own feeling is this war will be conducted on entirely different principles, there will not be the opportunities for bloodsuckers to make blood money which existed during the so-called Great War.

I'm much interested in this "cash and carry" proposition. For the name of God! This country cannot stand by and watch England and France destroyed the only other two countries standing for something in the world.

Despite his admiration for Roosevelt, Dumaine's roots were firmly planted in Republican soil. Early in 1935, Dumaine began working zealously for his friend Frank Knox, onetime publisher in Manchester, New Hampshire, but then in Chicago with the Daily News. Dumaine gave a large dinner with carefully picked important guests for Knox at the Parker House on October 14, 1935, and continued to work for his nomination until the Republican National Convention in 1936 selected Alfred Landon as standard-bearer. Disappointment of their hopes did not affect the friendship or the common interest in the welfare of the country. Knox wrote to Dumaine, July 10, 1937:

> My dear Fred,
>
> .... Please disabuse yourself that I have any political ambitions. I had my fling so far as personal participation in it is concerned. I am, however, just as deeply interested in the preservation of American institutions as I ever was, and I think the prospects for beating this crowd of half-baked radicals in Washington looks very much better.

This declaration released Dumaine, and he cast about for another likely inheritor of the prophet's mantle, finding him in Thomas E. Dewey whom he described as "Thirty-seven, has wife and two children, works early morning until midnight; has 120 daily indictments and 72 assistant district attorneys."

> May 24, 1939: Home from New York on five o'clock. John Sargent on train says Roosevelt is candidate for third term, with, probably, [U. S. Senator] Dave Walsh as Vice-President.

By February of 1940 Dumaine was lamenting and wrote in his diary that "ten years ago incomes were taxed on an average of 6 percent; now 24 percent," and buttonholing all his friends for subscriptions to Dewey's campaign. "Young, confident, virile—doubt if he makes the grade," he predicted sorrowfully. He went to the Republican National Convention at Philadelphia for the week of June 24 and came home so dejected that he telephoned ahead to be met at the airport by his favorite dog of the day, the big German Shepherd Liebo.

> Monday, June 24, 1940: To Philadelphia, staying at Bellevue Stratford. Governor Harold E. Stassen of Minnesota elected Temporary Chairman. He's ineligible for President, only thirty-three.
>
> Friday, June 28, 1940: Wendell Lewis Wilkie, Indiana-born, citizen of New York, president of Commonwealth and Southern,

nominated on sixth ballot early this morning. Took ten o'clock train to New York, one o'clock plane to Boston. Robert came in bringing Liebo; drove me home.

Wednesday, July 17, 1940: Roosevelt sweeps Democratic Convention for third-term nomination as President, in violation of one of the oldest traditions of the United States. Eighty-two-year-old Senator Glass nominated James A. Farley and threw chief issue in face of delegates when he laid down Jeffersonian policy that no President should serve three terms.

Roosevelt recaptured Dumaine's support by three actions: the appointment of Felix Frankfurter as a justice of the United States Supreme Court; the bipartisan appointments of his friends Frank Knox to secretary of the Navy and Henry Stimson to a war post in the cabinet; and, third, the Lend-Lease bill. After the Knox appointment, Dumaine resumed contributing to the Democratic campaign funds. He gave $250 the week before the November 1940 election and contributed again for the next Jackson Day dinner in 1941.

You know by nature I'm a Republican; also my views about the Chief. Anything one can do to give him a second's peace of mind and comfort is a pleasure. I'm adding my widow's mite.

His allegiance to Roosevelt continued until the president's death, the last letter from Dumaine to "the Chief," after the latter's return from Yalta, being dated only a month before his death.

In 1942, Dumaine was writing to Sir George Roberts in England:

I'm fond of Roosevelt. He's really a wonderful man, physically handicapped as he is. Some weeks ago when in Washington, he sent word to come and see him. You know he works all night, stays late in bed. I went there at ten o'clock, he was still in bed. I sat on the bed and had an old-time man-to-man visit.

For ten years now he's carried the burden of this great country on his shoulders. There was no apparent change, bright, alert, and with a memory like "all outdoors."

Really, disregarding whether you agree with all his policies (I don't), he will go down in history as one of the world's greatest characters.

Broadly speaking, the financial world is against Roosevelt, and many of my business friends observe with humor my voting for him. They forget much legislation, started by Teddy Roosevelt, passed by Congress, was inspired and probably justified by the ethics and methods of a dozen or more men who were able to amass untold fortunes, entirely unjustified. All this, over the years, has brought about a movement too much the other way, and now with war requirements, capital in the United States is getting the rap.

The date of Dumaine's bedside chat with Franklin D. Roosevelt was April 3, 1942. Dumaine had arranged a dinner the night before at the Shoreham Hotel in Washington, taking with him from Boston Frank Buxton and Charles P. Curtis, Jr. At the meal, in a private dining room, were two Supreme Court justices, Frankfurter and Byrnes; Secretary of the Navy Knox; Undersecretary John J. McCloy; and Louis Kirstein of Boston. The president happened to have paged Frankfurter on the telephone. Learning that Dumaine was in town, the president made the appointment for the next morning. Dumaine recorded his memory of it.

Drove to the White House, shown upstairs promptly, in a few minutes into Chief's room. He was sitting up in bed and called out, "Hello, Fred. I'm delighted to see you; want to take a look and not hear you over the telephone." Recalled his visit to Groton ten years ago. Could see no indication of his aging or lack of energy. Told him it was wonderful how he had stood all these ten years. Mentioned nudist talk around, told him I'd been looking for a nudist without success. Seemed to amuse him.

Also spoke of lunching recently with Al Smith whom I asked what the hell had happened to him and the Chief. It was simply the Chief had pulled a party and failed to invite him.

Silly! Like Bill Taft's letter to Teddy, mentioning Brother Charlie before Teddy. I said Al was friendly and very complimentary; seemed to please the Chief.

He spoke complimentary of Knox. I said, "Good man, doesn't know anything about boats beyond a canoe."

"No," said the Chief. "He's learning. When Badger [of North Carolina] was Navy Secretary, they took him on board a naval vessel; he looked down the hatch and remarked, 'She's holler!'" Very pleasant few minutes, all to credit of Felix. MacIntyre met us at the stairs on way out. Looked pale and poorly.

During the conversation with the president, Dumaine had quoted to him a saying of Abraham Lincoln's which Roosevelt professed not to know. Dumaine, on his return to Boston, had a copy of the quote framed and sent to the president. The text read:

> If I were trying to read, much less answer, all the attacks made on me, this shop might well be closed for any other business. I do the best I know how, the very best I can; and I mean to keep on doing it to the end. If the end brings me out all right, what is said against me will not amount to anything. If the end brings me out wrong, ten angels swearing I was right would make no difference.
>
> A. Lincoln

Roosevelt's acknowledgment to "Dear Fred," said, "That is a mighty nice quotation and delightfully printed and framed. I am hanging it up in my office that all may read." Dumaine's copy had long hung in his Boston office, an encouragement and an expression of his own philosophy.

In his letter to Sir George, Dumaine made the following observations:

> Found the Chief in bed, and, like everyone else, received the impression I was the most important man in the country.... We talked, not one word about government or national affairs — of mutual friends (or were before they decided to leave this world) and, as you know, he likes to joke.

> Seriously the world is staking its all on this man and there could be no greater disaster than to have something fatal happen to him.

> I have turned into a Roosevelt Republican.

F.C. Dumaine in his 70s

CHAPTER XVIII

The Last Hurrah — Control of the New Haven

Dumaine admired Edward French's 1940 feat in persuading bond-holders and stockholders to a voluntary reorganization of the Boston and Maine Railroad. Essentially the plan followed the pattern Dumaine had not been able to achieve for the Amoskeag Mills. The Reconstruction Finance Committee advanced $26 million in cash to the troubled railroad. The fewer bondholders who insisted on cash, the greater working capital left for the railroad. Dumaine offered more than moral support, voting all of the bonds he controlled in favor of the reorganization. His diary on the subject reads as follows:

> Tuesday, March 26, 1940: Luncheon, Ned French, returning to office. Handed French $1.3 million B&M bonds for deposit, also proxies for 447 shares. To New York on five o'clock. Told A. J. County by telephone Penn Road proxies must vote for B&M plan. All New England Governors today are putting out statement supporting the B&M plan.

In a New Haven board meeting three years later, Dumaine commented on the merits of reducing that railroad's funded debt:

> Wednesday, February 17, 1943: New Haven board meeting. Several directors absent. . . . [I] proceeded to explain, since 1937 and including 1942, New Haven Railroad spent $51 million paying accumulated bond interest, which, if used to purchase bonds in various years at average price, would have secured and canceled $151 million par value of bonds having an accumulation of $12 million. In other words, for $51 million,

209

company's debt would have been reduced $160 odd million. Result is company has total bonds outstanding $240 million. Had purchases been made as stated, company would have only $90 million odd, or less debt than Boston & Maine.

This seemed to make no special impression on board; as matter of fact, I don't think they understood the figures. On whole, very unsatisfactory situation. It was quite apparent management had no sympathy in situation, waste of time to discuss these figures, Hall intimating legal difficulties would make it impossible, etc.

This difference of opinion between Dumaine and other New Haven board members would ultimately contribute to Dumaine being dropped from the board. To a great extent Dumaine's desire to reduce funded debt as he succeeded in doing in the Waltham Watch situation may have been a reaction to the fact that it was the Amoskeag Manufacturing Company bondholders that ultimately caused that great firm to finish in bankruptcy. Had they been willing to accept the refinancing offer, which was similar to that approved in the B&M reorganization, jobs at Amoskeag would have continued through World War II.

The outbreak of the second world war brought about an increased demand for rail. Dumaine took note of this in writing to his lifelong friend, George Moses, former Senator from New Hampshire.

...All railroad securities seem to be on the up during the last few weeks. Of course, railroads never before have had their present opportunities. It's the only industry in the country, probably any country, where profits are. . . unusually large. Roads blessed with good managements which are using these large earnings to purchase their own securities, thereby very materially reducing their structures, of course will have an easier time when things are normal and less interest to earn.

For many years the portfolio of the Amoskeag Company had contained 1,358 shares of the Boston Railroad Holding Company, receiving until 1937 the 4 percent guaranteed dividend. In 1942 additional purchases were made as the opportunity offered until Amoskeag Company owned 3,663 of the 24,150 outstanding publicly owned shares. DUMAINES, the family trust, held 222 shares, and Nuelle, through the Delaware and Hudson Railroad, (B&M maintained a substantial traffic exchange with the D&H at Mechanicsville, New York) also acquired large holdings in The Boston Railroad Holding Company. Ex-Governor Joseph B. Ely was counsel and adviser and Charles Francis Adams, so long associated with Dumaine, was, like Dumaine, a director of the New Haven Railroad and a trustee of Amoskeag Company. Mr. Adams was also a member of the Protective Committee for Holders of Railroad Holding Company Publicly Held Preferred Stock. In late 1944 these stockholders were endeavoring "to bring about among stockholders distribution of Boston and Maine stock held by the Boston Railroad Holding Company," since the reorganization plan of the New Haven under consideration contemplated termination of the New Haven's obligation to guarantee dividends and par amount on publicly held shares. The New Haven Railroad held 247,759 shares.

Once Amoskeag, the DUMAINES Trust, and the Delaware and Hudson acquired their preferred stock holdings of the Boston Railroad Holding Company, they petitioned the court for the appointment of a receiver to sell the assets. Since the dividends were in arrears, the court might find that the holding company should be liquidated. If this were to happen it would not impact on operations or on employment. It would simply result in a transfer in the ownership of the B&M stock held by the Boston Railroad Holding Company. However, since preferred stock is higher in the pecking order over common stock in the case of a liquidation, the common stock holdings of the New Haven would receive nothing until the preferred stock was to receive all past dividends and the full face value of the stock. This was an additional conflict between Dumaine and other New Haven board members.

> August 22, 1944: Discussed with Charlie Adams Boston Railroad Holding situation and proposed request to Supreme Court for ruling, Amoskeag's position and mine. He agrees perfectly proper for me to explain whole Boston Railroad Holding picture from its inception to the New Haven board, as I suggested, is the way to approach the subject.

> October 23, 1944: Boston Railroad Holding directors' meeting held at 199 Washington Street. Reelected officers. Voted 1,000 odd stamped shares owned by Holding Company in favor of New Haven plan and favored payment to the New Haven of any excess there may be after satisfaction of publicly owned shares. I did not vote.

Dumaine's decision not to vote against the motion may have been a result of a conflict of interest because he was a member of the New Haven board who was opposed to New Haven's plans. Later that month, New Haven's counsel, appearing before the Massachusetts Railroad Committee intimated that the Delaware and Hudson's and DUMAINES' interest in the Boston Railroad Holding Company were purely speculative.

In the Interstate Commerce Commission's poll of shareholders in November 1944, both DUMAINES' and the Amoskeag Company's shares were voted to reject the New Haven reorganization plan. This action by Dumaine further alienated him from the other board members.

There was another bone of contention in the tug-of-war between the Dumaine faction and the Buckland-Hall faction over the New Haven Railroad. This was the $2.2 million worth of Boston and Providence Railroad bonds which came into Dumaine's hands in 1945, and the $2.3 million of Old Colony Railroad bonds acquired in 1944 by the Amoskeag Company. Many years earlier both of these old railroads had been leased by the New Haven Railroad. Dumaine went in debt to a New York bank to buy the B&P bonds that a Boston bank was selling.

> June 25,1945: Bought $2.17 million Boston and Providence bonds from the Provident Institution for Savings at 104. It was intended to make this purchase by the Dexter Trust. Shawmut lawyers felt the terms of the Trust prevented the purchase and loan and it was therefore made by DUMAINES [trust].

> August 20, 1945: Borrowed of Manufacturers' Trust Co. New York to take up $2 million Boston & Providence bonds, note for two years, rate 1 ½ percent; 10 percent margin to be kept good.

New Haven directors wanted authority from I.C.C. to discontinue passenger service on the Old Colony Line. Dumaine was strongly opposed to abandonment of the Old Colony Railroad, which served thousands of commuters into Boston and many more thousands of vacation-bent people from all over America to Cape Cod. One reason he bought the Old Colony bonds was to give his group a voice in the final decision.

> January 19, 1945: Peabo Gardner reports John Hall said to be bitter over Boston Railroad Holding and Old Colony Railroad opposition. Quite vocal on these questions.

Mr. Hall soon became more than vocal. In March of 1948, he wrote a letter to the Boston press discussing the Boston Railroad Holding Company situation. The letter addressed Dumaine's attempt to secure the dissolution and liquidation of the holding company. Citing both the Amoskeag Co. and the DUMAINES Trust together with their ally, the Delaware & Hudson Co., he concluded their motive was to realize a gain on their investment in the preferred stock of the company.

Dumaine made no public answer. Perhaps he blew off steam when he recorded in his diary the total of fees paid to the firm of which John Hall was a member by the various Dumaine concerns and the New Haven Railroad. It came to considerably more than the $314,000 which Mr. Hall had estimated to be the gross profit likely to be made by the Amoskeag Company stockholders on their 3,663 shares of Boston Railroad Holding Company.

On February 20, 1948, the Massachusetts Supreme Judicial Court upheld the validity of the legislature's decision authorizing receivership of the Boston Railroad Holding Company and sale of its assets, including the Boston and Maine stock. The dissolution was not completed until March 6, 1953, two years after Dumaine's death. However, much transpired relative to Dumaine and the New Haven between those dates.

Dumaine was preparing for his last great endeavor ⏤ to stabilize the finances of the New Haven Railroad. It was late in 1945 before he took anyone into his confidence about buying control of the New Haven Railroad. He sent for J. Harold Stewart, an accountant.

"You've heard of an old man's folly?" barked Dumaine. "Well, I'm an old man. Would you say I was crazy if I bought the New Haven?"

"I'd say most old men were crazy to do it," answered Stewart, "but not you, F.C. You'd be crazy like a fox."

"I'm ready to do it," declared Dumaine. "Here's the portfolio of all holdings in DUMAINES and the Amoskeag Company. I want you to take this to Washington, show it to Mahaffy of the I.C.C., and get his opinion as to whether the government will raise any stink about me being president of the New Haven.

"When two men know a secret, it ain't a secret anymore," growled Dumaine. "I've told you, but I trust you, and Mahaffy can keep his mouth shut, too. You go down and show that portfolio to him."

Stewart made the trip, and while there was no written commitment, Dumaine soon knew that the I.C.C., in addition to no objection, would be glad if someone ⏤ Dumaine *or anyone* ⏤ could get the New Haven back to running efficiently.

In seeking the blessing of the I.C.C. to acquire control of the New Haven Railroad, Dumaine was admitting to himself and to Stewart that his purchase of the $2 million worth of Boston and Providence bonds in 1945 had been speculative and might be vulnerable. It was frankly a controversial matter. Old and good friends ⏤ among them Governor

213

Joseph B. Ely and John T. Hall — had opposed the purchase. Dumaine obstinately bought them outright with DUMAINES trust money, instead of parceling them among the Amoskeag, Dexter, or Coolidge trust funds he managed.

With all the bitterness that had grown in the battle over the reorganization of the New Haven Railroad, the question of continuation of service on the Old Colony Line, and the liquidation of the Boston Railroad Holding Company, it was inevitable that Dumaine would be dropped from the board of directors at the annual meeting in April 1947. What could not be foreseen by the board members who voted to remove Dumaine was that by May of the following year Dumaine would have the controlling interest and become chairman of the board.

About the same period that he acquired the Boston and Providence bonds, Dumaine met for the first time a young New Yorker, Patrick B. McGinnis:

> July 8, 1942: New York. Dinner, Biltmore. Bill Snow, Henry J. Dietrich [L. F. Rothschild & Co.]; Patrick B. McGinnis [Pflugfelder, Bampton & Rust, 61 Broadway, N.Y.]; Buck. McGinnis, specialist in railroad reorganization, seems to know his onions.

> July 17, 1942: Patrick B. McGinnis [Pflugfelder, Bampton& Rust, N.Y.]. Gave him order to spend $100,000 of Amoskeag money in purchase of New Haven bonds he recommends strongly. He's of opinion in bankruptcy proceedings, reporting purchases unnecessary.

In 1943, at the age of 77, Dumaine was suffering much from recurring prostate trouble and the lung condition of bronchiectasis. He felt so ill that he reviewed his *Last Will and Testament*. Satisfied with its terms, he executed a codicil stating he desired to make no change.

His negotiations as to the sale of Waltham Watch to the Guilden interests in New York had advanced to the point where Dumaine knew that soon he would have several million dollars in cash. He also knew that in the family trust DUMAINES he had provided for the future of his children and grandchildren and had made separate provision for lifetime income for Bessie Thomas and for his wife, Louise Gould Dumaine. There was every excuse, but in Dumaine's mind no good reason, for his accepting the opportunity offered to retire and enjoy tranquil life as a country squire at Groton with his dogs and horses.

> April 7, 1943: Offered Jack Morgan's holdings in the J. P. Mor-

gan Company, 18,750 shares at $200. Morgan is paying $6 or 3 percent return. Rather high-priced it would seem. George Whitney likely to be the controlling factor at Morgan's.

J.P. Morgan, Jr., had died on March 13, 1943. The J.P. Morgan shares were offered to Dumaine at less than the going market price of $206. Dumaine would have from the Waltham Watch sale more than the $3.75 million necessary to buy the Morgan stock, and the income would be at least $100,000 a year. It was a gilt-edged investment and yet another reason to retire to Groton. Whether the decision to pass on the offer was because he felt the price was too high or because he was anticipating the New Haven purchase is uncertain.

The New Haven Railroad was approaching the termination of its court control during reorganization. On September 12, 1947, Judge Carroll Hincks in Federal District Court, New Haven, Connecticut, approved discharge of the railroad as a debtor under the reorganization plan approved by the court and the Interstate Commerce Commission. The plan had been bitterly debated for twelve years.

In 1935, when the railroad went into receivership, the corporation had a theoretical capitalization of $489 million that consisted of $157 million of common stock, $49 million of preferred stock, and $283 million of bonds. As might be expected, the market value of the securities was significantly less based on the operating performance.

When the railroad came out of bankruptcy, the book value of New Haven's investments in securities of subsidiary and leased lines was written down from $176 million to $22 million. As a result, all of the original $157 million common and $49 million preferred stock of the New Haven was eliminated. The $283 million that bondholders received was 30 percent or $85 million in fixed interest bonds, 58 percent or $159 million in contingent-interest bonds, and 14 percent or $39 million in new preferred stock. Unsecured creditors of the old New Haven received new common stock with a face value of $107 in return for their obligations.

Even these reduced capitalizations represented an overvaluation of the organization as a going entity, since all of the securities had market values below their stated par. The fixed interest bonds sold at approximately 80 percent of their par value, or $68 million, the contingent interest bonds at approximately 40 percent of their par value, or $62 million, the preferred stock at 20 percent of their fair value, or $8 million. The common stock sold at an even lower percentage for a market value of about $12 million. Thus in 1947 the entire market value of the New Haven amounted to $150 million of which $20 million represented equity.

An even more interesting situation arose because of the voting rights of the stock. The bankruptcy decree stated that, for at least the first five years, the preferred stock would elect two-thirds of the company directors. The net result was that through a relatively small investment in new preferred stock one could control the New Haven.

This left Dumaine in an interesting position. While his original holdings of New Haven preferred stock were now worthless, his $2 million Old Colony bonds, which were replaced with new bonds and preferred stock of the New Haven, had a growing importance.

Most of the other original bondholders of New Haven and its allied railroads bonds were insurance companies. When they received the new distribution, they sold their preferred shares. Since they assumed that these sales would be absorbed by a diverse group of investors, they did not anticipate that anyone would capitalize on this opportunity.

In its January 31, 1948 issue, the United States Investor noted:

> The Amoskeag Company, with a strong board of prominent Bostonians, owned 12,900 shares of the old New Haven preferred, wiped out in the reorganization; and $2.2 million principal amount of obligations of the Old Colony railroad, slated under the reorganization plan to have a strong voice in operation of the road during the next five years at least, for it has . . . a total of 50,000 or 11 percent of the 453,428 shares of the 5 percent convertible issue, with 878,815 shares reserved for conversion of income bonds. Under provisions of the new preferred, holders, voting separately as a class, are entitled to elect two-thirds of the board of directors during the five-year period.

If anything, the above observation underestimated the strategic position that Dumaine had attained. In his 1969 book titled *The New Haven Railroad, Its Rise and Fall*, John R. Weller comments on both the speed and economy of the Dumaine takeover:

> Thus, in a few months the Dumaine interests had acquired 125,000 shares of the new preferred, and, with the shares held by the McGinnis group, this made up more than half of the 391,000 outstanding. Less than one-half of the ultimate $107 million of new common as yet had been distributed, but this made little difference because the preferred had control. It was

216

estimated that the Dumaine-McGinnis group had paid about $22 each for their preferred shares, bringing their total cost of obtaining absolute control to somewhere between $4 to $4.5 million. . . .

August 12, 1948, was the date set for the meeting to reorganize. That day, Dumaine boarded the train in Boston to attend the meeting. For years he had traveled the Shore Line from Boston to New Haven at least once a week. Usually it had been a through trip to New York or Philadelphia for board meetings and business or to Washington for conferences on tariffs, or wage-and-hours, or regulation of the textile industry. However, this ride was unique. Frederic Christopher Dumaine, son of a broom maker, was riding to the meeting in which he would be named head of the great New York, New Haven and Hartford Railroad.

Two decades earlier, with Robert Winsor, W. W. Atterbury, and A. J. County, he had almost achieved it. The stock market crash, Winsor's death, and his own "foolish debt" in tying up $1 million trying to salvage Winsor's estate in the Kidder, Peabody reorganization had blocked him from getting control in 1930. Now the dream was coming true. Unfortunately, many old friends were no longer there to take joy with him in the moment.

Many years before, when he began the shrewd campaign of strategic purchases and plans culminating in this ride to New Haven, Dumaine had viewed the field and picked the younger man he meant to be the working head of the New Haven under him.

> May 4, 1942: Long conversation with [Laurence F.] Whittemore. Working on Moore's Falls situation [flood control]. . . Having controversy with Serge Semenenko in Brown [Company] situation. Semenenko has been difficult, looking for $35,000 fee in bankruptcy proceedings. Brown and Canadian interests in bad humor. Canadians own one-half or more of entire Brown capital. Unless opposed, they might start some kind of action. Brown Company in need of good man for president. Whittemore not a candidate. Advised Whit to stay with railroad, not take Brown presidency even if offered on silver plate. While none of my business, had reasons for making statement.

Legend grew and was embroidered that on August 12,1948, when Dumaine went to New Haven to take charge of the railroad, he "rode in a day coach and carried a ham sandwich in a brown paper bag for his lunch."

C.F. Adams and F.C. riding the coach to the New Haven board meeting.

It was true that he rode in a day coach, buying tickets for the friends or assistants who accompanied him, telling them jocosely, "If you want a Pullman seat, you'll have to pay for it yourself."

The brown paper bag, however, actually contained a clean shirt and a supply of cigars. August in New England is famed for its dog days of oppressive heat and humidity. Dumaine knew he would need a clean shirt by the time he reached New Haven. His lunch that day was the lobster dinner served in the New Haven offices to the directors.

There had been dickering behind the scenes before the meeting. Dumaine had finally agreed to a compromise that John L. Hall be elected a director for the common stockholders, on the understanding that Hall would retire from the board at the April meeting.

The unfortunate Howard S. Palmer, former president of the New Haven, an earnest salaried railroad executive, paid the usual penalty for backing the wrong horse. The retiring New Haven directors, at their last meeting before handing over the reins to Dumaine, voted a $35,000 a year pension for life to Mr. Palmer, he being 63 years old. The new directors, handpicked by Dumaine, in December of 1948, rescinded their predecessors' vote and made a maximum annual pension of $10,000 for retired executives. Of course, Dumaine himself, as he had done in rehabilitating Waltham Watch in 1923, was taking no salary until dividends were earned.

At the August 12 meeting, only three of the sixteen "temporary" directors were retained: Charles Francis Adams; Morgan B. Brainard, president of the Aetna Life Insurance Company; and Allenton F. Brooks. Mr. Brainard would say, later, "The policies initiated by Dumaine, if time had permitted, would have made the New Haven a successful New England institution." Banished from the board were longtime directors like E. G. Buckland, Howard S. Palmer, and James L. Richards. The board members elected at that meeting to represent the preferred stockholders included many individuals who had served on Amoskeag and other company boards with Dumaine.

Frederic C. Dumaine was elected chairman of the board and named a member of the executive committee. Dumaine temporarily assumed the role of president, having already lined up Laurence F. Whittemore for that position.

In April 1949, Fortune magazine ran a feature article on Dumaine entitled "Capture of the New Haven." The article began with:

> The history of any great U.S. railroad is loaded with classic stories, but one of the latest is one of the best. It tells how a frail and shrunken curmudgeon of eighty-two rode from Boston to New Haven - and glory - in a day coach with a brown paper bag in his hand, and how he reversed the trip in a railroad compartment with the railroad in his pocket. The abducted railroad was the New York, New Haven and Hartford; the sly old citizen with the flair for drama was Frederic C. Dumaine, a financier famous, in a special way, in New England, but little known elsewhere.

The article went on to relate the history of both Dumaine's career and the New Haven. It later raised the question: since the New Haven had more than its share of troubles and Dumaine was well along in years, "Why, then, did Dumaine buy it?" In response to this question it suggested the following:

> Perhaps Dumaine, being smarter than most, can see a way to make fast money from his railroad, and to hell with the long view. That is what enemies like to believe. Perhaps moneymaking is not his interest this time. Perhaps he is thinking of his son and heir, Buck Dumaine. Perhaps he is unconsciously motivated by the fact that he has never been accepted socially by the top level Boston financial men who have long followed his

business advice. Perhaps he is simply getting even with those who pushed him from the New Haven Board of Directors in 1947. This would be characteristic Yankee cussedness. Perhaps, although his critics snort at the thought, he is telling essential truth when he says that he pocketed the New Haven because he wanted to take control from the outlanders of New York and Connecticut and give the good folk of Massachusetts an overdue break.

As noted earlier, J.P. Morgan is often quoted as saying, "A man does something for two reasons, a good reason and the real reason." While the real reason may have been the potential to profit from the project, the good reason was that he wanted to end the loss to investors of the New Haven and restore its operating efficiency to serve the New England public and industry. This writer believes that Dumaine would accept this characterization. However, he would be inclined to add the following: For one to be successful in accomplishing the end, in the real reason (i.e., making a profit) there must be a good reason (i.e., the need to improve upon bad management.) This seems to be the code that Dumaine followed throughout his business career.

F.C. Dumaine had some uplifting ideas to keep the New Haven on its track.

CHAPTER XIX

Putting the New Haven Back on Track

Dumaine was not a lawyer, but he had a nose like one of his own hunting dogs for a legal issue. He sensed one in the tangle of Boston and Providence Railroad and New Haven accounts, so he spent money for experts to wade through reams and volumes of figures going back fifteen years. Dumaine employed J. Harold Stewart as accountant and Charles L. Kades, a New York tax expert. The Treasury Department validated their reasoning and figures.

Instead of the New Haven owing back taxes of more than $22 million, the government awarded a refund of $7.8 million, and the Joint Committee of Congress, which scrutinizes such abatements, confirmed it.

Technically, the original error had been a question of bookkeeping, a mix-up between the losses of the New Haven and its leased line, the Boston and Providence. Incidentally, halfway through the preparation of the case, Kades and Stewart informed Dumaine that if the correct principle was established and maintained, the Old Colony Railroad, also under lease to the New Haven, would owe the government some $3 million.

"The hell with that," said Dumaine. "If the principle's right, there's bound to be some chips hewing down to it. Go ahead."

Prior to the hearing set by the Internal Revenue Service, certain friends of Dumaine hinted that in their political experience in the 1940's,

221

it was advisable to spread some "sugar" around Washington. They offered, if supplied with funds, to put it where it would do the most good. Dumaine called in Stewart and Kades, told them of this proposition, and flatly ordered them to see to it that no gifts were dispensed to secure a favorable decision.

"By God, we're right, and justice that has to be bought ain't worth having," he raged.

The final decision on the matter substantiating New Haven's claim would not be handed down until shortly before his death.

After taking over the New Haven, Dumaine's preoccupation was to squeeze out the water and trim off the fat that had brought the New Haven to its financial straits. His first act as temporary president was symbolic of this goal. At the September 29, 1948, directors meeting, he reported:

"A round table costing $2,500, installed in a large room only to be used once a month. Arrangements made to dispose of this unnecessary and expensive furniture; sublet room."

Within a year, he had authorized and negotiated the sale of twenty-seven parcels of unused real estate of the New Haven, which brought in $296,000 in cash, beside saving taxes. He found customers for unused rolling stock in Mexico and in Israel; he gave up the Grand Central office used by the New Haven president and sublet it at a profit.

No detail was too small for him to explore. He discovered an item in the accounts for storage at $300 a month of a vast surplus of Irish linens in a warehouse and sold them to the Pullman Company for $11,000. He pushed the sale of superfluous real estate, but dressed down a man for buying 100 metal "For Sale" signs at $17 each. "Wooden board or cloth signs would have served the purpose; the money spent for the metal signs would have paid the interest on 4,000 New Haven bonds," snapped Dumaine.

He discovered in the inventory that the Readville shops were storing eighty-three bells from old steam locomotives; diesel engines rapidly were replacing steam power. Dumaine received a bid for the bells at $15 each. However, he wisely paid $20 each for refurbishing the bells he bought as presents for his old friends.

The railroad owned some waste land in South Boston near the waterfront and the railroad yards. Dumaine called Archbishop Richard J. Cushing of Boston, whose charitable undertakings he admired, and offered him the land—for the legal token of one dollar—on which to build a church. Dumaine would die, though, before the Chapel of Our Lady of Good Voyage was built and consecrated.

On his trips to New York, F.C. continued to ride in day coaches so he could count noses to assess passenger traffic and observe conditions. He was as happy fussing over his railroad as a 12-year-old boy with a new bicycle. Best of all, the directors backed him on his lifelong creed of not paying unearned dividends.

> September 28, 1949: New Haven directors' meeting.... Unanimously voted not to pay preferred dividend at this time. To Boston on 5 o'clock train; six cars including diners and buffets. Passengers, 402, all told. 840 people added to payroll account 5-day week. Net of $210,000 a month. Adding payroll tax, makes $224,000 a month, about 2-3/4 million a year.

He was squirreling away in a special account the proceeds of cash sales of superfluous property. His aim was to accumulate enough to retire securities to reduce the top-heavy setup of the New Haven so that it could earn and pay dividends. When asked about his intentions, he stated, "Lot of people bought these New Haven securities because I've made a few companies successful. Never made money in the stock market; made a few pennies picking up defunct concerns, putting them on paying basis." It was his way of defining the leading motive of his character — the desire to see industry in New England "run right."

In evaluating Dumaine's performance over the first year of operation, Fortune noted:

> Dumaine has so far taken no salary. He has set a limit of $10,000 on the pensions of retired executives, past and future. Two thousand persons have already been cut from the payroll at an annual saving of more then $6 million.

Those who attacked Dumaine for his actions in the strikes at Amoskeag and Waltham took this latter point as an indication of his antilabor view. Others suggested that the elimination of 2,000 jobs in the short run may contribute to the continuation of the many thousand remaining jobs into the future.

The Fortune article went on to list economies including the selective reduction in traffic in unprofitable areas while attempting to maintain essential service. In reference to the Old Colony Line, whose service Dumaine had long supported, Fortune noted:

> On the Old Colony, recent schedules eliminated 45 weekly, 41

Saturday, and 28 Sunday runs. (President Whittemore announced that the remaining trains will take care of 80 percent of the passengers.)

Since the Old Colony last year lost $3.8 million, the New Haven has every right to cut off Old Colony passenger service at any time. But Dumaine is reluctant to lose the good will gained for the road when he announced he would operate the service as long as he could. He is hoping that the towns concerned will lower railroad taxes and that the Commonwealth will buy the South Station, thus lessening the heavy expense burden for the using railroads. Those who know Dumaine believe he will be able to negotiate some such deal.

Dumaine made no pretense of being an expert railroading man. He called in the operating executives and asked for their cooperation, promising if they would run the railroad efficiently, he would manage its finances honestly. He availed himself of the technical experience of veteran employees.

Dumaine's insistence on economy was notorious. Laurence Whittemore told him one day, "Fred, you can hear a dollar bill falling on a carpet in the next room."

"You bet I can, if it's being wasted or going into the sewer," retorted Dumaine.

He kept his ears skinned back, listening for wasted New Haven dollars, but Bill Snow was the only one to whom he confided what he meant to do with his own dollars.

"After we get this Providence matter settled," he said to Snow, referring to the $2 million of Boston and Providence bonds, "that's all I owe money for; pay that off. I'll have some cash I don't care about. I thought I'd start a little trust fund, income to go to the New Haven employees' Credit Union as long as it might be in existence."

Dumaine did not live long enough to collect the money for the Boston and Providence bonds, so his trust fund for the employees did not become a reality. He did collect some choice abuse over the bonds in 1950 when the New Haven stockholders voted, 464,846 to 84,639, to buy in the Boston and Providence debentures of which the family trust DUMAINES held $2 million in stock.

In 1950 people who would have shed no tear had Dumaine lost a couple of million dollars became vociferous on learning that Dumaine would make a profit on his judgment. The press ran sensational, if blatantly inaccurate, stories. The Providence Journal, learning from some stockholder that requests mailed out for proxies before the annual meeting contained a frank statement that F.C. Dumaine and William B. Snow had a financial interest in the matter, ran a story that Dumaine and Snow were each about to make $1 million personally. According to the Journal, Dumaine had bought up debentures for $2 million and proposed to make the New Haven pay $3.2 million for them. Only the Boston Traveler, which took the trouble to interview Buck Dumaine for the facts, reported that the difference represented interest owed by the New Haven Railroad, accruing since 1938. In 1950, through nonpayment of the interest by the New Haven since 1938 under the lease which the New Haven had originally taken in 1896, the Boston and Providence was insolvent and in receivership. Its forty-four miles of track, stations and rights-of-way were an indispensable link of the Shore Line used by the New Haven between Boston and New York and by the Pennsylvania between Boston and Washington. To Dumaine it seemed clear and simple that the New Haven should buy the B&P to untangle the financial mess and operate the trackage economically.

His view was not shared by 11 percent of the New Haven stockholders, according to the vote at the 1950 annual meeting. One man from Washington, D.C., Eugene Havas, representing 1,323 preferred shares, told the press that if the New Haven had $3 million, it should be paid out in dividends. "When money is being paid out in the way that is proposed instead of in dividends, I feel we are being cheated," he was reported as saying. Mr. Havas cast his votes on a write-in ballot for John L. Hall and Howard S. Palmer as directors, but Dumaine and the directors he endorsed were all reelected. A Time news article in the April 24, 1950 issue, used the Havas remarks as a springboard for an article captioned, "An Embarrassing Situation."

> Boston dowagers once dismissed Frederic Christopher Dumaine, 84-year-old president and chairman of the New York, New Haven and Hartford Railroad Co., in a single frigid sentence: "Mr. Dumaine is the sort of person who spits in the fire." When he heard of the remark, F.C. turned to a friend and asked blandly: "Well, what the hell? Doesn't everybody?"

> Last week, hardfisted, hardheaded old Fred Dumaine disdainfully spat on the hot fire stirred up under him at the New Haven's annual meeting. Stockholders were asked to approve the purchase of the outstanding 5 percent debenture bonds of the long-bankrupt Boston & Providence Railroad Corp. for $3.2 million. Who owned the debentures? None other than Chair-

man Dumaine and a few of his friends. They had bought the bonds for $2.2 million in 1945 when Dumaine was just a New Haven director. Now they stood to clear a $993,200 profit on the deal.

To former Massachusetts Governor Joseph Buell Ely, who represented Dumaine at the meeting (the old man's physician had told him to stay home), this was "an embarrassing situation." But to dividend-hungry stockholder Eugene Havas the situation was far worse. "Nothing like this has happened since the days of Fisk and Gould!" he yelled. "This is shameful... But Dumaine and his friends have voting control of the railroad, so the stockholders had to agree to give them their profit."

Dumaine, as was his way, took no notice of the personalities and inaccuracies. He was too busy discussing railroad legislation with U. S. Senator Charles W. Tobey of New Hampshire, who visited Dumaine at Groton.

April 22, 1950: Tobey. Discussed question of doing all possible to eliminate government present tax of 15 percent on railroad tickets; secure its elimination, leave freight tax where it is. On [St.] Lawrence waterways, explained my experience in shipping business for many years. It will be absolutely impossible for a regular Atlantic Ocean ship operating between Europe and New York to spend the time going up to the Lakes in the St. Lawrence waterways. The time it would take would cost more than the receipts. Tobey commented little about Waterways. Tobey says we're living on a keg of dynamite.

Dumaine inherited two other insolvent concerns on taking over the New Haven in which his outlook had differed from that of the old board of directors, the Old Colony and South Station. The old board of New Haven directors had secured permission of the I.C.C. to abandon passenger service on the Old Colony division whenever receipts fell below a stipulated sum. Dumaine was deeply resolved that it would be a hardship and injustice to the population of southeastern Massachusetts to permit such abandonment. While he understood the inroads made by the automobile on commuter traffic, he assured South Shore residents that he wanted to continue service on the Old Colony division.

August 23, 1950: I want to give the Cape some kind of decent service. If they'll show me how the outfit can receive their money back on any service they want, they'll have it. I have a little sentiment about Cape Cod. Came into this thing to bring its control back to this area. Never could understand why a million prospective customers couldn't have some service without losing money.

South Station, built by the Boston Terminal Company, organized in 1896 to erect the structure on land of the old New England railroad, also had a sentimental as well as a practical interest for Dumaine. He remembered when the first trains of the Old Colony division had abandoned the old Kneeland Street station to run into the tracks and platforms of South Station at midnight of December 31, 1898.

South Station was the terminal for trains of the New Haven, the Pennsylvania, the Boston and Albany, the New York Central, and the Old Colony. Once it had been Boston's pride, but in fifty years it had become smoke-begrimed, shabby, rundown. Now the South Station was in the federal courts. As of February 1, 1947, the $14 million principal of Boston Terminal Company bonds was due and not paid, and no interest had been paid by the New Haven since October 30, 1939. The 1896 statute of the Massachusetts legislature empowered bondholders to collect from the participating railroads any loss suffered by bankruptcy of the Terminal Company. By 1949, total claims of bondholders for principal and back interest amounted to $21 million. The New Haven Railroad seriously had been considering making Back Bay Station (on lease from the Boston and Providence) its Boston terminal unless rental relief at South Station was forthcoming.

The City of Boston was a creditor, too, for back taxes. One of Dumaine's first thoughts was to keep the New Haven running into South Station. He told the New Haven Railroad executives:

> Some of your owners who have invested in this outfit have a notion with a tax like that, we ought to be arranging to discontinue the use of the South Station. I kind of hate to lose it, personally.... Someone who is competent ought to be telling us how we could operate without the South Station.

> We set the money aside [in the Special Account] until we have these two problems, the South Station terminal and the Providence R.R. settled, thinking perhaps the money would be useful for the system.

Dumaine had known politicians and watched politics from the days of James G. Blaine through Franklin D. Roosevelt. He knew when appropriations were running low and when municipal payrolls or bond issues had to be met. His timing for combating excessive municipal taxes on South Station was excellent when he met with the former newspa-

227

per boy who had asked what he intended to do with the apple core some 60 years earlier.

December 22, 1948: Called on Mayor [James Michael] Curley [of Boston]. With five attorneys, offered to pay $3.1 million to settle taxes through '49 plus $200,000 per annum. No agreement reached.

Monday, December 27, 1948: Called on Mayor Curley 11:30 A.M. concerning future city taxes. Made no progress whatever. They say the railroad officials agreed to the $300,000 annual payment. Told him distinctly I couldn't see my way clear to obligate the company indefinitely for so large a payment.

December 30, 1948: With Whit, called at the Mayor's office one o'clock. Gave him check for $3.1 million, cleaning up all city claims to the end of 1949.

Dumaine tried to arrive at a mutual understanding with the railroad operating heads. He instituted regular conferences in his office, which he had moved to Room 440 in South Station. He would start the ball rolling with one of his sharp tongued comments, and then listen, catching information and ideas later put down in his diary. A typical remark would be "Whenever I go on trips over the New Haven line, I see row upon row of empty cars. If the cost is $20,000 every day, that would be about $7 million a year — about pay the interest on our bonds." In the first year of Dumaine's management, a net saving of $2 million was effected on empty "foreign" cars at $1.50 a day per car.

Safety was a point he constantly stressed. He had never forgotten the Bussy Bridge wreck he had witnessed as a youth. The accident on the Boston and Providence had put the railroad in bankruptcy and led to its lease to the New Haven. "We cannot have accidents like the old Bussy Bridge wreck on the Boston and Providence in 1887. The claims on that accident practically put that railroad out of business. There are five bridges between New York and New Haven, all built around 1895, all overloaded. What would new bridges cost?" he asked.

He wanted the directors to take a personal and informed interest in the railroad's operating problems, too, and initiated them by bringing to a board meeting in August 1949 Frank J. Doolan, who had been with the railroad since 1904 and by 1947 was Assistant to the President. Dumaine told the directors:

I was a director in the New Haven for 20 years. I never saw anybody except Frank Wall once or twice at a board meeting to

228

explain something about ships used to run down Buzzards Bay to Nantucket. Mr. Doolan here is responsible for operating this railroad. He's never been asked to a director's meeting. I have a notion some of the directors would like to meet some of its operating men. If you have any questions about the railroad, I'm sure, so far as he is able, Mr. Doolan would like to give you an answer; if not able, he'll take it up for you.

With all his emphasis on economy, he would not have any skimping on maintenance. "Don't neglect roadbeds or anything to do with safety. That's not money saved," he warned his men.

The first eighteen months, with Whittemore as president, Doolan as top operating executive, and Dumaine chipping in his two cents' worth here, there, and everywhere, showed the old man in top form. In eighteen months — through economies along with sales of surplus material and land — a reserve fund of $7 million was yielded. Dumaine still wanted to reduce New Haven's liabilities by purchasing the road's own securities.

> March 21, 1949: Pat McGinnis telephoned. Told him under no circumstances would I pay more than 40 and 60 for New Havens. He said he couldn't afford to allow New Haven securities to decline ruthlessly. I'd be pleased to see them go to 5, and, with the money we have, buy the whole of them. I had put quite a considerable amount in this situation, the lower they went, the better it would be, as far as I was concerned. There was no argument.

But there was an argument — the old argument over and over again — in the Amoskeag Manufacturing Company, the Waltham Watch Company — now the New Haven. It was an argument between those to whom securities were only something from which you drew cash, and people like Dumaine to whom a mill, a factory or a railroad was something that must be efficiently useful and not overburdened with debt before it could pay dividends.

"He was a wonderful, loyal, kindhearted friend, but a cuss to work for," said Laurence F. Whittemore. "His point of view stemmed from his early upbringing. Times had changed, but he could not reconcile himself to the shift in viewpoint to that of the minority stockholder."

Over the Labor Day weekend of 1949, Dumaine, had "the worst attack ever," as he noted in his diary. The distress in breathing lasted from Sunday morning until Monday night without relief, but his strong will would not let him give in. He insisted that his Betty go for the hunting season in Ireland. He was proud that she was to ride as Master of the Hounds of County Wexford.

His people were worried about him. Sunday, November 20, 1949, Buck went over to Groton from his home in Weston to insist the doctors put his father in the hospital. F.C. yielded, but remembering where his good friend Dr. Billy Brooks was a resident, selected Brooks Hospital in Brookline. F.C.'s wife, Weesie, was then in the Massachusetts Memorial Hospital. Thanksgiving came and went, the first time in eighty-odd years F.C. had not eaten Thanksgiving dinner at home. Every day he had his secretary, Jo, at his bedside for dictation. Amoskeag Company or New Haven officials came in for conferences.

Dorothy Wayman, in an interview with Whittemore, related the following:

> The Brown Company again wanted Whittemore as president and were pressing him for an answer. Whittemore himself wanted to avoid the open rupture he knew must come if he pressed Dumaine to pay a dividend at the annual meeting in April. He went out to Brooks Hospital after Thanksgiving.
>
> The split that led to my resigning as president of the New Haven was over his policy of reserving cash to pay off bonds and put the road on its feet. Stockholders were pressing for dividends and recent court decisions seemed to support their position. He had this special account of liquid cash and I said to him, "We'll have to show that money." His answer was, "'Damn 'em; it's none of their business.'" I was too fond of him to have an open break at the next annual meeting, so I got out.

Dumaine dictated a long diary entry about that day's events. Imperturbable, faithful Carolyn Johanssen, who had been with him for forty years, never fumed a hair when he swore at her, or gave in an inch when he was in error. It was an office routine to see Jo march out of the private office, pick up the big Webster's International Dictionary, and lug it in to Dumaine's desk to prove a point. She never argued, she just showed him. Once she collected a handsome apology, to everyone's surprise. She had filled out an insurance claim for Tim Splaine, after a bale of hay fell on him. To the question "Occupation?" Jo had typed in "Hostler." Dumaine, glancing over it before signing as employer, exploded. "Blankety-blank, Jo! Thus and so and double asterisks! There's no such word in the English language. Tim's a stableman, damn it." Webster backed up Jo — and Dumaine apologized to her.

Five-Star General Douglas MacArthur campaigned in 1948 aboard a New Haven train.

Now in the hospital dictating the diary pages, Dumaine betrayed how sick he really was. For the first time in thousands of pages, tens of years, he put down that he could not remember whether, a few hours earlier, he had told something to Whittemore or only thought of it later when he lay alone, reflecting.

Two days later he had his way about going home to Groton. He had decided to take over the title of president of the New Haven himself for the little time left to his earthly span. That way he could keep the controlling group intact, and Buck could probably succeed him when the time came. He confided his decision to the diary:

> I don't want to make a mistake picking man for permanent president. I can hold down the job, sign papers. See if this man Doolan is good enough. Let him run it for a while. We'll see how good Doolan and McGill are.

> November 29, 1949: Harry McGill at hospital. [Told him] I'm going to give you a lecture. The New Haven, up until 1948, was run like other railroads. I've taken a liking to you, think you're honest, know enough to keep your mouth shut. If you do, you are more than the average fellow on this system. Up to

'48, the New Haven was run by proxy, 10 shares here, 10 shares there. A group of men put $4 million in there, bought control. They're going to insist it be run like an up-to-date industry. That's never been done. Unless we can make the railroad earn money enough from fares and freights and that sort of thing to pay expenses, it will cease to operate, go back into receivership—and you'll be out of a job. I probably put the most money in there; the group appointed me to represent them. They expect to get results. So do I.

The challenge of becoming president of the New Haven was like a tonic to the old man. In a rare newspaper interview with John J. Carey of the Boston Post in 1950, Dumaine gave the following candid statement of his goals and policies relative to the New Haven. The interview highlighted the balance between cutting costs and improving the quality of service. For the reader interested in adjusting the numbers for inflation, all values should be multiplied by 7. For the reader interested in adjusting for inflationary and real growth in the economy, all numbers should be multiplied by 30.

For the reader not interested in getting bogged down in numbers, it is sufficient to say that all values were significant.

> Why are these newspapers sniping at me for when I am trying to rebuild the New Haven railroad so that it can provide a real service to the community? Why should they continue to censure me for getting rid of those who put the road in bankruptcy, and who would put it there again if they followed on the way they were going? There simply was too much deadwood in the organization, gathering together in the past 40 years, and it had to be removed.

> It has always been my ambition to try and bring control of our local railroads back to Boston and New England interests, and that is what my associates and I are trying to do with the New Haven.

> The waste and extravagance of the old management which has been superseded is almost incredible. The former president maintained three enormous, sumptuous offices, one in New York, one in New Haven, and one in Boston. Around him he gathered a hierarchy of assistants, secretaries and traveling secretaries, and each of his assistants had secretaries all the way down.

> These former presidents received salaries ranging from $60,000

to $75,000 a year with additional expenses connected with the president's office running up to more than $50,000 a year. We have cut this all out. I don't receive a cent of salary either as president or as chairman of the board of directors, when I could reasonably charge $50,000 to $60,000 a year for each job. The only way I can make any money out of my investment in the New Haven will be when all the other stockholders make money, by making the road prosperous and profitable.

After building a magnificent building in New Haven, costing well over $2 million, the old management was still spending $175,000 a year for outside office rents, and of this, $120,000 was being spent in New Haven alone. In New York, we were paying $25,000 a year rent for one parcel of office space. We have leased this space for $36,000 a year of which one-third goes to the New York Central and one-third to the New Haven. The net gain for us, therefore, is the $25,000 a year we were paying out plus $12,000 we are receiving, a total gain of $37,000.... [In Boston, three offices] have been closed and we have saved nearly $60,000 a year without any appreciable impairment in service so far as we can see....

I don't pretend to know how to run a railroad, but I know something about business and a railroad must be run as a profitable business or it can't run at all.... Around New York Harbor we found tugboats, lighters and wharves, some of which had not been used for several years and might never be used again. But they were kept in service at a high cost in wages and taxes. One wharf that had been condemned for several years was being maintained with three watchmen and plenty of taxes. And now some of our critics are screeching about why should we let men [management] go who were responsible for such waste. We have cut down the cost at New York Harbor by $500,000 a year, and this is not peanuts even for a big railroad....

When a department head wanted $1 or $2 million, the old management apparently signed the voucher without carefully examining the needs for these big expenditures. Now we call them in and ask for their work sheets to see just how much they need. We do not refuse any request for the operations and maintenance of the road. We, on the word of outside railroad authorities, have as good as the best railroads in the country, and some say the best of all.

Some of these department heads have come to us asking for

233

big sums for purchases when on examination we find they have already on hand supplies enough to last two years or more. At the big shops in Readville, for example, we found $100,000 worth of repair parts for engines that had been scrapped years ago....

When we took over control, the road's inventory amounted to $10 million. We have cut this to less than $5 million and everything is in better shape, with the supplies being currently used whereas a lot of the old stuff had become obsolete.

We found $4 million worth of scrap iron along the road. We sold $2.4 million of this for cash last year, and we have cashed in $1.6 million more so far this year.

We found that we had 6000 parcels of real estate on our hands not used for railroad purposes. We are cashing this in at the rate of $400,000 a month.

The cost of running the Grand Central Station at New York has been reduced by $1 million a year, of which one-third is for the New Haven's account.

Restaurants on which we were losing $30,000 a year have been leased to outside parties for $25,000. Food and service are better then we were providing and we are $550,000 a year better off.

By the end of the year, Dumaine's health had deteriorated considerably. On December 8, he was driven from Groton to Boston for the Woodchuck Club luncheon. He had Doolan as his guest, introducing him to Paul and Joe Draper, Dick Ely, and Ned French.

With stableman-hostler Tim Splaine as nurse-valet, Dumaine went into the Parker House in Boston to host a dinner for the New Haven directors the evening prior to their board meeting on February 20. In that meeting, he was successful in getting his way on the Boston Terminal and Boston and Providence questions. That morning he was taken back to Groton to get comfort again in his old red wool shirt and red tassel cap in his father's armchair. The following week, aided once more by Splaine, Dumaine went to Boston for the testimonial dinner for his friend and associate through sixty years, Charles Francis Adams.

The exertion tired F.C. so much that he could not be at the annual meeting of the Amoskeag Company the next morning, where it was recognized that his stewardship since 1925 had brought the investment company safely through the shoals of the depression in which so many

234

companies were wrecked. The market value of its securities in 1950 was estimated at $25 million, and the Amoskeag Company had never missed paying a dividend in a quarter of a century of the country's worst financial years. The achievement demonstrated Dumaine's formula for success — if he had a free hand in management, he not only could earn dividends, but he would also pay them. In 1950, the Amoskeag Company preferred stock paid its regular $4.50 dividend and the common $3 a share.

It was the twenty-seventh of March before Dumaine was well enough to go into his Boston office for the first time since November. Dumaine's health was failing: he had wasted away to under a hundred pounds and was subsisting on oxygen and raw eggs in brandy. Still he fought on to realize for the railroad his goal of efficient operation that would result in triple benefits — to the community, the employees, and the investors. His faith in the potential of America and of Americans had never failed. He had put his own cash and persuaded his friends to back him, when reorganizing a New England transportation entity that, under former management, or mismanagement, was on record as having lost to investors some $600 million. He did it at no personal profit, taking no salary, paying himself and his associates no dividends. Dumaine believed that a railroad was an artery supplying lifeblood to the industries and people of New England.

Three days before Dumaines' death, Clarence Barnes, former Massachusetts attorney general, called on Dumaine. He came to report the final cash settlement arranged on behalf of the Boston friends who had joined Dumaine in 1930 in subscribing $5 million to rescue Robert Winsor's old firm of Kidder, Peabody. The old man was glad to have that business wound up; he had long ago taken as a bad debt his own loss of $700,000. On this Thursday in May 1951, he wanted to talk only about the New Haven and his plans for it.

As Barnes said good-by, Fred Dumaine called after him, "If the Lord gives me a couple of years more, I'll make the New Haven the finest railroad in the country." Dumaine would not be granted those years. His eldest son, Buck, would have to take on the responsibility.

F.C. on his favorite horse, Pat Rooney.

CHAPTER XX

The Horseman Is Home From The Hunt

Frederic C. Dumaine, who had spent seventy-one of his eighty-five years under the name Amoskeag, realized that his death was imminent. He wanted to die in a manner similar to his father: among loved ones in a familiar environment.

Mrs. Dumaine — Weesie — suffering from hypertension since 1938, could not cope with the lack of servants and isolation at Groton during gasoline rationing. The big house was closed; she and Dumaine had an apartment at the Charlesgate in Boston. Old Tim Splaine and Bill Burke looked after the dogs and horses from the farmhouse on Farmers Row, Groton.

By 1943 Dumaine recognized that his wife would not be equal again to managing the large mansion at Groton. Six of his children now had their own homes, and the farmhouse, stables, kennels, and woods on the Groton estate he had earmarked for Betty. He listed the big house for sale, though it was several years before a buyer materialized. By the spring of 1944, Dumaine, homesick for his horses and dogs, moved out from the city to the small farmhouse on the estate. He was free, by then, of the chore of daily attention to Waltham Watch affairs.

237

He stayed alone at the Groton farmhouse, in a wing on the ground floor built in 1946. It contained a forty-foot paneled library with a view across the valley to Mount Wachusett.

There was a noble fireplace, comfortable chairs, his Currier & Ives prints, and old sporting prints of horses. Opening from this library was his bedroom and bath. In the bedroom stood the old chair where Christopher the broom maker had sat dying. On his bed slept the black cat. A screen door was installed between bedroom and library so that the red setters could be closed in or out.

In 1949, Lawrence Whittemore found an apartment for him at the Hotel Lincolnshire on Charles Street, at the foot of Beacon Hill in Boston. Dumaine liked it because it had a view over the rooftops westward up the Charles River, with the granite towers of the bridge to Cambridge. He would divide his time between the apartment in Boston and the farmhouse in Groton.

In December 1950, his daughter Betty came home from Ireland for Christmas and daughter Cordelia came up from New Jersey. It was like one of the old Christmases, with children and grandchildren dropping in. But by New Year's he was having bad days again, so bad that he could not even talk over the telephone to his office. Edward F. Williams, one of the New Haven directors, himself convalescent, rode to Groton on January 21 and found Dumaine unable to go to New York for the January New Haven directors' meeting. The old man now was sleeping nights sitting upright in his father's armchair.

Breathing was becoming difficult and recourse to oxygen was frequent. Through the spring of 1951 it became his routine to be driven to Boston Sunday evenings, stay at the Lincolnshire suite, attend conferences there or at his office until Thursday noon, join his intimate associates for the Woodchuck Club luncheon at the Parker House, and return to Groton for a long weekend of rest.

He held the last meeting of DUMAINES that he would attend at the Lincolnshire on May 22, 1951. Albert H. Wiggin of the Chase National Bank of New York, his friend from boyhood, had died the day before. For the DUMAINES meeting came Allan Forbes, Ned French, G. Peabody Gardner, H. E. Melzer, Charles B. Rugg, J. Linzee Weld, and Buck. They carried out Fred Dumaine's wish by electing Charles P. Curtis, Jr. trustee and new president of the family trust. The day was a Tuesday. On Wednesday and Thursday morning F.C. held conferences in his office on New Haven matters, but became too ill to attend the

238

Thursday Woodchuck Club luncheon. They drove him back to Groton.

He was taken with a sinking spell, and his sons, Buck and Spike, started to carry him to his bedroom.

"No, no!" he gasped. "Put me in Father's chair. I think I'm going out."

He rallied that time with oxygen. His daughter Cordelia came from New Jersey on Friday to help Betty. On Saturday afternoon, as he sat in the library in his old red shirt and red tasseled cap, the red setter dogs at his feet, Cordelia rolled up his sleeve to give an injection. He suspected a transfusion.

"No, I don't want to take any more of your blood," he muttered.

Early in the evening of May 27, Betty came to get him to bed. For three months now this daughter, trained as a nurse, had been sleeping on a cot in the hall outside his door, ready for any need. His dogs took their usual place in the corner of the bedroom. The black cat was curled at the foot of his bed.

"No. Put me in Father's chair," he said.

"Later, Daddy," answered his girl. "You lie down and rest a little and I'll come back and help you to Grandfather's chair."

"All right. I guess they've done all they can for me," he acquiesced.

As she eased him on to the pillows, the big black cat lifted its head and its eyes grew large. With an eerie cry, the cat bolted from the room.

"What's the matter with that cat?" muttered Dumaine.

When Betty came back to help him to Christopher's chair, death had come first. Frederic Christopher Dumaine had died, peacefully in his sleep, on May 27, 1951.

There was a brief service for the family and cremation at Mount Auburn Cemetery in Cambridge on Tuesday. The funeral, at the Groton farmhouse, was at half-past four on Wednesday afternoon, Memorial Day. A hundred and fifty friends and kin gathered by invitation. Louise Dumaine was too ill to be present. Elizabeth Thomas, once Dumaine, now Mrs. Clark was present with the seven children she had borne him, their wives or husbands and fifteen grandchildren.

Also in attendance were men and women who had worked with Dumaine in the Amoskeag Mills, the Waltham Watch factory, the shipping companies, and the railroads of New England. There were judges of the courts, bankers, lawyers, clergy, editors, surgeons, labor leaders — a cross-section of the New England he had loved and labored to make sound.

The former rector of the Episcopal Church at Concord, Rev. E. P. Daniels, officiated. After the service, the urn was transported to Dumaine's final resting place in a Concord buggy driven by hostler-stableman Tim Splaine and pulled by Dumaine's 34-year-old mount, Jake. Following a brief grave side ceremony, the urn was placed beneath a rough-hewn granite millstone on a slope overlooking the Nashua River.

The funeral cortege proceeds to the final resting place of Frederic C. Dumaine.

Twelve Rules Of
Money, Success, Love And Happiness
As Prescribed By
Frederic C. Dumaine

Rule 1 - A New York Multi-Millionaire says, "The secret of making money is never to refuse to sell at a profit, even if the profit is small, for the profit is yours. You are in the clear with that, and you can reinvest again." Many people go broke or lose money by holding out for big or bigger profits. F.W. Woolworth (the 5 and 10 cent store owner) made many millions of dollars with small profits and volume sales.

Rule 2 - Never let anyone waste your time. Time is the essence of your life. Napoleon Bonaparte often said, "Time is everything." The millionaire and loafer have the same amount of time each day: it's twenty-four hours each day and night for everybody.

Rule 3 - The best book, song, poem, or play has not been written yet. The best sales or business idea or plan has not been made yet. The greatest invention has not been discovered yet. There is always room for you — to dare and do, to conquer and master. You can do what no one has done before. Success begins with you and your mind.

Rule 4 - Have nothing to do with idlers, persons with vulgar minds, double-crossers, cheaters, and discouragers. It's always best to ask such persons not to come around any more. You do not need them.

Rule 5 - Business is coming competitive again now; soon it will be highly competitive. Study people and their wants. Charlie Schwab made millions of dollars out of steel. He said he made plenty of money, because he looked for and studied men who would and did buy steel.

Rule 6 - Sure you are going to make mistakes ⏤ that is, if you do anything. Mistakes are going to be your part, but let us learn the secret of mistakes, so that we will really know life. In the 15th century, Wang Yang Ming, the great Chinese philosopher said, "The sages do not consider that making no mistakes is a blessing." They believe, rather, that the great virtue of man lies in his ability to correct his mistakes and continually to make a new man of himself. Or as Goethe said, "Wisdom is only found in truth." Admit to yourself the wrong, profit by the cause of the mistake, so in the future you will know how to avoid or overcome it.

Rule 7 - Happiness begins in the mind and ends with joy in the heart. As Dandemis says, "Do not terrify your soul with vain fears, neither let your heart sink because of the phantoms of imagination." Remember that as fear invites failure, so he who hopes helps himself. You are entitled to the best in life, Always read the best of books, poems, see the best of plays, enjoy the best of music, associate with the best of people. Let "Trashy Persons Go" or "Forever Be Trash." Have quality in your life at all times.

Rule 8 - The greatest words you can ever say to the person you love are "I Love You". There are Power and Glory in these three words. Use them often. Show how much kindness, sweetness, truth and originality you can put in your love. Love begets love; hate begets hate. It's not the quarrels that count; it's seeing each day how much love you can bestow on the one of your affection ⏤ THAT'S WHAT COUNTS. A little love is a whole lot of Heaven here on Earth. You give in order to get.

Rule 9 - Successful men and women are ones who keep on trying. Success is failure turned inside out every time. As the old saying goes, "A Winner Never Quits and a Quitter Never Wins."

Rule 10 - If you know and feel that you are right, then, by all means, go ahead on the venture, whatever it is. People called Noah, Christopher Columbus, Henry Ford, and Goodyear were "crazy" when they started their work.

Rule 11 - You are different from all other persons in this world. Use, cultivate, exercise that difference. The secret of finding and knowing yourself is realizing that difference is an asset and not a liability.

Rule 12 - Change is the most permanent thing in life. Welcome it; do not hold back from it. There is nothing fixed or stationary in life. The majority of persons think they can keep life or business or love in the same old way, day in and day out. Life is constantly on the move. Henry Ford, twenty-eight years old, repaired bicycles in Detroit. He asked the butcher to credit him for a Thanksgiving turkey. The butcher refused him credit. At night when he went home he worked on the first Ford-to-be. He changed his mechanical ability from bicycles to automobile. Today, as you watch the Fords go by, he has made millions of dollars. Think "big thoughts" ⁻ they will grow; so will you ⁻ GROW WITH THEM.

Frrederic C. Dumaine at age 65.

Chronological Summary

1755   Louis-Michel Maingot, F.C. Dumaine's great-great-grandfather, emigrated from France as a member of the Queen's regiment stationed in Canada. Louis-Michel Maingot and his descendants were given the "dit" or second surname, Dumaine, meaning from the French Provence of Maine.

1760   The British captured Montreal from the French. Louis-Michel Maingot-dit-Dumaine was released from service and remained in the Provence of Quebec.

1805   Benjamin Prichard built first textile mill in Goffstown, N.H., on land ultimately annexed by Manchester, N.H. The property was later reorganized under the name of the Amoskeag Cotton & Wool Manufactory.

1815   Amoskeag Cotton & Wool Manufactory closed.

1824   J.E. Thayer, forerunner of investment banking house Kidder, Peabody and Co. organized in Boston.

1825   Partnership formed by Samuel Slater, Larned Pitcher, Ira Gay, Dean Oliver, Lyman Tiffany and Willard Sales under the name of the Amoskeag Manufacturing Company. The partnership acquired the property of the Amoskeag Cotton & Wool Manufactory.

1831   The partners of the Amoskeag Manufacturing Co. incorporated the business. This was first of five sister corporations organized in Manchester, N.H. by the Boston Associates, a name given to wealthy merchants responsible for constructing textile mills throughout New England.

1834   Boston Stock Exchange organized by J.E. Thayer and 13 other local brokerage houses.

1835   Amoskeag Manufacturing Co. began construction of canals to supply water power to mills to be built on the east side of the Merrimack River in Manchester.

1837   Francois-Xavier Maingot-dit-Dumaine, F.C.'s great-grandfather was killed by Canadian government forces in the Papineau Rebellion, in which French Canadians rose up against the "injustices" of the royal government.

1839   First Stark Mill completed. Second of five sister corporations built by the Boston Associates in Manchester, N.H. The company employed daughters of "Yankee" farm families. The women lived in company boardinghouses built by Amoskeag.

1840   First Irish operators in Manchester began working in the Stark Mill.

1844   New York and New Haven Railroad incorporated. Construction of rail line completed in 1848.

1846   First Manchester Mill completed. Third of five sister corporations built by the Boston Associates in Manchester, N.H.

1849   Amoskeag Manufacturing Co. built its first locomotive. A total of 232 would be built over the next ten years, at which time the business was sold to the Manchester Locomotive Works.

1850   Dennison, Howard & Davis formed in Roxbury, Massachusetts. (Forerunner of Waltham Watch.) The firm's eventual success was a result of development of intricate special purpose watchmaking machinery by Aaron Dennison.

1851   Amoskeag Manufacturing Co. awarded first medal for superiority of goods at the London World's Fair.

1853   Dennison, Howard & Davis name changed to Boston Watch Co.

1854   Boston Watch Co. moved to Waltham, Mass.

1856   Ezekiel A. Straw was chosen as Amoskeag Manufacturing Co. agent, or chief manufacturing officer. First of three generations of family to serve in that capacity.

1857   Boston Watch Co. property sold at bankruptcy auction to Royal E. Robbins for $56,000. Dennison brought back as factory superintendent.

1858   Christopher Dumaine, F.C.'s father married Cordelia Roberts, a widow with three daughters, in Chelsea, Massachusetts. Both of Dumaine's parents had immigrated from Canada.

1859   Boston Watch Co. name changed to American Watch Company. Beginning of "Golden Age" of profits and growth.

        Amoskeag Manufacturing Co. built its first steam fire engine. A total of 550 would be built over the next eighteen years, at which time this business was also sold to the Manchester Locomotive Works.

1860   Langdon mill incorporated. Fourth of five sister corporations built by Boston Associates in Manchester, N.H.

1862   Dennison out as factory manager at Boston Watch Co.

1864   First French Canadians began working in Amoskeag Mills.

1865   Kidder, Peabody & Co. organized by Henry Kidder and Francis and Oliver Peabody, three former clerks in the Boston investment banking firm of J.E. Thayer & Brother.

1866   Frederic C. Dumaine born March 6 in Hadley, Mass.

1872   New York & New Haven acquired and merged the New Haven & Hartford to form the New York, New Haven & Hartford, often called the New Haven. For the remainder of the century, the company's program was aimed at controlling all regional railroads and steamship lines.

1874   Manchester mills sold at auction, severing Amoskeag interests in that sister corporation.

1876   T. Jefferson Coolidge becomes treasurer, or chief executive officer, of Amoskeag Manufacturing Co.

1878   Kidder, Peabody & Co. becomes American agent for London banking firm Baring Brothers & Co. Ltd.

        Christopher Dumaine, F.C.'s father, died. F.C. began working at Henry Pettingall's drygoods store.

1879   Amory Manufacturing Company organized. Last of five sister corporations organized by the Boston Associates in Manchester, N.H.

Robbins warned in Boston Watch Co.'s annual report of increased competition.

1880   F.C. Dumaine began working for Amoskeag Manufacturing Co. as an office boy in the Boston office at $3.00 per week under Lucius Manulius Sargent and T. Jefferson Coolidge.

1885   Herman Straw, second of three generations of Straws, appointed agent at Amoskeag Manufacturing Co.

Boston Watch Co. name changed to American Waltham Watch Co. to reflect residence. In 1906, the name was shortened to the Waltham Watch Co.

1886   Jefferson mill built by T. Jefferson Coolidge for Amoskeag Manufacturing Co. even though management knew labor costs were lower in the South. The company established the policy of remaining a Manchester firm.

1887   Langdon mill merged into Amory mill, reducing the number of independent mills in Manchester from five to four.

1888   F.C. Dumaine moved to Boston in order to go to night school, whle working at Amoskeag Manufacturing Co.'s Boston office during the day.

1889   F.C. sent to Manchester to learn the manufacturing end of the textile business.

1890   F.C. Dumaine saw his first United States president when Benjamin Harrison toured Amoskeag Manufacturing Co. in August.

1891   F.C. sent back to Boston as a buyer for the Amoskeag Manufacturing Co.

1892   J.P. Morgan became a director of the New Haven and appoints Charles S. Mellen president. Under their leadership the company invested heavily in trolley lines and electric street railroads and acquired 90% of water transportation in New England.

F.C. Dumaine moved to Amoskeag Manufacturing Co.'s selling and accounting department.

1895   F.C. married Bessie Thomas April 13.

1897   Mary Dumaine, F.C. & Bessie's first child, born April 19.

1898 F.C. appointed treasurer of Amory Manufacturing Company.

1900 Elizabeth Dumaine, second child, born January 3.

Cordelia Dumaine, F.C.'s mother died June 23.

1901 Harriet Dumaine, third child, born March 12.

Stark Mill sold to U.S. Cotton Duck trust, a firm that was attempting to form a trust in duck cloth by acquiring mills in the North and the South.

1902 F.C. (Buck) Dumaine, Jr., fourth child, born September 5.

F.C. Dumaine given responsibility for reorganizing Fore River Ship and Engine Company at Quincy, Massachusetts.

1903 Manchester Mills acquired by T. Jefferson Coolidge, returning that property to control by Amoskeag interests. F.C. appointed treasurer and given responsibility for refurbishing the mills.

Dumaine hires Admiral Francis T. Bowles, the Navy's chief of construction, as president and operations manager of Fore River.

1904 *U.S.S. Rhode Island* launched at Fore River Shipyard on May 24. Bessie Dumaine christened the ship. The *U.S.S. New Jersey* launched that fall.

1905 F.C. Dumaine appointed treasurer of Amoskeag Manufacturing Co.

The Amory Co., which had previously absorbed the Langdon Mills, and the Manchester Mills were merged into the Amoskeag Manufacturing Co. The Stark Mill was the only one of the five original textile mills that was not combined under Amoskeag.

U.S.S. Vermont and the *Spray*, a steam trawler, launched at the Fore River Shipyard. The *Spray*, built for Dumaine's Bay State Fishing Co., was an unsuccessful venture for two years when fished by foreign crew familiar with trawler fishing but unfamiliar

Frank G. Webster becomes head partner of Kidder, Peabody following death of Frank Peabody.

1907 Cordelia Dumaine, fifth child, born February 17.

The New Haven acquired 40 percent of B&M stock (effective control.)

1908   Brandeis claimed the New Haven was not only a monopoly, but it was wasteful and inefficient. Attempted to impose legislation forcing NH to sell B&M. Not successful.

F.C. becomes a director of the Boston and Maine Railroad.

F.C. becomes a director of the Old Colony Trust Company.

Dumaine hires Gloucester fisherman Michael Greene to captain *Spray*. On first trip he returns with a boat full of deep-sea flounder, a fish not in favor in New England. The fish were distributed free to leading Boston hotels, compliments of Dumaine, with the caveat, "This is a sample of the best English sole, famous in all European restaurants." The product was immediately successful. Over the next five years, Fore River built eight more trawlers for the Bay State Fishing Co., the name given to Dumaine's new enterprise.

1909   F.C. and Bessie combined business [Fore River] and pleasure trip to London.

F.C. Dumaine constructs the Coolidge Mill in Manchester, substantially increasing Amoskeag's textile capacity.

Boston Railroad Holding Co. formed to control New Haven's Boston & Maine shareholdings. F.C. Dumaine named BRHC's president.

Mellen now president of B&M and Maine Central as well as the New Haven.

Dumaine had increasing concern with conduct associated with Fore River soliciting contracts to build battleships for Argentine government.

1910   Christopher Dumaine, sixth child, born April 6.

Dumaine met with U.S. President Taft concerning political pressure to have Argentine government contracted with the New York Shipbuilding Co. instead of Fore River.

1911   Amoskeag reorganized as a voluntary trust.

Series of New Haven train wrecks occurred over a three year period.

1912   F.C. and Bessie visited the Taft White House. They declined an invitation to stay over Saturday night to attend the opera, instead the elected to return home for Sunday horseback riding with their children.

Thomas Park Dumaine, seventh and last child, born August 21. Thomas Park's name was later legally changed to Pierre.

Dumaine establishes Amoskeag employee welfare system: clinics, dental care, visiting nurses, technical school, social clubs, stock purchase plan and building lots for residential houses.

New Haven needs new financing for past and current expansions.

1913   Fore River Shipyard sold to Charles M. Schwab's Bethlehem Steel Co.

J.P. Morgan died. Mellen replaced as president of New Haven by Howard Elliott (from Northern Pacific)

New Haven and B&M both needed rate increases based on labor and material inflation. New Haven's December dividend passed. First time in 40 years.

1914   Year of maximum physical output of Amoskeag mills.

Bessie, F.C.'s wife, became active in Women's Suffrage Movement.

Consent decree reached by the New Haven calling for B&M and the trolleys to be managed by five trustees under the Boston Railroad Holding Co. The steamship lines were sold at a loss.

1916   F.C. and Bessie separate. Bessie moves to Cambridge. The four oldest children remained with F.C. The three youngest lived with their mother.

Bay State Fishing Co. sold to New York interests for a profit of $1.5 million.

1917   Edward Pearson became New Haven's chief executive officer.

1918   Government took control of all railroads during World War.

Buck Dumaine, between academic years, was sent to Amoskeag mills for a summer job .

1919   Amoskeag profits reached all time high associated with wartime production.

F.C. and Bessie divorced.

Robert Winsor replaced retiring Frank G. Webster as senior partner at Kidder, Peabody & Co. A period of extreme conservative management and passive solicitation of new business started.

251

1920   DUMAINES Trust formed for F.C.'s children and grandchildren.

Parker Straw succeeded his father Herman as agent at Amoskeag in June. He was the third generation of Straws to hold that position.

1920   All railroads in operated in difficulty due to increased competition from trucks, autos, and buses. The ICC adopted policy of supporting consolidations. New Haven wants to be independent of B&O, NYC & Penn. At the same time it wanted to head a New England system. B&M wanted to be independent of New Haven.

1921   Amoskeag's earnings of $1.3 million fell short of dividend requirements of $2.5 million resulted in a reduction in surplus of $1.2 million.

Waltham Watch Co. neared bankruptcy. Banks appointed G.K. Simonds general manager.

1922   Amoskeag's nine-month strike.

Amoskeag acquired Stark Mill property when its management decided to concentrate production in the South.

1923   Waltham Watch reorganized by Kidder, Peabody & Co. F.C. Dumaine became president and treasurer.

Abbot v. Waltham Watch Co., et al. Suit was brought by original stockholders upset with details of reorganization. Court found for Waltham Watch.

Under Dumaine, Waltham Watch Co. retired $1 million debt from proceeds of inventory liquidation.

F.C. married Louise (Weesie) Gould on December 3.

1924   Five-month strike began at Waltham Watch Co. in response to attempt to cut wages 10 percent. Amoskeag suffered a $2.9 million loss before payment of dividend.

1925   Amoskeag reorganized into Amoskeag Company, a holding company, and Amoskeag Manufacturing Company, an operating company, to appease stockholders concerned that future losses would erode past profits accumulated by Amoskeag.

New Haven Railroad began a period of five years of operating profitably.

1926   Waltham Watch Co. showed first profit since reorganization and write off. Earnings $1.3 million. Company began to retire some of its bonds, both classes of preferred stocks and class B common stock. By 1928, approximately a third of both classes of preferred and class B common were retired.

1927 Waltham Watch Co. earnings were $872,000; $240,000 paid to 7% prior pfd. stock; no other dividends. Board awarded Dumaine $75,000 for services through July 1. Dumaine on salary from that date forward.

Curtis, Sanger & Co. of New York, offered to purchase Amoskeag Company with intent of closing mills and liquidating property, which was refused by directors.

Dumaine refinanced Amoskeag Manufacturing Co. with intent of preventing liquidation of Manchester facilities by subsequent corporate raiders. Over two thirds of Amoskeag Company stockholders accepted offer to swap their shares of holding company for $52 in cash a $40 bond of the manufacturing company and a share of the manufacturing company.

Five-year period began during which Amoskeag was to operate at a level of approximately 50 percent of capacity in an attempt to minimize operating losses.

1928 In July, Dumaine meet with Arthur V. Davis, president of Aluminum Corporation of America, in an attempt to convince Davis to construct an aluminum plant on the Merrimack, thereby to provide jobs and allow Amoskeag to partially liquidate mills. Davis concluded that water power was not sufficient to justify construction of the plant.

John Pelly (Central of Georgia) became president of New Haven following Pearson's death.

1929 Parker Straw, the third of three generations of Straws that served as agents, resigned on January 18.

Stock market crash and beginning of "The Great Depression." This aggravated Amoskeag's tenuous position and eventually resulted in losses at Waltham Watch Co.

Because labor agreed to accept wage reductions Amoskeag was able to successfully bid on profitable sales contracts. Profit of $1.1 million earned for the year. One third of profits was paid out as a bonus to labor in the form of savings deposits in various Manchester banks.

1930   Robert Winsor and Frank G. Webster, two of F.C.'s friends and principals of Kidder, Peabody & Co. died in January. In November, Dumaine was asked to help bail out Kidder, Peabody & Co., which was in need of a substantial cash infusion. With the assistance of the House of Morgan, Dumaine manages to raise $5 million of which almost $1 million was his own. The new creditors formed Commonwealth Corp. to oversee loan. Dumaine was president and one of five directors of Commonwealth Corp.

Merrimack River Savings Bank, one of the banks authorized to receive employees' bonuses, closed. Amoskeag covered loss to employees who still had bonus deposited in the bank.

Penn System has 23 percent ownership of the New Haven, which was effective control.

Depression had impact on New Haven's revenue and earnings.

1931   Frank G. Webster, succeeded in gaining control of Kidder, Peabody & Co. for his son Frank Jr., his son-in-law Chander Hovey, and Albert Gordon, a Harvard Business School classmate of the younger Webster. Dumaine and other individuals and corporations lost the $5 million loaned to Kidder, Peabody & Co.

1932   F.C. Dumaine was present at Groton School in October when Franklin Delano Roosevelt was campaigning for president.

FDR elected president in November to take office the following March.

1933   Congress passed Roosevelt's National Industrial Recovery Act.

1934   Dumaine discusses the textile labor problem with F.D. Roosevelt at the 50th *Anniversary of the Groton School.*

1935   New Haven filed for reorganization under Sect 77 bankruptcy.

In February, Dumaine spoke to the Cotton Textile Code Authority urging for equality of wages between the North and the South under the National Recovery Act.

In the spring, Amoskeag began closing mills. By September, most production rooms were closed and employment was below 1,000 workers. Dumaine emphasized that workers must accept competitive wages and production for Amoskeag to reopen on a profitable basis.

Dumaine met with Reconstruction Finance Committee, a part of Roosevelt's New Deal, attempting to seek funds to reopen mills.

On November 12, the Textile Advisory Board, a committee appointed by New Hampshire Governor Styles Bridges and headed by Bishop John Peterson, submitted its report, calling for greater production efficiency, further tax relief, and greater cooperation between Management and labor. The committee opposed Dumaine's position on the necessity of wage cuts.

December 24, Amoskeag, with bonds in default, filed for protection under the bankruptcy act while it attempted to restructure its financing in order to reopen the mills.

1936   March 9, Amoskeag Manufacturing Company submitted plan for refinancing to reopen the mills. The proposal required a majority of bondholders to trade in their bonds for preferred stock.

March 11-12, the Merrimack River overflowed Amoskeag Dam wiping out bridges and causing $2.5 million dollars of damage to the mills. Amoskeag Manufacturing Company still was willing to go along with refinancing plan.

March 17, Amoskeag Company, the holding company, which owned 32 percent of the manufacturing company, was willing to accept the manufacturing company's reorganization plan even after assessing the impact of the flood.

March 24, Dumaine met with Manchester bondholders, who were undecided whether to accept the refinancing or to try and force bankruptcy.

April 6, Court hearing was held on reorganization. Manchester bondholders of $1.1 million bonds, critical for the refinancing to be successful, remained undecided.

April 16, Dumaine met again with Manchester bondholders.

During May, Manchester and Boston newspapers stated Manchester bondholders willing to go along with refinancing.

June 7, Buck Dumaine stated that Manchester bondholders reneged on agreement to go along with refinancing.

June 9, Amoskeag Manufacturing Company withdraws reorganization plan since, "...the assets of the company will be depleted by reason of the fact that so many bondholders have elected to withdraw cash... particularly in New Hampshire...."

July 21, The Amoskeag Manufacturing Company declared insolvent in Federal District Court. Dumaine, Joseph Carney of Reconstruction Financial Committee, and W. Parker Straw were named co-trustees of the bankruptcy.

Manchester citizens formed Amoskeag Industries to purchase the mills and related property. They subscribed $500,000 in cash, obtained $2.5 million from Public Service Company of New Hampshire, for the power plant and water rights. The remaining $2 million paid to Amoskeag Manufacturing was loaned by Manchester savings banks.

1938   F.C. contacted War Department and telephoned President Roosevelt concerning the conversion of Waltham Watch Co. to war production.

1939   Buck Dumaine replaced F.C. as treasurer of Amoskeag Company, the holding company. F.C. assumed the position of president.

1940   February 1, Final summary of bankruptcy of the Amoskeag Manufacturing Co. All creditors paid in full. The remaining surplus was paid as a liquidation dividend to stockholders.

Airlines started inroads into railroad passenger traffic.

1941   Waltham Watch Co. employees organized by AFL.

Suit filed by Waltham Watch Co. stockholders calling for payment of dividends on class A common and 6 percent preferred. Decision called for payment of dividends for years 1939-41.

Elgin, Hamilton, and Waltham companies were indited for violation of Sherman Antitrust Law.

1942   Production of civilian watches at Waltham halted in favor of war work.

Dumaine visited President Roosevelt at the White House and, in an attempt to cheer up the president, quotes Abraham Lincoln. Dumaine subsequently had the quotation matted, framed, then sent to President Roosevelt, who wrote Dumaine, "I am hanging it up in my office that all may read."

1943   At Waltham Watch Co., all but $378,000 of the $1.7 million 7 percent prior preferred was retired.

Waltham Watch fined $33,860 for hiring girls under the age of 18 in order to fullfil government military contract.

1944   Dumaine sold his Waltham Watch Co. stock to Ira Guilden and left management.

Waltham Watch was presented with the Army-Navy Production Award for high achievement in producing material needed for war.

1946   F.C. retired as president of Amoskeag Company but continued as chairman of the board until his death.

1947   New Haven's 1934 reorganization completed, total capital reduced from $489 million to $385 million. All stock wiped out. New capital $195 million debt; $39 new preferred stock; $107 common stock. Market values of both classes of stock were substantially below par values. Dumaine voted off the board.

1948   Dumaine wins control of New Haven board through Amoskeag, DUMAINES Trust. and Pat McGinnis. Dumaine was successful because he was acquired a majorityof the preferred shares that elected 2/3 of board for first five years out of bankruptcy. Control obtained with $4 to $4.5 million.

Over the next three years, the New Haven, under Dumaine, earned profits of $22.5 million as a result of cost reductions and liquidation of excess real estate.

1949   Waltham Watch Co. files for reorganization. Dumaine offered to reorganize the firm taking no salary. An alternative reorganization was selected.

1951   New Haven stockholder suit demanded resumption of dividends

May 27, Death of Frederic C. Dumaine.

Marin Maingot
m. circa 1710
Madeleine Choquette

Michel Maingot
m. 01 October 1733
Marie Levasseur

Louis-Michel Maingot-dit-Dumaine
1735-1794
m. 11 January 1762
Marie-Anne Fontaine

Louis-Francois Maingot-Dit-Dumaine
1771-1804
m. 22 September 1794
Marie-Euphrosine Soly

Francois-Xavier Maingot-Dit-Dumaine
1803-1837
m. 15 September 1828
Adelaine Lescualt

Dumaine

Joseph Dumaine
1829-?

Stephanie Dumaine
1833-?
m. 11 April 1854
Noel Lussier
m. (2) 23 April 1864
Adolphe Tetu

Philomene Dumaine
1837-?
m. 06 February 1860
Hypolite Audet

Pierre Dumaine
1831-?

Christopher Dumaine
1835-1878
m. 14 May 1858
Cordelia Roberts

Frederick-Christopher Dumaine
1866-1951
m. 13 April 1895
Elizabeth Thomas
m. (2) 3 December 1923
Louise Sylvester Gould

BIBLIOGRAPHY

Books

Brown, George Waldo. *The Amoskeag Manufacturing Company.* Manchester, N.H. Manchester, N.H.: Amoskeag Manufacturing Company Print Shop, 1915.

Carosso, Vincent P. *More Than a Century of Investment Banking: The Kidder, Peabody & Co. Story.* New York, N.Y.: McGraw-Hill, Inc., 1979.

Chernow, Ron. *The House of Morgan, an American Banking Dynesty and the Rise of Modern Finance.* New York, N.Y.: Atlantic Monthly Press, 1990.

Clark, John B. *History of Manchester.* Manchester, N.H.: Mirror Office, 1875.

Coolidge, T. Jefferson. *The Autobiography of T. Jefferson Coolidge.* Boston, Mass.: Houghton Mifflin Company, 1923.

Creamer, Daniel and Coulter, Charles W. *Labor and the Shut-Down of the Amoskeag Textile Mills.* New York, N.Y.: Arno and the New York Times, 1971.

Hareven, Tamara K. *Family Time and Industrial Time.* Cambridge, Mass.: Cambridge University Press, 1982.

Hareven, Tamara K., and Randolph Langenbach. *Amoskeag: Life and Work in an American Factory-City.* New York, N.Y.: Pantheon, 1978.

261

Harlow, Alvin F. *Steelways of New England*. New York, N.Y.: Creative Age Press, Inc., 1946.

History of the Amoskeag Strike. Author Unknown. Manchester, N.H.: Amoskeag Manufacturing Company Print Shop, 1924.

Hearden, Patrick J. *Independence and Empire: The New South‚s Cotton Mill Campaign*. DeKald, Ill.: Northern Illinois University Press, 1982.

James, Henry. *Richard Olney and His Public Service*. Boston, Mass.: Houghton Mifflin Company, 1923.

Kenison, Arthur M. *Dumaine's Amoskeag: Let the Record Speak*. Manchester, N.H.: Saint Anselm College Press, 1997.

Landes, David. *Revolution in Time: Clocks and the Making of the Modern World*. Cambridge, Mass.: Harvard University Press, 1984.

Moore, Charles W. *Timing a Century: History of the Waltham Watch Co*. Cambridge, Mass.: Harvard University Press, 1945.

Potter, C.E. *History of Manchester*. Manchester, N.H.: C.E. Potter, Publisher, 1856.

Sanderson, Edmund L. *Waltham Industries: A Collection of Sketches of Early Firms and Founders*. Waltham, Mass.: Waltham Historic Society, Inc., 1957.

Spading, R.V. *The Boston Mercantile Community and the Promotion of the Textile Industry in New England*. New Haven, Conn.: Yale University - Ph.D. Thesis, 1970.

Wayman, Dorothy G. "Dumaine of New England." Unpublished manuscript, 1958.

Weller, John L. *The New Haven Railroad: Its Rise and Fall*. New York, N.Y.: Hastings House, Publishers, 1969.

Articles and Pamphlets

"Amoskeag Manufacturing Company," *Stories of Certain Massachusetts Industries*. Boston, Mass.: reprinted from the Boston Globe, 1915.

"Boot Hill Tales from the Corporate Graveyard," *Audacity*, Spring 1993, p. 63.

"Capture of the New Haven," *Fortune*, April 1949.

Dexter, Lewis. "History of the Stark Division of the International Cotton Mills." Manchester, N.H. privately printed, 1921.

District Court of the United States, District of Massachusetts, "Amoskeag Manufacturing Company Bankruptcy Hearings," No. 58,599, 1936.

"Embarrassing Situation, An," *Time*, April 24, 1950.

"Great Career Closes, A," *American Textile Reporter*, June 14, 1951.

Langenbach, Randolph. "The Amoskeag Millyard: Am Epic in Urban Design." *Harvard Alumni Bulletin*, April, 1968.

"New Englanders Again Control New Haven R.R.," *Business Week*, July 26, 1948.

Sabath, Adolph J., Chairman, "Investigation of Real Estate Bondholders' Reorganizations." U.S. Congress, House of Representatives, Public Hearings Before a Subcommittee of the Select Committee, Sept. 30, Oct 1 & 2, 1934.

Saunders, D. "Frederic Dumaine: Upstreaming the Profits," *Forbes*, July 13, 1987.

Straw, William Parker. *Amoskeag in New Hampshire: An Epic in American Industry*. New York: Newcomer Society of England, American Branch, 1948.

Sweezy, Alan R. "The Amoskeag Manufacturing Company," *Quarterly Journal of Economics*," Vol LII, No. 3, (May, 1938.)

Tilden, Leonard E. "New England Textile Strike." *Monthly Labor Review* 16 (May) 1923: 13-36.

"Waltham Mess, The," *Fortune*, April 1949.

Wayman, Dorothy G., "Unpublished Notes on Dumaine's Diary"

Newspapers

Amoskeag Bulletin, Manchester, N.H.

Boston American, Boston, Mass.

Boston Globe, Boston, Mass.

Boston Herald, Boston Mass.

Boston Post, Boston, Mass.

Boston Record, Boston, Mass.

Boston Traveler, Boston, Mass.

Hartford Times, Hartford, Conn.

Manchester Leader, Manchester, N.H.

Manchester Mirror, Manchester, N.H.

New Haven Journal-Courier, New Haven, Conn.

New Haven Register, New Haven, Conn.

New York Journal American, New York, N.Y.

New York Times, New York, N.Y.

United States Investor, New York, N.Y.

Wall Street Journal, New York, N.Y.

Waltham News-Tribune, Waltham, Mass.

Worcester Telegraph, Worcester, Mass.

Company Records

Amory Mills

Amoskeag Company

Amoskeag Manufacturing Company

Langdon Mills

Manchester Mills

Waltham Watch Company

Index

A

B

D

E

F

270

M

N